*The Women of Provincetown, 1915–1922*

# The Women of Provincetown, 1915–1922

CHERYL BLACK

The University of Alabama Press
TUSCALOOSA AND LONDON

9  8  7  6  5  4  3  2  1
10  09  08  07  06  05  04  03  02

Typeface: ACaslon

∞

The paper on which this book is printed meets the minimum requirements of
American National Standard for Information Science–Permanence of Paper for
Printed Library Materials, ANSI Z39.48–1984.

**Library of Congress Cataloging-in-Publication Data**

Black, Cheryl, 1954–
The women of Provincetown, 1915–1922 / Cheryl Black.
p.  cm.
Originally presented as the author's thesis (Ph. D.—University of Maryland,
College Park, 1998).
Includes bibliographical references (p. ) and index.
ISBN 0-8173-1112-2
1. Provincetown Players. 2. Women in the theater—Massachusetts—Provincetown—
History—20th century. 3. American drama—Women authors—History and
criticism.  I. Title.
PN2297.P7 B58 2002
792′.082′0974492—dc21
2001003850

British Library Cataloguing-in-Publication Data available

*Cover illustration:* "Provincetown Playhouse 1920," by Marguerite Zorach. Private
Collection, Courtesy Kraushaar Galleries, New York.

*To LR, my partner in all things,
and to Nathaniel, our most successful collaboration*

# Contents

# *Illustrations*

# Graphs

# *Acknowledgments*

This work was begun seven years ago as a dissertation topic, and during those years many individuals, organizations, and institutions have lent their support in countless ways. Two scholars have been especially important to this project. Patti P. Gillespie, my longtime mentor and friend, directed the dissertation with her inimitable, ruthless enthusiasm and has generously continued to lend her experience, insight, knowledge, humor, criticism, encouragement, and support through every step in the process of turning the dissertation into a book. Robert K. Sarlós has generously shared with me his abundant store of material and intellectual resources over the years (as well as a very fine apricot brandy—the closest we could get to "Provincetown punch" on short notice). I am especially indebted to Professor Sarlós for his close reading of at least two versions of the work-in-progress, his invaluable critical commentary, and his continuing interest and encouragement.

I am also indebted to Judith Barlow, Jackson Bryer, Roger Meersman, Deborah Rosenfelt, and Catherine Schuler for reading various manuscript drafts and offering insightful criticism and encouragement. I gratefully acknowledge individuals who have alerted me to relevant sources: Jackson Bryer, Kenneth Cameron, Leona Rust Egan, Drew Eisenhauer, Michael O'Hara, Robert K. Sarlós, and William Vilhauer. For assistance in locating or granting permission to publish photographs, I thank Linda Briscoe, Daphne Cook, Valentina Cook, Daniel L'Engle Davis, Anne Easterling, Dee Garrison, Kathleen Kaplan, Mimi Muray Levitt, Paula Scott, and Jonathan Zorach. At the University of Missouri, Columbia, I am grateful to the reference librarians and staff of Ellis Library for their able and gracious assistance and to my Theatre 267 students (WS2000) who so enthusiastically explored the Provincetown past with me and brought the plays to life in classroom performances.

I wish to thank the curators, librarians, and staffs of the libraries and museums whose special collections were crucial to my research: Judy Markowitz and Beth Alvarez, Mckeldin Library, University of Maryland; Bryan D. Rogers and Laurie Deredita, Shain Library, Connecticut College; Levi Phillips and John Skarstad, Shields Library, University of California, Davis; Marie-Héléne Gold, Radcliffe Library; Jennifer Lee, Butler Library; Kathleen Manwaring, Syracuse University Library; Alfred Mueller and Patricia Willis, Yale Collection of American Literature; Fredric Wilson and Annette Fern, Harvard Theatre Collection; Marvin Taylor and Helice Koffler, Fales Library; Stephen Crook, Berg Collection of New York Public Library; Tom Lisanti and Jeremy Megraw, New York Public Library for the Performing Arts; Marty Jacobs, the Museum of the City of New York; Michael Redmon, Santa Barbara Historical Society; Margaret Kulis, Newberry Library; Margaret D. Hrabe, Barrett Library; and Peter Blodgett, Huntington Library.

At the University of Alabama Press, I am grateful for the assistance and support of Nicole Mitchell, Curtis Clark, Jennifer Horne, and Suzette Griffith and for the meticulous editing of Jonathan Lawrence. I would like to thank the editors of *Theatre Survey* and the *Journal of American Drama and Theatre* for permission to incorporate material in this study previously published in those journals.

I would like to thank CaSandra Brooks, Jeff Jones, Kathleen Brant, Suzanne Hayes, Michael Kelly, and the Santvoord family—Van, Sandra, Vincent, and Sonia—for their gracious hospitality during research trips to New York and Provincetown. Finally, this book would never have been completed without the unflagging and cheerful assistance of my husband, LR Hults, who has so frequently during the past seven years set aside his own work (or recreation) to help me with "the Provincetown project."

Every attempt has been made to obtain permission to reproduce copyright material and to make the proper acknowledgments.

*The Women of Provincetown, 1915–1922*

# Introduction

Women . . . have been involved in greater numbers and in a greater variety of jobs than are indicated in the theatre history books.
—Helen Krich Chinoy, *Women in American Theatre*

In the first two decades of the twentieth century, an American Bohemia emerged. Essentially a state of mind representing a radical departure from traditional American customs and beliefs, this metaphoric locale eventually became a geographic reality. By the second decade of the twentieth century, Greenwich Village had become the cultural Mecca for the radical element in America: anarchists, socialists, Freudians, free lovers, and feminists. At about the same time, the Villagers adopted the Cape Cod fishing village of Provincetown, Massachusetts, as their official summer home.

In the summer of 1915, Village Bohemians who transplanted to Provincetown included labor journalists Mary Heaton Vorse and John Reed; *Masses* editors Floyd Dell and Max Eastman; Eastman's wife, lawyer Ida Rauh; theatre designer Robert Edmond Jones; postimpressionist painters Marsden Hartley, Charles Demuth, Brör Nordfeldt, and William and Marguerite Zorach; and novelists Hutchins Hapgood, Neith Boyce, Susan Glaspell, and Glaspell's husband, former classics professor George Cram "Jig" Cook. This group was a special one, closely related by personal and professional ties and part of the cultural leadership of Greenwich Village. Horrified by the recent outbreak of war in Europe, they yet hoped for a spiritual revolution in America that would result in equality and harmony among the country's divided classes, sexes, and races.

As a community of politically engaged artists and intellectuals, the Greenwich Village/Provincetowners were convinced of the relationship between art and politics. Although painting, poetry, and literature were much more commonly represented in the group, theatre dominated the talk that summer. There was reason for enthusiasm: inspired by Europe's independent theatre movement, small subscription theatres had recently opened in Chicago, Boston, and New York. Despite differences in specific structures and policies, these "little theatres" universally opposed commercialism in the theatre. The Greenwich Village/ Provincetown group had already begun to experiment with various types of political performances: lectures, demonstrations, suffrage films, and most famously, the Paterson Strike Pageant of 1913, a re-creation of a silkworkers' strike staged by John Reed and Robert Edmond Jones at Madison Square Garden.

The idea grew, during long liquid conversations among the dunes, that the theatre was vitally important to America's spiritual and social regeneration. Crucial to such regeneration was the development of a native drama and communal creation: an American theatre, like that of ancient Athens, should be a unifying cultural force, expressing "a spirit shared by all."[1] Talk led to action. Cook and Glaspell, in collaboration, and Neith Boyce had each recently completed a one-act play, and they decided to stage them at the seaside cottage leased by Boyce and her husband, Hutchins Hapgood. Considering the group's lofty ideals for the drama, their first two plays—*Constancy*, which satirized a love affair between Reed and Mabel Dodge, and *Suppressed Desires*, which lampooned the Village's current obsession with psychoanalysis—may seem modest achievements. For the Provincetowners, however, the personal was always political, and individual regeneration was a prerequisite to social regeneration: "Without self-knowledge . . . our political and economic effort is useless."[2] The first performance was so successful that the group immediately commandeered Mary Heaton Vorse's fish wharf and converted it into a rustic theatre. Two additional plays were hastily written, energetically performed, and enthusiastically received. The Provincetown Players had begun operation. The following summer (1916), the Players welcomed an unknown Eugene O'Neill into their midst and staged ten new one-acts and four revivals at their Wharf Theatre. Newcomer O'Neill shared the Provincetowners' general disdain for bourgeois conventions but lacked allegiance to any particular political theory or goal. He differed from his new associates also in his serious ambition for a career in the theatre. That fall twenty-nine individuals formally organized as "The Provincetown Players: The

Playwright's Theatre" and rented a space at 139 Macdougal Street.[3] They remained in Greenwich Village for the next six years, producing nearly one hundred plays by more than fifty writers, achieving a legendary status along the way.[4]

Scholars of theatre and drama generally recognize the Provincetown Players as one of the most influential theatre groups in America. Provincetown historians have credited the group with a number of contributions, including the development of a noncommercial theatrical tradition, the discovery of two significant American dramatists (O'Neill and Glaspell), the promotion of a nonhierarchical organizational structure and racially integrated casts, and the introduction or advancement of numerous scenic innovations.[5] Robert K. Sarlós has concluded that this company was "the single most fruitful American theatre prior to the Second World War: it introduced more native playwrights, had a greater impact on audiences and critics, and a longer life than any other similar group."[6] These achievements are impressive and undisputed. This study, however, proposes that the Provincetown Players has another, largely unacknowledged claim to fame as one of the first theatre companies in America in which women achieved prominence in every area of operation. At a time when women playwrights were rare, women directors rarer, and women scenic designers nearly unheard of, Provincetown's female membership excelled in all these functions.

More than 120 women were associated with the Provincetown Players.[7] Of those, approximately 40 were important, regularly active members who performed a multiplicity of functions. Thirteen of the company's 29 founders were women; 16 of its 51 playwrights were women; 7 of its 19 executive committee members were women; 6 of its 28 scenic designers were women; its leading costume designer was a woman; its leading actor was a woman; and its leading director was a woman.[8] The company's best-known female member, playwright Susan Glaspell, was second only to Eugene O'Neill in productivity and critical reputation. Although most of these women did not make lasting careers in the theatre, their affiliation with the Provincetown Players allowed them to make significant contributions to the development of modern American drama and theatre. Examining their careers offers new insights into the character and contributions of one of America's most influential theatre companies, at the same time illuminating one of the most important eras in American theatre history, one that marks the emergence of theatre direction and design as theatrical specializations and the introduction and development of new styles in playwriting and acting.

The story of Provincetown's women has been fleetingly suggested by existing general histories, but none have highlighted the achievements or experiences of women.[9] To date, scholarly attention has focused on dramatic criticism, with Glaspell receiving the lion's share of that attention.[10] In fact, the women of Provincetown have received more attention from literary critics than from theatre historians. Although these scholars have begun to pose historical questions (e.g., What is the relationship between women playwrights and women directors? How do we account for the pattern of participation by playwrights?), the studies that would answer these questions have not been undertaken. Only a handful of articles on the theatrical contributions (acting, directing, designing, etc.) of Provincetown women have been published.[11] Although one scholar has recently asserted that "the role of women in the Provincetown Players cannot be overestimated,"[12] the precise nature and extent of women's roles at Provincetown is still generally unknown. To fully document the artistic contributions of these women and to assess the significance of those contributions is one objective of this study. Theatre history, no less than general history, has frequently been reduced to the doings of great men. As Provincetown's membership included a considerable number of celebrated men, including O'Neill, Cook, Reed, and Jones, it is not surprising that its women have been slighted. Although I do not dispute the significant contributions of these men, I wish to bring the achievements and experiences of women center stage, an objective that necessarily shifts men's experiences and contributions to the periphery.

The experiences of the women of Provincetown, however, are significant not only because of what these women had to offer the theatre, but also because of what the theatre had, or has, to offer women. Exploring their experiences as artists and as women within a network of women artists whose associations were personal as well as professional leads inevitably to an investigation of gender ideology, feminism, and sexism in Western culture. Investigating specifically what it was like to be a *woman* at Provincetown continues a tradition of research begun by Rosamond Gilder's *Enter the Actress* in 1931 and rejuvenated in the late twentieth century by a number of works, including Chinoy and Jenkins's *Women in American Theatre* (1981), Albert Auster's *Ac-*

*tresses and Suffragists* (1984), Tracy C. Davis's *Actresses as Working Women* (1991), Charlotte Canning's *Feminist Theatres in the U.S.A.* (1996), and Catherine Schuler's *Women in Russian Theatre* (1997).[13] The experiences of Provincetown's female membership add to our understanding of how women have used and have been used in the theatre.

Previous historians' tendency to overlook women's achievements, as well as the significance of those achievements, can perhaps be traced to their failure to recognize first-wave feminism as an important part of the cultural and historical context in which this organization developed. All previous full-length historical studies of the Provincetown Players look primarily to the aesthetic influences of Europe's independent theatre movement and the political influences of anarchism and socialism to explain the origins and character of the Provincetown Players.[14] Yet the modern feminist movement was born in Greenwich Village in the 1910s, and a considerable number of Provincetown's members, male and female, were at the forefront of the movement. The relationship between feminism and the Provincetown Players has also been suggested, not by theatre historians, but by social historians, who have identified several members of the company as feminist activists,[15] and by literary critics, who have identified feminist themes in many dramas by women.[16]

Contemporary chroniclers of the little theatre movement also treated the movement as primarily an artistic phenomenon, inspired by aesthetic experimentation largely disassociated from social or political events.[17] Recent scholarship by social and theatre historians, however, has begun to demonstrate a strong relationship between women's theatre activity and social activism during this era, especially Karen Blair's insightful analyses of pageantry and the little theatre movement as manifestations of Progressive Era reform initiatives.[18] In 1922, George Kelly's popular play *The Torch-Bearers* fixed a false but enduring stereotype in the minds of the American public: the "little theatre woman" as pampered, pompous, talentless, and brainless. Blair's identically titled study successfully subverts this stereotype in its presentation of hardworking and talented women who used the arts "to effect their vision for social change in America."[19]

Blair gives minimal attention to the Provincetown Players; in fact, she specifically laments theatre histories' tendency to recognize only the Provincetown Players and Eugene O'Neill in their accounts of the little theatre movement: "In our reverence for this contribution to American commercial theater, we have forgotten that the Provincetown Players was not a unique phenomenon, but was representative of a larger movement."[20] I have positioned the Provincetown Players specifically within the tradition Blair explores, as a cultural manifestation of larger social movements, especially first-wave feminism.[21] To explore the relationship between these movements and the Provincetown Players and to analyze the impact of these movements on women's participation is a second objective of this study.

In order to illuminate the complex interplay of the personal, political, and aesthetic that existed within this organization, I have framed the examination of women's theatrical contributions within two contextual chapters that examine their political, personal, and artistic endeavors within a changing historical context. Chapter 1 introduces the women of Provincetown and places them in their social and historical context at the time of the company's creation. Chapter 7 examines the postwar context and provides a brief overview of the post-Provincetown lives and careers of the company's female leadership. The intervening chapters examine the achievements and experiences of groups of women in a particular theatrical practice: managing, writing, performing, stage directing, and designing. Wishing to stress collaboration and interrelationships, I have organized those chapters to illustrate the interdependent relationship that generally exists between these various functions, a structure that I hope also serves to reveal how women's achievement in one area facilitated achievement in another.

# I

## Creating Women

We were no lost generation. We had faith—we were creating a new world, we were creating a new theatre.

—Ida Rauh, interview with Louis Sheaffer

*Through the streets of Greenwich Village, a strikingly handsome Ida Rauh—her friends have told her she resembles the lions in front of the Fifth Avenue Library—rides in a rented limousine, tossing birth control pamphlets out of the window.*

*In the capitalist utopia of Lawrence, Massachusetts, short story writer Mary Heaton Vorse witnesses firsthand the conditions in which striking factory workers live: rooms with no windows, rats in the hallways, filth everywhere, and inadequate food, fuel, and toilets.*

*Into a flaming torch positioned directly in front of the White House, Louise Bryant and seventy-five members of the National Woman's Party (the "IWW of the suffrage movement") ceremoniously feed copies of the president's speeches, and finally, his effigy.*

*From the window of her more than usually bohemian apartment at Fifty-seventh and Sixth, postimpressionist painter Marguerite Zorach, whose fauvist-cubist contribution to the Armory Show has been ridiculed by America's philistine critics, drops dead rats into parked limousines.*[1]

The women who committed these subversive acts have several things in common: they all rejected comfortable or privileged backgrounds to ally themselves ideologically with the working class; they were all living in Greenwich Village in 1916; and they were all charter members of the Provincetown Players.[2] Understanding the times in which they lived is crucial to understanding why they wished to create and sustain an experimental theatre company; examining their experiences as women is crucial to appreciating their achievements as artists.

In the years before World War I, revolutionary impulses in art and politics were being fed by a crosscurrent of intellectual and philosophical ideas: Edward Bellamy condemned America's economy as "a great coach on which a few rode in luxury";[3] Charlotte Perkins Gilman asserted that social custom, not biology, relegated women to inferior status; Havelock Ellis and Ellen Key linked procreation to sexual pleasure; Sigmund Freud and Carl Jung probed levels of consciousness; and Albert Einstein shattered the existing perception of perception. Friedrich Nietzsche had recently died, taking God and traditional Christian values with him. Critics of America's socioeconomic system ranged from progressive liberals who sought to modify the existing system to anarchists who demanded the complete abolition of industrial capitalism and all government institutions. The struggle for gender and racial equality also gained momentum during these years as a new generation of leaders initiated diverse strategies to gain civil rights. As historian Oscar Handlin observed, "Progressivism" was as much a mood as a political party, a common conviction that "new times called for new measures. . . . In the presidential election of 1912, no candidate called himself a conservative."[4] The progressive mood affected culture as well as politics; in the same year that one million Americans voted for a Socialist presidential candidate, W. C. Handy brought the blues to Memphis, Maurice Browne and Ellen Von Volkenberg brought the little theatre movement to Chicago, and Max Eastman and Floyd Dell brought "feminism, fun, truth, beauty, realism, freedom, peace, and revolution" to the pages of *The Masses.*[5]

In Greenwich Village, theatres and the magazines that reviewed them were "little," verse and love were "free," and everything else was "new," especially women. According to Hutchins Hapgood, "When the world began to change, the restlessness of the women was the main cause of the development called Greenwich Village, which existed not only in New York but all over the country."[6] But it was in Greenwich Village that the restlessness of women cultivated a new idea—part social theory, part philosophical perspective, part political action, part religion—that came to be known as "feminism." Nancy Cott has characterized first-wave feminism as a significant new phase in women's emancipation, broader in scope and more radical in purpose than the nineteenth-century "woman movement": "To some extent Feminism was a reaction against an emphasis in the woman movement itself, the stress on nurturant service and moral uplift. . . . When the woman movement of the 1910s stressed woman's duties, Feminists reinvigorated demands for women's rights."[7]

"Feminist" was a newly coined term in the 1910s,[8] and anyone who wanted to see one, advised Heywood Broun, should come to the Village, where the town was filled with "real, rampaging ones."[9] They were fairly easy to spot—they were the ones with short hair and no corsets, who smoked in public and said "damn" right out loud. And if they were not on the street or on a soapbox, they could be found at one of their many newly formed organizations: the Liberal Club, the Lucy Stoner League, the Feminist Alliance, the Woman's Peace Party, the Women's Trade Union League, the Equality League of Self-Supporting Women, the Men's League for Woman Suffrage, the National Woman's Party, the American Birth Control League, and Heterodoxy, a discussion club for women with unorthodox views. In the Village, "Heterodite" was a synonym for "feminist";[10] the club "epitomized the Feminism of the time."[11]

Greenwich Village feminists read everything, appropriated what they found useful, and ignored the rest. They agreed with Charlotte Perkins Gilman that "woman's place was everywhere" and with Crystal Eastman that peace was prerequisite to a new egalitarian society.[12] Many accepted Edward Carpenter's assertion that a socialist economic system was essential for women's equality, but others applauded Emma Goldman's refusal to wait.[13] They embraced the new sexual theories of Swedish psychologist Ellen Key, who insisted on women's right to sexual fulfillment and to maternity, with or without marriage, and of Havelock Ellis, who focused on satisfactory heterosexual relations and promoted changes in marriage and divorce laws.[14] Ellis, along with Carpenter, Key, and Goldman, established a new sexual ethic popular with early feminists because of their radically liberal attitudes toward sex and sexual pleasure. Freudian psychoanalysis helped feminists discover any hidden complexes that might interfere with newfound sexual freedom, and Margaret Sanger's "birth control," another newly coined term, promised freedom from unwanted pregnancy. Feminists even co-opted Nietzsche's "will to power" to conceptualize superwomanhood. Greenwich Village feminists resisted commitment to any one political, ethical, economic, or aesthetic dogma; for most of these women, the essence of feminism lay in "daring to live exactly as they wished."[15]

Almost without exception, Provincetown's female founders epitomized these restless and radical women. Mary Heaton Vorse was "one of the gay, warmhearted girls . . . who turned twenty early in the century and felt it was up to them to be doing something about saving the world."[16] Discovering at the age of nineteen that "an awful gulf" existed between herself and her genteel New England neighbors, Vorse left her native Amherst for Paris.[17] She studied art, but became a writer of short stories featuring "new woman" protagonists, eventually settling in Greenwich Village. Vorse was instrumental in fostering a sense of community among the Villagers since at least 1906, when she discovered Provincetown as a summer retreat and cofounded the prototype of Village radical organizations, the "A" club, a cooperative housing venture at 3 Fifth Avenue, where "everybody [was] a Liberal, if not a Radical— and all for Labor and the Arts."[18] In addition to her lifelong commitment to labor journalism, Vorse was also a pacifist, a contributing editor of *The Masses,* and a charter member of Heterodoxy. Despite her demanding career, she struggled to create a fulfilling domestic life. After a miserable first marriage to writer Albert Vorse, who drank too much, worked too little, and chased other women, she chose a more promising partner in Joe O'Brien, who was both a labor journalist who shared her radical politics and an "eager stepfather" who stayed home with the children while Vorse covered the Women's International Peace Conference.[19] As the sole support of four children, Vorse was keenly interested in new parenting strategies, and in 1913 she introduced the revolutionary educational theories of Maria Montessori to the Greenwich Village/ Provincetown community. The new methods encouraged individuality rather than conformity (the toddler version of Nietzsche, perhaps), and Vorse and other Provincetown parents hastened to "release the spontaneous interests" of their children.[20] Her brief, happy marriage to O'Brien ended with his death in the fall of 1915, just after the couple had shared one summer season as Provincetown Players. After O'Brien's death, Vorse engaged in several "free unions" within the Greenwich Village/Provincetown community, including one with short story author and playwright Wilbur Daniel Steele, who later married Provincetown cofounder Margaret Thurston Steele, and playwright Norman Matson, later common-law husband to Susan Glaspell.[21]

Like Vorse, Ida Rauh was a force in the Village: "half-Nietzschean, half-Marxian, half-anarchist, believing in free love and a freed proletariat."[22] Contemporaries have remembered her as languorous of move-

Mary Heaton Vorse. Courtesy Schlesinger
Library, Radcliffe Institute, Harvard
University.

ment but indomitable of will: "when a woman of Ida Rauh's character
and will power is determined to act, she can move mountains—and she
did."[23] Although well educated and widely talented, Rauh did not settle
on a single career, but used her private income to finance various social causes, including the Women's Trade Union League, the National
Labor Defense Fund, Heterodoxy, the Lucy Stone League, and the
"Woman's Freedom Congress" of the Women's International League,
as well as uncompensated artistic pursuits, including poetry, sculpting,
and acting. Her interest in the theatre predated Provincetown; she was
a cofounder of the Washington Square Players, a company dedicated
to producing American, as well as European, plays of quality. Rauh
scorned the bourgeois practice of marriage, at least until she was thirty-
five, when she met the equally languid and equally erudite Max Eastman, brother of feminist theorist Crystal Eastman. Eastman must have
seemed a likely prospect. He was editor of *The Masses*, founder of the
Men's League for Woman Suffrage, a poet with a Ph.D. from Columbia University, and "handsome as a faun."[24] Moreover, he was politically
educable; Rauh had converted him from utopian to Marxian socialism.

Ida Rauh. Courtesy Schlesinger Library, Radcliffe Institute, Harvard University.

Eastman, however, had not contemplated parenthood, and the birth of their son Daniel in 1912 alarmed him: "By its arrival I was permanently trapped and shackled."[25] Even more disconcerting was his discovery that Rauh's idea of modern marriage included monogamy. When Eastman fell in love with actress Florence Deshon in 1916, his marriage to Rauh ended bitterly.[26] After Eastman's departure, Rauh began an intimate, probably sexual, relationship with Jig Cook, who was married to Susan Glaspell at the time.

Glaspell's background was both middle class and midwestern. She was born in Davenport, Iowa, and graduated from Drake University in Des Moines in 1899. Glaspell quickly made a name for herself as a newspaper reporter, covering in 1900 the murder trial that inspired her most famous play, *Trifles*. In Davenport she encountered new social theories at the Monist Society for freethinkers, founded by Cook and Floyd Dell. By the time she moved to Greenwich Village in 1913, Glaspell was a successful novelist whose fictional heroines were, if not radical revolutionaries, at least on the verge of new social and personal relations. She joined Heterodoxy and the Lucy Stone League, and in 1914 she declared in print her allegiance to socialism and woman suffrage.[27] Glaspell's personal life is dominated by her relationship with Cook, whom she met in Davenport in 1907. In addition to being a member of Davenport's first family, which clearly made a mark on Glaspell's small-town class consciousness, Cook was by most accounts a charismatic combination of Nietzsche, Thoreau, Plato, Dionysus, and Jesus. Even though Cook was waiting for a divorce from his first wife in order to marry his second, he and Glaspell began a relationship that ultimately led to their marriage in 1913. According to Hapgood, Glaspell had, "with the determination of every woman in love, taken [Cook] away from his then wife and children."[28] Glaspell's devotion to Cook, which one contemporary described as "fatuous," is perhaps hard to understand.[29] He had failed at two marriages and a number of careers; he drank to excess; and he was a notorious womanizer, accused by Province-town actress Kirah Markham of operating a "producer's office couch."[30] And yet, Cook clearly was a charismatic leader whose enthusiasm inspired others: "a figure of gigantic creative energy, superhuman, with a Promethean fire shining in his face."[31] He was also an ardent lover, once responding to Glaspell's suggestion that they might meet in Italy by assuring her that he would "go to Hell to meet her."[32] That Cook loved Glaspell and championed her work seems indisputable. They collaborated on two plays, and theirs is one of the rare instances of male/female collaboration in which the male contribution is erased. Cook's name was and is frequently omitted as a coauthor of *Suppressed Desires.* Despite—or perhaps because of—her "fatuous" devotion to Jig, Glaspell commanded great respect, both as an artist and a human being: "she was always Susan Glaspell, she was never Mrs. Cook."[33]

Like Glaspell, Neith Boyce began life in a small midwestern town. At age ten she moved to California, where her father cofounded the *Los Angeles Times.* Boyce had a lonely childhood; her siblings died in an epidemic, and her parents withdrew emotionally. She turned to writing and retained an aloof, slightly pessimistic outlook for the rest of her life. When she was twenty-seven she became the first woman reporter on New York City's *Commercial Advertiser.* In New York, she joined Heterodoxy and built a successful career as a novelist. Boyce's fiction, like that of Glaspell and Vorse, depicted the lives of middle-class "new woman" protagonists in conflicted personal relations. Boyce herself re-

Susan Glaspell, photograph from
a painting by William L'Engle.
Courtesy Schlesinger Library,
Radcliffe Institute, Harvard
University and Daniel L'Engle
Davis.

solved to avoid intimacy altogether: "it was much better to observe
other people's love affairs and write about them."[34] But her cool objec-
tivity could not withstand the determined pursuit of her *Commercial
Advertiser* colleague Hutchins Hapgood. When Hapgood met Boyce,
he was bowled over by her classical beauty but dismayed to find her "a
very charming piece of congealed ice."[35] Boyce was not, however, as inaccessible as she appeared. She enjoyed Hapgood's zest for life and she
shared his interests in radical politics and art. In 1899 she agreed to
marry him—keeping, of course, her own name and her career. The marriage was a turbulent one in which Boyce struggled to maintain a protected emotional distance from Hapgood's passionate excesses. Hapgood, like most Village men, was an ardent proponent of free love and
had been "psyched" to rid himself of any lingering libido-repressing
complexes. Theoretically, both partners were free to enjoy extramarital
relations, and Hapgood enjoyed a number of them, including one with
Provincetown actress Mary Pyne. When Boyce attempted flirtations,
however, Hapgood became violently jealous. Although Hapgood complained of Boyce's reserve, she was not indifferent to Hapgood's affairs:
"I assure you I never think of your physical passions for other women
without pain."[36] Boyce and Hapgood had four children, and although

Neith Boyce. Courtesy Yale Collection of American Literature, Beinecke Rare Book and Manuscript Library, Yale University.

Hapgood was an affectionate father, Boyce was the primary caregiver. According to their daughter Miriam, Hapgood did more than most fathers of his generation in bringing up his children, but he often criticized Boyce for not devoting enough time to the house, the children, and their domestic welfare. Hapgood was often away gathering material for his sociological studies while Neith remained at home, trying to work, sometimes with the help of servants, but constantly interrupted.[37]

Marguerite Thompson Zorach was a native Californian, also born into middle-class comfort, and also not "temperamentally suited to teas and Monday afternoon clubs."[38] In 1910 she abandoned her plan to attend Stanford in order to study art in Paris. There she saw, and was immediately fascinated by, the unconventional use of color and line in Matisse, Picasso, and others working in the fauvist or cubist style. Thompson began to paint in a uniquely innovative form that combined the saturated color of fauvism with cubist composition. In 1911, Thompson's professional and personal lives collided when she met fellow art student Lithuanian-born William Zorach. Marguerite, William recalled, was wearing a black silk turban with a big red rose in the center and painting "a pink and yellow nude with a bold blue outline. She knew what she was doing—but I just couldn't understand why such a

Marguerite Zorach with
Tessim Zorach, 1915.
Courtesy Jonathan Zorach.

Stella Ballantine. Courtesy Schlesinger
Library, Radcliffe Institute, Harvard
University.

nice girl would paint such wild pictures."[39] As Rauh had persuaded Eastman to political radicalism, Thompson led Zorach to aesthetic innovation, urging him to abandon impressionism and to "let his colors go wild."[40] William quickly converted to what he and Marguerite referred to as "postimpressionism," and the two artists' styles became almost indistinguishable. The Zorachs married in 1912 and by 1913 had left their rather squalid digs on Fifty-seventh Street for their famous "postimpressionist studio" at 123 W. Tenth Street. Transforming their home into a work of art, the Zorachs hung yards of unbleached muslin, painted the floors red and the walls yellow, and decorated the hallway as a garden of Eden, with a life-sized Adam and Eve and a red and white snake draped around the trunk of a tree.[41] Both Marguerite and William exhibited at the Armory Show of 1913, which introduced to America European painters Kandinsky, Matisse, Picasso, Brancusi, Bracque, and Duchamp, and at the Forum Exhibition of Modern American Painters in 1916. Marguerite, who was the only woman represented in the Forum Exhibition and the only artist not to have a statement printed in the catalog, tried to create a partnership with her husband that was both domestic and professional:

> There is a tendency in men to transform the loved one into a mother image. . . . I had that tendency but Marguerite would have none of it. She was not going to be any man's mother. To her, marriage was a partnership; share and share alike, the good, bad, difficult, the joys . . . work, ideas, accomplishments were to be shared. She was happy to do the cooking, to make her clothes and the children's, and in the very early days she made my shirts out of pongee silk. But she felt that the care of the house and children was the responsibility of both of us.[42]

Modern marriage to Marguerite also meant monogamy, though William had what he described as "romantic" affairs. Unfortunately, we have only his word that Marguerite was not jealous of his amours, but only "annoyed" or "amused."[43]

Stella Comyn, Emma Goldman's beloved niece, was an early convert to anarchism. She was only ten in 1901 when police interrogated her concerning her aunt's relationship with presidential assassin Leon Czolgosz.[44] Stella remained loyal to Emma and anarchism for the rest of her life, helping to publish the anarchist journals *Mother Earth* and

*Blast*. Comyn was also a feminist who cofounded Heterodoxy in 1913, and an actor whose interest in theatre predated Provincetown; she worked with Rauh and a number of other future Provincetowners in the Washington Square Players' first season.[45] Unlike many of the era's anarchists, Comyn married; unlike most feminists, she took the name of her husband, actor Edward J. ("Teddy") Ballantine, and took on most of the domestic responsibilities within the marriage. Stella Ballantine was a fervent Montessorian whose son Ian's spontaneous interest in violence once got him locked out of the O'Neill household for trying to kick Agnes Boulton O'Neill in the stomach.[46]

Louise Bryant was the only female founder of the Provincetown Players who was not a firmly established member of the Greenwich Village community, having just arrived from Portland, Oregon, in the spring of 1916 to live with John Reed. Bryant had no trouble, however, fitting in with the radical crowd. At the University of Oregon, she was considered a "fast girl" who wore lipstick, flirted, and dressed flamboyantly. In Portland she was a sexually liberated suffragist who read *The Masses* and contributed poetry and sketches to *Blast*. When she married Portland dentist Paul Trullinger in 1909 she kept her name, her career as a social editor and fashion illustrator, and her private studio. Why Bryant married Trullinger remains a mystery, but she left him without a backward glance when she met Reed. Trullinger, with what was apparently typical consideration, sent her violets on the day she left him (she wore them to the train station) and waited until after she had gone to have a nervous breakdown. The famously inconstant Reed was convinced he had met his soul mate: "She's two years younger than I, wild and brave and straight, and graceful and lovely to look at . . . an artist, a rampant, joyous individualist, a poet and a revolutionary."[47] Bryant had in fact underestimated her age by four years and overestimated her professional achievements, a trend toward personal reinvention that continued throughout her life. Bryant's arrival in Provincetown caused a stir, especially after she managed to capture O'Neill's attentions without losing Reed's. Reed's friends worried that Bryant was using him to advance her career as a journalist; O'Neill's friends marveled that she was able to keep him sober; and everyone was agog when Reed and Bryant married in November 1916. Reed explained that marriage was necessary for Bryant's economic security, in case he died after the kidney surgery he had scheduled that fall. Bryant also cited their need to

Louise Bryant. Courtesy Sheaffer-O'Neill Collection, Shain Library, Connecticut College.

travel together and her desire to have a child: "I don't want to make it hard for a child over anything so silly as marriage."[48] For Max Eastman, Reed and Bryant's personal relationship had achieved a beauty so perfect, it was art: "It was a companionship in what philistines call adventure, a kind of gypsy compact. And that will to live, to be themselves in the world, and be real, and be honest, and taste the whole tang of it, was more to them than writing, it was more to them than any particular practical undertaking, even a revolution. It was as though they had agreed to inscribe at last two audacious, deep, and real lives in the book of time and let the gods call it poetry."[49]

Less information is available on the lives of the remaining charter women; however, with the possible exception of Alice Hall, who seemed to be living a fairly conventional existence with Professor Henry Hall and their children, all founding women were well-educated wage earners engaged in professional and/or personal partnerships with men in the company. Myra Musselman Carr was a painter and sculptor who cofounded the Modern Art School in Provincetown with actor Freddie Burt. Lucy Huffaker was a writer who later married director Edward Goodman. Margaret Thurston Steele, a "racy girl with a strong sense of humor,"[50] was a painter married to playwright Wilbur Daniel Steele. Margaret Nordfeldt, married to postimpressionist painter and designer Brör Nordfeldt, was a homeopathic doctor. Nancy Schoonmaker, married to Edwin Schoonmaker, was a journalist, suffragist, and pacifist.

Excepting Louise Bryant, all the women had long-standing personal and/or professional relationships with each other, and almost every woman was in a close personal and/or professional relationship with one of the male founders. But these thirteen charter members were part of a much larger network of radical artists and anarchist/feminist activists. Provincetown's charter women attracted like-minded women, who flocked to Macdougal Street during the next six years.

Edna Kenton was one of two women in the company who published feminist theory. In two articles, published in 1913 and 1914 and designed to appeal to a general readership, Kenton drew on Nietzsche, Gilman, Goldman, Freud, Ellis, Key, Montessori, and the editorial policy of *The Masses* to come up with a composite perspective on the "woman question." In her first article she called for a "world-wide readjustment of human relationships" and defended militant feminism as a means to that end: "Women have never lived in an environment created by themselves for themselves, but in this man's world, under codes not their own, according to ideals set up for them in no way borne out by facts."[51] Her second article promised, on behalf of feminism, and in this order, "fun to men, greater scope to women, better parents to children, and more charm to life." In this article, Kenton distinguishes actual women and men from the social constructions "Woman" and "Man," what she calls "capitalized impersonalities." Kenton's feminism is, in that sense, "anti-Woman"—that is, against socially constructed Woman—and feminism's fundamental aim is a quest for authentic identity: "[Feminism] is her conscious attempt to realize Personality; to make her own decisions instead of having them made for her; to sink the old humbled or rebelling slave in the new creature who is mistress of herself."[52]

Kenton certainly epitomized this new creature. Born in Springfield, Missouri, in 1876 and educated at the University of Michigan, Kenton was by 1916 a successful novelist as well as an influential critic and editor. Along with future Provincetown colleagues Floyd Dell, Jig Cook, and Lucian Cary, all then working as critics in Chicago, Kenton supported the revolt against genteel traditions in fiction and was especially influential in her opposition to de facto censorship by critics of

Edna Kenton, John Reed, and
Ethel Plummer. Courtesy Harvard
Theatre Collection.

Theodore Dreiser's early novels.[53] Kenton's astute criticism earned great
respect from the era's most noted writers. Waldo Frank, after Flaubert
to George Sand, addressed her as "cher maitre."[54] Dreiser trusted her
implicitly: "I shall always send my work to you in uncertainty and re-
joice when you approve."[55] In New York, Kenton helped found Heterodoxy and was instrumental in organizing the Feminist Mass Meetings
in Cooper Union, where featured speakers included Dell and Eastman
and topics encompassed "The Right to Work," "The Right to Her
Convictions," "The Right to Organize," "The Right to Ignore Fashion," and "The Right to Keep Her Own Name."[56] Although the "beautiful and bookish" Kenton never married, she had a long, intimate relationship with lawyer and Provincetown actor Justus Sheffield.[57] Jig
Cook, who named her distinctive laugh "Risus Ednae Kentonae,"[58] was
also, apparently, an admirer: "Writing to you gives me an uncanny desire
to see you. Have my sins (which I am trying hard not to mention or
think of) well, my sins—would they make you cold and distant if we
came within handshaking range?"[59]

Provincetown's second feminist theorist, Mina Loy, agreed with Kenton that the present perception of woman was an "impersonality." Dismissing "economic legislation, vice-crusades and uniform education" and exhorting women to "seek within yourselves to find out what you are," Loy proposed a radical solution to the problem of sexual double standards: "the *unconditional* surgical *destruction of virginity* throughout the female population at puberty."[60] Born Mina Gertrude Lowy in 1882 (she changed her name to Loy in 1903), a British citizen of Hungarian Jewish descent, Loy arrived in New York in October 1916. A futurist who had had affairs in Italy with both Filippo Marinetti and Giovanni Papini and had served as a nurse in a military hospital to relish the blood and noise of war, Loy was a radical's radical. The *New York Evening Sun* immediately featured the beautiful and brilliant poet (her second husband claimed she was "too intelligent to have friends") as the prototypical "Modern Woman," and the Players lost no time in inviting her to join them onstage.[61] Loy introduced futurist poetry to New York; her "Pig Cupid" was on everyone's coffee table:

Spawn of Fantasies
Silting the appraisable
Pig Cupid   his rosy snout
Rooting erotic garbage[62]

Loy, who was married first to painter Stephen Haweiss and then to professional boxer Arthur Craven, was one of the few Provincetown women to avoid sexual liaisons with the men in the company. According to William Carlos Williams, she was "too smart to involve herself, after a first disastrous marriage, with any of us."[63] As a eugenicist who considered it a duty of women of superior intelligence to produce children, Loy had four during her two marriages.

Like Loy, with whom she developed a close personal friendship, Djuna Barnes was noted for striking looks, intimidating wit, and a radical lifestyle. Bohemia was nothing new to Barnes, who had grown up in a bizarre household consisting of her suffragist, spiritualist, free-loving grandmother, her similarly free-spirited, polygamous father, her mother, and her father's mistress, Fanny. In fact, Barnes's father, Wald, whom she described as a "messianic reformer" who "imagined a world of musicians and poets, free from societal constraints and religious oppres-

Djuna Barnes and Mina Loy. Courtesy
Papers of Djuna Barnes, Special
Collections, University of Maryland
College Libraries.

sion," sounds remarkably like Jig Cook.[64] By 1915, Barnes was well known
in the Village as a newspaper reporter, illustrator, and modernist/futurist
poet:

> They gave her hurried shoves this way
>     And that.
> Her body shock-abbreviated
> As a city cat.
> She lay out listlessly like some small mug
> Of beer gone flat.[65]

Barnes avoided political labels, but she seemed to support suffrage, once
allowing herself to be force-fed in order to write convincingly and
sympathetically of such treatment of England's militant suffragettes.[66]
Barnes's sexual—as well as political—identity defied categorization: "I
might be anything, if a horse loved me, I might be that."[67] Before her
Provincetown days, Djuna enjoyed, or endured, an arranged "marriage"
to a much older man, a three-year engagement to a German aristocrat,
and another common-law liaison with radical writer Courtney Lemon.
Within the Provincetown community, Barnes shared a house at 86

Edna St. Vincent Millay.
Courtesy Library of Congress.

Greenwich Avenue with Ida Rauh, Berenice Abbott, Charles Ellis, James Light, and Susan Jenkins, had affairs with Light and Lawrence Vail, and had an intimate friendship, possibly sexual, with Mary Pyne.[68]

Somewhat less experimental than her sister poets, Edna St. Vincent Millay nevertheless became an instant celebrity with the publication of *Renascence* in 1912:

> The world stands out on either side
> No wider than the heart is wide;
> Above the world is stretched the sky,—
> No higher than the soul is high.[69]

Millay was slow to appreciate modernism in painting, as well, describing all the cubist works in the Armory Show of 1913 as "piles of shingles."[70] If artistically conventional, however, Millay was unquestionably sexually adventurous. Her first sexual partners were women at Vassar,

Evelyn Scott. Courtesy
Photography Collection, Harry
Ransom Humanities Research
Center, The University of Texas
at Austin, and Paula Scott.

and she also seemed drawn to bisexual men. She did not, however, discriminate against heterosexual men, including Provincetowners John Reed, Rollo Peters, and Floyd Dell, to whom she was briefly engaged.[71] Dell claimed to have "cured" Millay of homosexual impulses, but he found her rapid transition to flaming heterosexuality equally dismaying, and their relationship languished.[72]

Evelyn Scott (born Elsie Dunn) was another sexual outlaw. Never legally married, she eloped, just before her twenty-first birthday, with a married man (Frederick Wellman, who took the name "Cyril-Scott"). After several years as social exiles in Brazil, where Scott gave birth to a son and wrote a play later produced by Provincetown, they moved to Greenwich Village. There she had affairs with, among others, poet and Provincetown actor William Carlos Williams.[73]

Perhaps the company's most committed anarchist was Eleanor Fitzgerald, a tall, striking redhead of Scotch-Irish descent who grew up on a farm in Madison, Wisconsin. Fitzgerald began working at sixteen, first as a teacher, then as a nurse at the famous Battle Creek sanatorium, and finally as a booker of Chautauqua tours. After meeting anarchists Ben Reitman, Emma Goldman, and Alexander Berkman in Chicago,

Eleanor Fitzgerald and Buff.
Courtesy Papers of Djuna
Barnes, Special Collections,
University of Maryland
Libraries.

Fitzgerald embraced the anarchist movement. She served as assistant editor for both *Blast* and *Mother Earth,* spoke on behalf of labor unions, and raised $150,000 for political prisoners. Also a Heterodite and a Freudian, Fitzgerald had her cherished tramp collie Buff psychoanalyzed. Although she never married, Fitzgerald carried on a long relationship with Alexander Berkman, whose affections she shared with Goldman, Becky Edelson, and others.[74]

The roster of socially, aesthetically, and/or sexually radical women who worked with the Players is nearly inexhaustible, but it includes the courageous young anarchist Becky Edelson, imprisoned for labor agitation when she was fifteen; tall, tawny-haired Christine Ell, also an anarchist and owner of the famous restaurant above the theatre, gregarious, greatly beloved, and notoriously unfaithful to her husband, company stage manager Louis Ell; darkly beautiful Kirah Markham, who carried on nearly simultaneous affairs with Floyd Dell and Theodore Dreiser before marrying Provincetown designer Lloyd Wright in 1916;[75] playwright Florence Kiper Frank, a University of Chicago graduate who challenged women playwrights to write about the "problems of feminism";[76] playwright and poet Mary Carolyn Davies, a lanky Oregonian who had attended the University of California, wrote poems expressing "girl consciousness," and edited the modernist little magazine *Quill;* Alice Woods Ullman, a well-known illustrator and novelist; Bosworth Crocker, a playwright married to critic Ludwig Lewisohn; and Sophie Treadwell, a graduate of the University of California who became the first American woman war correspondent (later, the author of *Machinal*). Other Provincetown Heterodites include Kenton's sister, Mabel Reber, married to Provincetown stage manager and carpenter Neil Reber; Edith ("Daisy") Haynes Thompson, who owned a Village furniture shop; professional actors Helen Westley and Margaret Wycherly; and Grace Potter, a suffragist and psychoanalyst who had studied with Jung and Rank.[77]

The Provincetown Players not only coexisted with this cultural revolution, they helped create it. For the women in the community, however, who matched their male counterparts in educational and professional achievement but were yet socially unequal, the need for a new world was especially urgent. As Louis Sheaffer has noted, the revolution "promised most to and demanded most from women."[78] The restlessness of women was at this time fundamentally optimistic, for they lived in a time when social, psychological, and political theorists were providing a steadily increasing theoretical basis for the continuing advancement of their sex. The Provincetown women, most born between 1875 and 1895, were the first generation of American women to reap the benefits of greater educational and professional opportunities. For the most part, they were expatriates from a privileged economic class (Rauh was one of the few who did not earn a living), far to the left of the "progressive" political continuum and overwhelmingly committed to feminism. Almost without exception, they were well-educated, independent professionals working as writers, painters, poets, doctors, journalists, actors, and restaurant and shop owners. They were extraordinary women, widely talented, rich in experience, and intellectually, artistically, and personally adventurous.

Educational and professional achievement had political implications: with every law or medical degree or journalistic byline earned, with every poem published or portrait painted, women supported Gilman's assertion that "woman's place was everywhere." But personal choices had political implications as well. The right to control one's sexual

Kirah Markham. Courtesy Billy Rose Theatre Collection, New York Public Library for the Performing Arts, Astor, Lenox and Tilden Foundations.

Mabel Reber. Courtesy Schlesinger Library, Radcliffe Institute, Harvard University.

Edith Haynes ("Daisy") Thompson.
Courtesy Schlesinger Library, Radcliffe
Institute, Harvard University.

Helen Westley, photograph by
Nickolas Muray. Courtesy
Papers of Djuna Barnes, Special
Collections, University of
Maryland Libraries and Mimi
Muray Levitt.

Grace Potter. Courtesy Schlesinger
Library, Radcliffe Institute, Harvard
University.

life, the right to sexual pleasure, the right to choose or reject marriage, motherhood, or heterosexuality—these were, as indeed they still are, political freedoms that have been politically and/or legally mandated. The sexual double standard was part of an unjust social system that feminists were determined to abolish. Revolutionizing relations between men and women and women and children was an extremely important aspect of self-transformation, of "sinking the old slave" and becoming "new creatures." This project of self-transformation, of self-creation, was fundamental, radical, and affected every aspect of their existence.

Provincetown's women began their experiments in new human relationships by challenging the old. Having joined men in work, they attempted to join them in play. They asserted sexual equality by resisting, delaying, or attempting to restructure marriage and by engaging in free-love unions. As diligently as they set out to remake marriage, Provincetown's women were struggling to reform maternity by experimenting with various parenting strategies. The new world these women desired was to be an egalitarian utopia where absolute personal freedom led to absolutely unfettered artistic expression. It is, perhaps, in the attempts by these women to readjust their personal relationships—as lovers, wives, mothers—that their political objectives are most clearly manifested. The women of Provincetown were pursuing a formidable objective: to revolutionize all human relationships—to create a new world. Their every aspiration, including their desire to create an experimental theatre company, can best be understood as part of that objective. The heterosocial collective they helped found would become a proving ground for the new egalitarian society Provincetown's women wished to create along feminist ideals. Their stage would become a platform for feminist issues and an arena in which women and men enacted personal conflicts with wide-ranging social implications.

# Managing Women

I did my best, Susan, and I had the time of my life.
—Edna Kenton, letter to Susan Glaspell

Even so eccentric an organization as the Provincetown Players had to deal with the usual administrative concerns: establishing aesthetic, administrative, and financial policies, selecting plays and making up season bills, acquiring artistic and support personnel, developing an audience, fund-raising, bookkeeping, and publicizing. For the Provincetown Players, given the experimental nature of the association and its gifted, temperamental, and inexperienced membership, performing such tasks was a formidable challenge. And yet they met that challenge with remarkable success. The Provincetown Players survived for eight seasons, establishing and maintaining one of the most devoted subscription audiences in the history of American theatre. Relying almost exclusively on audience support, they stayed afloat financially, at the same time remaining remarkably faithful to their artistic goals. The artistic contributions for which the company is noted occurred within this organizational context, and a number of women were instrumental in creating and maintaining the company's artistic goals and administrative policies. Throughout the history of the Provincetown Players, in fact, many of these essential responsibilities rested primarily in the hands of women. From the initial conceptual meetings, which culminated in the creation of the company and the articulation of its artistic vision, to the final determination of the time and manner of its dissolution, women were consistently and significantly involved.

Although Provincetown's ideals of communal creation and artistic experimentation are generally most closely associated with Jig Cook's personal vision of a "beloved community of life-givers,"[1] several women in the group were instrumental in creating that community: Neith Boyce, Ida Rauh, Susan Glaspell, and especially Mary Heaton Vorse: "The spirit of the community . . . was due in no small measure to Mary Heaton Vorse and the tradition already established in her own rambling, endless, wonderful house, in which everyone of the group as a newcomer had been housed while househunting, and in which anyone in need of it could go and live. . . . Mary was one of those people who *lived* what she wrote and advocated, was at home with everyone, and made everyone at home."[2] Mary Heaton Vorse, however, recognized Glaspell's visionary role in the theatre's conception: "A great deal of emphasis has always been put, and rightly, on George Cram Cook as the moving power which gave the impetus to the group and which made 'the Provincetown' the remarkable theatre it was. Not enough has been said about Susan Glaspell and her quality of enthusiasm when a new idea absorbed her."[3] Glaspell, in turn, remembered Ida Rauh as one of the first to initiate "exciting talk of starting a theatre."[4] Neith Boyce was also an instigator: "I have been stirring up the people here to write plays."[5] It was Boyce, along with Jig Cook, who formulated the group's first policy statement: "One man cannot produce drama. True drama is born only of one feeling animating all the members of a clan, a spirit shared by all and expressed by the few for the all." According to Glaspell, "[Jig] and Neith Boyce said it together. He came home and wrote it down."[6]

Having articulated their vision, the Players next outlined the methods by which they would realize this vision. According to their constitution, written mostly by John Reed and adopted by the active membership on 5 September 1916, the Provincetown Players' primary objective was to encourage American playwrights by producing "American plays of real artistic literary and dramatic—as opposed to Broadway—merit." Administration, as well as artistic creation, was to be essentially collective. Active members, those "engaged in the production of plays," would, "as a body," select plays to be produced and determine important questions of policy. Deviating from a purely nonhierarchical structure, the members elected two salaried officers, a president, Cook, and a secretary-treasurer, Margaret Nordfeldt. These two officers, who were expected to devote full-time energies to the "club," along with three other elected officials, made up the executive committee, whose rather vaguely defined responsibilities were to "conduct the business of the club" and to submit questions to the active membership. The first members of this committee were Cook, Nordfeldt, Reed, Bryant, and Dell.[7]

The Provincetown Players' loyalty to collective egalitarianism began to wane as soon as the group moved to New York. Despite opposition from the idealists in the group, most notably Hutchins Hapgood, who perceived "death in organization," the group's more pragmatic members advocated change.[8] Chief among those who supported a shift toward hierarchy were two women: Ida Rauh, who volunteered to serve on a committee to solicit producers (i.e., directors) to work with the Players,[9] and Edna Kenton: "casualties were fewer and mayhem rarer among five autocrats than twenty democrats."[10] The pragmatists prevailed. During the first New York season, a number of committees were formed to concentrate power in the hands of fewer individuals. Throughout the fall of 1916, the company established a producing committee, a script revision committee, a bill-planning committee, a scenic committee, and a playreading committee. Women served on all these committees: Rauh and Sophie Treadwell on the producing committee, later chaired by company director Nina Moise; Marguerite Zorach, Alice Hall, and Margaret Swain on the scenic committee; Vorse, Glaspell, Boyce, and Kenton on the revision committee; and Bryant and Nordfeldt on the committee to devise season bills.[11]

Eventually, even these committees dissolved; no committee other than the executive committee is mentioned after the second season. Nor are there records of active membership meetings after April 1918, a circumstance that led Provincetown historian William Vilhauer to conclude that "much of the business organization and practically all participation of the active members in reaching decisions regarding the operation of the Provincetown ceased to exist."[12] As the active membership's role in decision making diminished, that of the executive committee grew. By at least 1918, the Provincetown Players was operating under a more or less traditional structure, with Jig Cook in a position roughly analogous to a contemporary artistic director and the executive committee roughly analogous to a contemporary board of directors. Power struggles between the executive committee and the remaining membership, as well as among the executive committee members themselves, began as early as the fall of 1916 and continued throughout the company's history. Membership in the executive committee changed throughout the company's existence, but it remained fairly evenly divided by gender.[13] In all, nineteen different individuals served the company as executive committee members. Seven were women. As executive committee members, these women wielded considerable influence, beginning with Nordfeldt and Bryant, elected in the fall of 1916. Nordfeldt had first participated with the Players as an actor, creating the roles of Mabel in *Suppressed Desires* (July 1915), Sally in *Joined Together* (December 1916), and Adora in *Sauce for the Emperor* (December 1916). But the Players presumably recognized, and needed, Nordfeldt's executive abilities. According to Brör Nordfeldt's biographer, it was Margaret Nordfeldt who handled tough negotiations with art dealers;[14] according to Edna Kenton, she did the same for the Provincetown Players: "We had a comfortable balance in our bank, thanks and thanks only to Margaret Nordfeldt's increasing watchfulness over all expenditures, however minor. What this meant to us we were still to learn, for after that first year she left us, and we never again found her equal."[15]

Nordfeldt's "competent grasp of affairs," however, conflicted with Cook's "rapt idealism," and she aroused his resentment by insisting that all receipts and expenditures pass through her hands.[16] Tension between Nordfeldt and Cook escalated when her husband openly challenged the preeminence of Cook and Rauh. Thus, when the Players demanded Brör Nordfeldt's resignation in March 1917, Margaret Nordfeldt resigned as well.[17] Among her strongest supporters were Edna Kenton, who regarded her resignation as "our first great misfortune,"[18] and Nina Moise, who later referred to the forced resignations of the Nordfeldts as "the massacre."[19] The Nordfeldts moved to Santa Fe, where Margaret later worked with the Santa Fe Players, organized by Ida Rauh in 1926. Nordfeldt returned to New York in the 1930s, where she practiced psychoanalysis until her death in 1968.

The indomitable Louise Bryant also seems a likely choice for leadership. Considering her newcomer status, Bryant's prominence during the summer and fall of 1916 is remarkable. In addition to including her in the first executive committee, the Players produced Bryant's play, *The Game,* three times in their first season and cast her in two leading roles.[20] Bryant's relationships with both Reed and O'Neill may partially explain her influence, but her own character and abilities must not be discounted. Bryant, who had previous amateur experience as a designer and actor, embraced the theatrical experimentation at Provincetown. Bryant impressed artist George Biddle as a commanding performer:

"Louise was a good deal like . . . La Passionar[i]a. Yes, she could take an audience by storm. It was her looks—her black hair, her high coloring, her white skin. And then, her emotion—she had a sense of her audience, and she could hold them."[21]

Never one to underestimate herself, Bryant claimed prominence within the group and clearly relished her responsibilities: "I was not only a director [leader], I was secretary, I acted, I put on plays, and I simply lived in the theatre or on the beach."[22] During the fall of 1916 Bryant was omnipresent at Macdougal Street, reading plays, attending casting sessions and rehearsals, and prompting performances.[23] Both Cook's request that Bryant support a candidate for membership and Alfred Kreymborg's assertion that his first play "was put on thanks to you two [Bryant and Reed]" confirm Bryant's early influence within the company.[24]

Like Nordfeldt, Bryant inspired resentment, and her influence diminished. In November 1916 she complained to Reed that "they have a play committee and we aren't in it."[25] Bryant, in turn, resented Rauh's influence: "We see lots of Ida and lots is too much."[26] Although both Bryant and Rauh were strong-willed women, competing for roles and general influence, other differences may have played a part in the conflict. Rauh was Jewish, and Bryant expressed anti-Semitic attitudes in letters to Reed, describing "a Jewish invasion" of Provincetown in June 1916[27] and once attributing Rauh's abrupt departure in the middle of a playreading to "true Jewish freshness."[28] Anti-Semitism may partially explain Bryant's differences with Emma Goldman, who famously remarked that Louise was not really a Communist, she only slept with one, and Stella Ballantine, who similarly maintained, in essence, that Bryant was not really a playwright, she only slept with one.[29] But resentment against Bryant, even when couched in political terms, seems fundamentally personal, and especially related to her sexuality/gender. Male Provincetowners have characterized her as a "bitch," a "nymphomaniac," and a "whore."[30] Max Eastman observed that she "was no housekeeper."[31] Vorse, like Goldman, questioned Bryant's political convictions: "Louise Bryant thinks the revolution is so everyone can have a fur coat."[32] In February 1917, Bryant, along with Reed, resigned from the company. They were succeeded on the executive committee by Edna Kenton and, ironically, by one whose influence Bryant most resented: Ida Rauh.

Rauh, who "lacked the yielding and surrounding instinct so notably possessed by water and other liquids,"[33] assumed power early on and encountered considerable hostility for doing so. As early as 1917, Brör Nordfeldt, for one, complained that "Jig and Ida were running things."[34] Like Bryant, Rauh was omnipresent at Macdougal Street, performing, directing, reading and selecting plays, and recruiting personnel. Two of Rauh's recruits, Eleanor Fitzgerald and Susan Jenkins, became important company members.[35] In the fall of 1919, when Cook took a leave of absence, Rauh, along with James Light, assumed Cook's responsibilities as director of the company.[36] Before the end of this season, however, Rauh left the Players to perform a role in the Theatre Guild's production of *Power of Darkness*. Although she performed in two Province-town productions during the spring of 1921, and her name remained on the list of executive committee members until September 1921, Rauh's presence at the theatre decreased sharply after December 1919.[37]

Rauh's absence may be partially explained by a general shift in influence that began during the watershed season of 1919–20. By 1919, many of the founding members had drifted away and newer, younger individuals had replaced them. Newer members James Light, Jasper Deeter, Charles Ellis, and Edna and Norma Millay differed markedly from older members like Cook, Rauh, Kenton, and Glaspell. A major source of contention between the two groups involved moving productions uptown and centered on motivations for the move. According to the older members, the new members' motives were tainted by material ambition.[38] In November 1919 Rauh was singled out for a particularly personal attack by Charles Ellis, who opposed her playing the female lead in O'Neill's *Diff'rent*. Apparently Susan Glaspell favored Rauh in the role, but Ellis, who was engaged to Norma Millay, promoted her sister, Edna: "Charlie Ellis let out at Ida. I've never heard anything like it . . . he had so much to say about her being too old—oh, he was horrid." Glaspell considered Ellis's attack "absurd . . . for while the girl is younger than Ida in the first act, she's older than Ida in the second." After conceding that Millay "will do well with it," Glaspell recorded, not surprisingly, that "Ida feels out of it, and unhappy."[39] Perhaps to end dissension, the company eventually cast Mary Blair, a friend and former classmate of Susan Jenkins's at Carnegie Institute, who, at twenty-five, was eighteen years younger than Rauh and three years younger than Millay. The character, Emma, is twenty in the first act and fifty in the

second. During the season of Rauh's relative inactivity, conflict accelerated between the two factions in the company, and in the midst of the
turmoil, as tension heightened and talk of reorganization surfaced,
Rauh officially ended her association with the Provincetown Players. On
10 September 1921 she voted by proxy to remove her name from the
executive committee.[40]

In addition to Rauh, two other leading women artists served on the
executive committee: Edna St. Vincent Millay and Susan Glaspell. Millay's tenure lasted from 1919 to 1921, Glaspell's from 1920 to 1922. There
is little evidence of specific executive action by Millay, but she maintained a significant degree of control over production of her plays, always staging them herself and casting herself or her sister in the leading
roles. Glaspell undoubtedly also used her executive powers to ensure
attention to her plays' productions. But she was also instrumental in
maintaining the company's noncommercial artistic goals and its exclusive commitment to American playwrights. She used her influence on
one occasion to stop director Jasper Deeter from violating the group's
ban on European drama: "A letter from Susan today shows me my presumption in the production of a non-native play for which I'm apolo-
gizing to each member of the executive committee. . . . the play was
immediately withdrawn and as there was further presumption in my
mind, the spring season has been ended."[41] Like Rauh and Millay, however, Glaspell was probably primarily occupied with her artistic contributions. In fact, throughout the history of the Provincetown Players,
only two members devoted themselves exclusively to "conducting the
business of the club": Edna Kenton and Eleanor Fitzgerald.

Kenton arrived in Provincetown, at Cook's invitation, in the summer
of 1916 and became an active member of the company on October 5. In
February 1917 she became a member of the executive committee, a tenure that lasted until the company ceased production in 1922.[42] Kenton,
who distrusted the group's original ideal of collective creation, whether
referring to artistic or business operations, became one of the strongest
promoters of hierarchy. In her history, Kenton made several references
to "idealism" versus "efficiency" or "competence"[43] in policy making, at
one point commenting wryly that "there is something to be said for the
'one-man' instead of the 'group' idea in drawing up a circular."[44] Kenton
also welcomed strong and individual stage direction: "We lacked leisure

in which the synthetic process might work out. What we needed was a tyrant—velvet gloved, if possible."[45]

Lacking specific theatrical experience, Kenton carved out a niche suitable to her literary talents, eventually developing skills that allowed her to pioneer the theatrical practice of literary management. She opposed the company's initial plan for democratic play selection as inefficient and favored transferring that critical responsibility to a select group. To some this change violated the company's collectivist principles, but Kenton reported flatly that "reading the plays aloud was impossible. After a final plea from Hutch Hapgood for democracy, efficiency triumphed."[46] A small committee that included Kenton and Glaspell assumed responsibility for reading plays, and eventually reading and selecting plays became a paid position for Kenton.[47] Although precise records do not exist, the Players were apparently overwhelmed with dramatic submissions.[48] Despite the volume, Kenton claimed that she and Glaspell read every play submitted.[49] Glaspell supported this claim by referring to "the nights Edna has sat over there reading plays no one else would read, and this in years when it wasn't a job for her."[50] Kenton was willing to do the work because she wanted to influence decisions. As one who sorted "possible" plays from "musts,"[51] she "lent a powerful guiding hand in the selection of plays."[52] Although few documents describe her approval or rejection of specific plays, evidence does show that Kenton, like Glaspell, consistently opposed the production of plays by European authors. Only twice in the history of Provincetown were there such productions, and both were instigated by men in the company.[53] Kenton was also an adamant champion of the company's noncommercial and experimental status, the only executive committee member who voted against moving *The Emperor Jones* to Broadway in 1920. For Kenton, the commercial success of *The Emperor Jones,* which set a new standard for Provincetown productions, was the "beginning of the end."[54] Cook and Glaspell confirmed Kenton's faithfulness to Provincetown's noncommercial status: "She, more than any other, had the purity of idea, the integrity. Hers was at times the only voice against alien gods."[55]

Kenton, who clearly developed a strong personal commitment to the Provincetown Players, took an active role in publicizing their achievements, thereby significantly contributing to publicity and audience development. Throughout its history, the Provincetown Players developed its audience by distributing seasonal circulars and publishing articles in newspapers and magazines. The circulars generally reiterated the group's aesthetic policies, described their proposed production calendar, and invited audience subscriptions. The first circular was more or less a group effort,[56] but the Players appointed Kenton and Lucian Cary to draft the announcement for their second season.[57] In April 1918, Kenton wrote a lengthy article for the *Boston Transcript* that provided the most complete and up-to-date record of the group's activities.[58] Like play-reading, publicity ultimately became a paid position for Kenton.[59]

The degree of Kenton's influence within the company shows most clearly through the events that unfolded during its last turbulent seasons. Kenton, who credited Cook and Glaspell with the success of the Provincetown Players, was disgusted by the rebellion smoldering among the newer members of the company, apparently fueled by O'Neill's increasing commercial success. Kenton urged Cook to return to New York and restore authority: "I do not believe that a 'row' is inevitable at all, if you come down. But bring Sue's proxy! . . . Nothing in all this matters to me but next year's policy and authority. . . . And let me say again that there need not be trouble over reorganization if we decide just not to have it."[60] Cook and Glaspell, however, seemed less willing than Kenton to continue the struggle. Divided and disillusioned, the Players announced an interim "rest" for the 1922–23 season. In February 1922, executive committee members Cook, Glaspell, Kenton, O'Neill, and Fitzgerald, along with company designer Cleon Throckmorton and attorney Harry Weinberger,[61] met and incorporated as the "Provincetown Players, Inc." Kenton explained that the motive for incorporation was "to hold the name and the idea of the Players" and that the motive for secrecy was to keep James Light out.[62] Cook and Glaspell sailed for Greece on 1 March 1922, giving Kenton their voting proxies.

The removal of Cook and Glaspell—and not just to Cape Cod, but halfway around the world—left a power vacuum in the Provincetown hierarchy that many tried to fill. According to Kenton, who has left a vivid, if one-sided, account of the events of the next two years in a flood of letters to Greece, James Light attempted to seize authority as soon as Cook and Glaspell sailed.[63] Kenton, however, was equally determined "to take Jig's place for the rest of the season."[64] Perhaps because Kenton had Cook's and Glaspell's proxies, perhaps because Light's sudden "leave of absence" in 1921 to chase Djuna Barnes had somewhat weakened his position, Kenton succeeded in thwarting Light's plans.[65] She later considered it one of her proudest achievements: "I kept James Light out and put the season through as planned before Jig sailed."[66]

Putting the season through as planned placed Kenton in conflict with several influential company members. Before Cook and Glaspell left for Greece, the company had planned to premiere Glaspell's *Chains of Dew* for the season's final bill. As soon as they were gone, however, Charles Ellis and James Light suggested *Taboo*, a new and exotic play by Mary Hoyt Wiborg.[67] When Kenton rejected this manuscript despite furious opposition from Light and Ellis, company designer Cleon Throckmorton and business manager Eleanor Fitzgerald suggested a revival of *The Emperor Jones*. Kenton squelched that plan as well: "I announced, without any counsel, to the public press, that *Chains of Dew* was going on. We were committed."[68]

Although subsequent events justified Kenton's dismissal of *Taboo*, which closed on Broadway after four performances, her high-handedness undoubtedly provoked resentment. Kenton, on the other hand, viewed those who flouted her, and through her Cook and Glaspell, as traitors. Kenton had always been heavily involved in several areas of operation, but now she expanded her sphere of influence, taking on duties that may have fallen to Cook or Glaspell as well as intruding on Fitzgerald's responsibilities. In addition to play selection and publicity, Kenton helped negotiate contracts and royalty agreements with agents, publishers, and producers, corresponded with Theodore Dreiser concerning rehearsals for his *Hand of the Potter*, and helped to cast and to engage a director for the production of *Chains of Dew*.[69] Kenton and Fitzgerald shared check-signing privileges,[70] and Kenton faithfully, sometimes ominously, informed Cook and Glaspell of all financial affairs, generally casting aspersions on Fitzgerald's abilities as she did so: "I leave it to Fitzie to write you about business . . . but in case she hasn't, the royalties on first week of the *Ape* were $500—second week the same—money in the bank is money wasted—according to Fitzie's philosophy, but we shall see what we shall see."[71]

In June 1922, Kenton announced to the public the company's plans for the interim, and she and Fitzgerald began to seek a suitable candidate to sublease the theatre. These negotiations became increasingly hostile and complicated as Kenton began to suspect a conspiracy, on the part of various "alien gods," to continue working *as the Provincetown Players* without Cook, Glaspell, or herself. When she and Fitzgerald finally agreed on commercial producer Alice Klauser, the problem was only postponed. Although Kenton had hoped for Cook and Glaspell's return and the continuation of the Provincetown Players in the fall of 1923, she considered their wishes paramount. When Cook and Glaspell cabled their desire for termination of the lease and the company in June 1923, Kenton accepted the dissolution as final and devoted the rest of her time with the Players to ensuring the theatre's "good death."[72] Meanwhile, O'Neill had been negotiating with critic Kenneth Macgowan and Robert Edmond Jones to reorganize the Provincetown Players with "new blood and lots of it" and to abandon completely the Players' methods of operation.[73] Kenton thoroughly distrusted Macgowan, whom she labeled "a weak, weak sister," and did everything she could to delay the process of reorganization. After months of Machiavellian evasion—"[Macgowan] and I had a little talk—in which he did all of it"—Kenton capitulated.[74] In November 1923, Kenton, Fitzgerald, and Weinberger granted Macgowan power as director of the Playhouse for the 1923–24 season.

The theatre space was now in new hands, but not quite new enough. For Kenton, the "good death" of the Provincetown Players required the sharp distinction, in the minds of the public, between the two companies. Such a distinction must, most significantly, include a new name for the new group. Reserving the name "Provincetown Players" for the older group became a sacred mission for both Glaspell and Kenton, especially after Cook's death in January 1924. The zeal with which Kenton discharged this mission parallels Macgowan and O'Neill's growing resentment against her. O'Neill was willing to drop the use of "Provincetown Players"—"in spirit and intention we had nothing in common with [the old corporation or the old name]"—but insisted on retaining "Provincetown Playhouse" as the name of the theatre building: "I don't see where sentiment can enter where the name of a building is concerned." O'Neill blamed Kenton for the friction: "if you had been willing last fall to be generous and turn over the theatre without strings to it to the new organization . . . there would have been no need for [the conflict]."[75] During the meeting at which the name "Experimental Theatre, Inc." was finally chosen, Macgowan accused Kenton of being "a thorn in his side" and objected to giving her a share in the common stock of the new corporation.[76]

Despite Kenton's assurance that she enjoyed the confrontation, and the months leading up to it—"I did my best, Susan, and I had the time of my life"[77]—the events of this meeting sparked an angry letter from Glaspell to Fitzgerald in defense of Kenton:

> I think Edna was treated abominably. Even if I hadn't had it in mind to resign, I should certainly have done it on this. I herewith do so. . . . [O]f all the people who worked for the Provincetown Players none ever worked more disinterestedly, more faithfully, nor to my mind to better purpose. . . . And she, in the last hour when Provincetown Players were Provincetown Players, is insulted like that.
>
> Fitzie, and all of you, for this letter is for all of you, from very deep down, I am through.[78]

The Provincetown Players had officially ceased to exist, but Edna Kenton had one more important task to perform. She resolved to write and publish a history of Provincetown Players in which its unique character, distinct from that of the Experimental Theatre, would be made clear. Although she published an article on the company's history in 1922,[79] she was unable to find a publisher for her book-length work, completed sometime around 1930. Instead, in 1931, Helen Deutsch and Stella Hanau, press agents for the Experimental Theatre, published their own history, an account that treated the Experimental Theatre as a continuation of the Provincetown Players.[80] Uncooperative to the last, Kenton refused requests from the authors for missing records, insisting, quite courteously, that hers were in storage and inaccessible.[81] Although Kenton was never again affiliated with a theatre company, she remained on intimate terms with her Provincetown associates. When the bankruptcy of her publisher in 1933 placed Kenton in serious financial difficulty, several Provincetown women, including Glaspell, Rauh, Lucy Huffaker, Grace Potter, Helen Westley, and Margaret Wycherly, rallied to her aid with an "Edna Kenton Fund."[82] Kenton published a number of books before her death in 1954, including a biography of her ancestor Simon Kenton and a critical edition of short fiction by Henry James.

Like Kenton, Mary Eleanor Fitzgerald ("Fitzie" to her colleagues) lacked any specific theatrical experience, using skills acquired in other pursuits to create not just a position with the Provincetown Players but a career in theatrical management that lasted for more than two decades, making her a pioneer, as a woman, in that field.[83] Through her work for political prisoners, Fitzgerald met Ida Rauh, who invited her to join the Provincetown Players.[84] The appearance, in the fall of 1918, of someone sympathetic to radical art and politics, with fund-raising and organizational skills, was a godsend. The Players had lacked such a person since Margaret Nordfeldt's resignation in March 1917. Fitzgerald accepted a part-time paid position, taking over the bookkeeping, records, the box office, and a "few other odds and ends."[85] Given her background, it is not surprising that Provincetown's mixture of art and anarchy appealed to Fitzgerald. As she later explained: "Then I went with the Provincetown Players full time, feeling that perhaps on a smaller stage (I had been reaching out for the whole wide world)—a few could be made conscious of decency, justice, and truth."[86] Goldman also saw a connection between Fitzgerald's radical politics and her theatrical career: "She attached herself to the theater not merely as a means of livelihood, but because she hoped she could continue advanced ideas by means of the drama and that she could make her life count for something, for something that would fill the gap your loss [Berkman's deportation] had created in her soul."[87]

During the fall of 1918, Fitzgerald divided her time between the Playhouse and the political prisoners' office. In 1919, after Berkman and Goldman were deported, she accepted a full-time position. Although her official title was secretary-treasurer, Fitzgerald was, according to Deutsch and Hanau, "really business manager, financier, general factotum and everybody's confidante."[88] Her duties included fund-raising, financing, bookkeeping, answering telephones, selling tickets, negotiating contracts, hiring support personnel, and supervising equipment installation. So extensive were Fitzgerald's responsibilities that by 1921 she had two assistants: Susan Jenkins, also recruited by Rauh in 1918, and Pauline Turkel, another member of the *Mother Earth* family. Turkel and Jenkins, both unpaid, seem to have operated out of a sense of loyalty to Fitzgerald.[89]

Friends and colleagues confirmed Fitzgerald's particular success at fund-raising: "she was wonderful at raising money since no one to whom she appealed could doubt her good sense or her competence";[90]

"Fitzie made people feel it was a privilege to help the Provincetown Players."[91] Just after her arrival in 1918, Fitzgerald, along with Cook, raised $1,000 in small sums (meeting a challenge for matching funds from philanthropist A. C. Barnes) to finance the remodeling at 133 Macdougal.[92] In 1920, Fitzgerald conducted a fund drive among subscribers to pay a $5,000 tax bill.

As an executive committee member, Fitzgerald helped make crucial decisions regarding productions. She strongly supported the production of Glaspell's *Inheritors* in 1921, over the objections of James Light and Charles Ellis, who feared its radical politics.[93] One of Fitzgerald's wiser decisions, although perhaps detrimental to her relationship with Cook and Glaspell, was her opposition to investing company funds in an uptown production of Cook's *The Spring*. Cook used his own money to finance the production, which opened on 21 September 1921. According to Kenton, it ran only four nights.[94]

In addition to her multiple official functions, Fitzgerald contributed immeasurably to the esprit de corps of the company. As Nilla Cook recalled: "[Fitzgerald] saw everyone's side with equal sympathy. . . . [She possessed] a delicate courtesy, a warm appreciation of the other person—without which I doubt if a single season of the Provincetown Players could have lasted!!! Her sense of humour, her unexcitable ways, her ability to see through problems people created for themselves were a mainstay of the New York Provincetown Players community."[95] Contemporaries generally employed maternal metaphors to describe Fitzgerald's relationship with the company. Deutsch and Hanau reported that Fitzgerald "seemed miraculously to be everywhere—in the box office, on Macdougal Street with *The Spring*, at the Princess with *The Emperor Jones*, at the Selwyn with *Diff'rent*, busy, smiling, capable. Many remember that energetic figure, in tan covert, usually, with a little brown leather hat, mothering her three casts. . . . She was everywhere, active and endlessly interested . . . the Provincetown was Fitzi's foster child."[96] For Djuna Barnes, Fitzgerald was "an eternal Eliza crossing the ice, and by main strength and gift of a pioneer right arm, has so far kept the baby [the company] from drowning."[97] O'Neill told her "all his troubles,"[98] and James Light attributed Cook's cooling toward Fitzgerald to her widespread nurturing: "Jig got sore because [Fitzgerald] wanted to take care of everybody, not just him."[99] In 1922, Cook blamed "motherhood" (along with commercialism) as one of the causes of the theatre's demise, and bitterly recommended to Kenton that she "get Fitzie a job in an orphan asylum."[100]

By 1921 the conflicting factions within the company had emerged, and Fitzgerald's allegiance was in question. As late as August of that year, Kenton apparently still hoped for Fitzgerald's support, reporting to Cook with satisfaction that "Fitzie is outraged by several with whom she sympathized. . . . Teddy [Ballantine] and Charlie [Ellis] will knife each other. . . . Fitzie is furious at them." Kenton even suggested that Cook and Glaspell go to London with the *Emperor Jones/Suppressed Desires* tour, assuring him that "Fitzie and I are in agreement."[101] Relations between the two women deteriorated, however, during the last, most contentious season of 1921–22. By this time Kenton was overtly hostile to the rebellious element, and she found Fitzgerald's failure to take sides against them unforgivable. During the spring and summer of 1922, Kenton bombarded Cook and Glaspell with allegations of Fitzgerald's disloyalty and incompetence: "Fitzie has been a great mistake. She was the business manager and she hasn't the first qualification for the job. . . . [H]er whole spirit is that of pleasing all—at the end of four years, she is almost worse with the bloodless revolutionists than the older generation."[102]

To Kenton, Fitzgerald's willingness to remain at the theatre during the interim no matter who rented it was the worst kind of betrayal. When, in fact, Fitzgerald did stay on, helping the new company with business and publicity and referring to "the Provincetown spirit" in their promotional letter, Kenton was outraged, and Fitzgerald was mystified and hurt by her reaction: "Why should the Provincetown Players not want to give this new group a bit of mutual sympathy?"[103] Cook's resentment toward Fitzgerald's indiscriminate sympathy, viewed by others as a positive trait, provoked a drunken telegram—"Fitzie is a goddamn Irish beauty liar"—and a somewhat more coherent letter of rebuke: "In any creative purpose, not to discriminate—between those who have and have not the gift, is deadly. . . . You subconsciously accepted the superiority to us of financially successful Broadway producers. When the tear—the rip—came, you were on the wrong side."[104]

Fitzgerald's universal benevolence is surely exaggerated; she did have a temper, and referred to some of the Provincetown group sardonically as "half-geniuses."[105] She resented and defended herself against Kenton's accusations: "I carried the burden of financing and seeing through that last season of 1921–22. . . . I saw that *The Hairy Ape* was carried through. Edna and I [saw that] *The Chains of Dew* [was carried through], and I stayed on the job seeing that the bills amounting to about $4500 or more were all paid and the slate clean so far as debts against the organization of the Provincetown Players was concerned."[106] She did not, however, share or understand the tensions between Kenton and Glaspell and the group that became the Experimental Theatre. Emma Goldman reported to Berkman that the controversy accompanying both the dissolution of the Provincetown Players and the organization of the Experimental Theatre drained Fitzgerald: "The theater gave her little else but responsibility, worry, everybody's trouble. She spent her time and substance in separating feuds, in explaining everybody's pettiness and jealousies. Until finally she became a nervous wreck."[107] Whatever distress Fitzgerald suffered because of her professional and personal ties at Provincetown, however, she maintained her position as business manager, eventually executive director, of the Experimental Theatre until 1929.[108] During these years the Experimental Theatre became a fully professional, union-affiliated organization, eventually expanding into the Garrick Theatre with a fund of $75,000. Fitzgerald, who saw "no antagonism between our kind of theatre and the commercial theatre," claimed that she consistently promoted artistic experimentation and encouraged new talent.[109] Throughout her tenure she stressed the continuity of purpose and achievement at the Playhouse, infuriating Glaspell in the spring of 1929 by inviting her to contribute "a few lines" to a promotional brochure celebrating the company's "fourteen year existence."[110] With or without Glaspell's endorsement, Fitzgerald refused to relinquish her heritage as a Provincetown Player or her belief in the consistency of her Provincetown career: "If I needed any proof of the truth and vitality of what I must call the Provincetown idea, I would find it in the fact that my belief in this kind of theatre, the theatre of opportunity for new talent, is as strong today [in 1929], after the curtain has dropped for the last time, as it was when I first joined the group. This was in November 1918."[111]

Ironically, Fitzgerald was just as upset about the Deutsch and Hanau book as Kenton was, but for different reasons. Although Fitzgerald agreed that the Experimental Theatre was a continuation of the Provincetown Players, she found the work "superficial" and the authors' portrayal of her patronizing: "They make me appear sentimental and muddled. Lord save us from our friends who think they know us."[112] Unlike Kenton, Fitzgerald had generously loaned the authors her Provincetown files, which she regretted.[113] Fitzgerald continued her career in theatre management through the 1940s, working for Broadway producer Robert Rockmore, the Theatre Union, the Federal Theatre Project, the Group Theatre, and the New School for Social Research.

Provincetown's original ideal of communal decision making was remarkably short-lived; throughout most of the company's existence, in fact, important decisions regarding play selection, casting, and other artistic and financial policies were determined by a small but powerful insider group. The individual makeup of that group shifted somewhat from season to season, but it always included at least a few influential women. A few of these, notably Glaspell and Millay, probably owe their influential positions to their artistic talent as playwrights and used that influence primarily to realize artistic goals. Others, like Kenton, Rauh, and Bryant, achieved influence primarily through force of personality and seemed interested in wielding influence across all areas of operation. Rauh was most likely also interested in retaining executive power to realize her own artistic goals.

The exercise of power within a community inspired by utopian ideals of collective creation is bound to be problematic. To some extent, the opposition faced by Provincetown's women executives came from philosophical anarchism, of both men and women, that opposed any authority whatsoever. Influential men, like Cook, also inspired resentment. But the exercise of authority by women is especially complicated by sexist assumptions because the traditional concepts of woman and power are anomalous. Given the unease that typically accompanies women and power, that these women experienced frustration and dissension is not surprising. Even for the Provincetown Players, a revolutionary subculture committed to undermining conventional values, making decisions and exercising authority—especially in heterosocial organizations— were new roles for women. At Provincetown, women were at least given the opportunity to rehearse these new roles. Considering the various ways in which Provincetown's women sought and maintained influence provides somewhat surprising insights into the historically conflicted relationship between women and power.

First, most were willing and able, even eager, to exercise authority. Kenton, Rauh, Bryant, and Nordfeldt welcomed responsibility. Although latter-day feminists tend to equate hierarchy with patriarchy and to associate collectivism with feminism, several of Provincetown's most influential women, all feminists, promoted hierarchy, making sure that they occupied influential positions within that hierarchy. Perhaps Kenton, Rauh, and others had already begun to learn what radical feminists in the 1960s had to learn all over again:

> He's the head of the SDS
> He believes in Liberation
> Unless you wear a dress.
> I make love
> And I make coffee
> But I can't make policy.
> Who's the garbage can
> Of the radical man?
> It's me.[114]

That is, in a "powerless" organizational structure that includes men and women, even in the most radical of communities, men are the default leadership. If conscious effort is not made to ensure authority, women "naturally" fall into subsidiary roles.

Most of these women encountered hostility; four of them aroused such a degree of hostility that they were actually squeezed out of the company or, in Kenton's case, denied membership in the new company formed by some of Provincetown's most important members. Anarchist aversion to sovereignty notwithstanding, sexism is almost certainly a factor in some of the problems these women faced. Certainly there was sexism, as well as irony, in male company members' calling Louise Bryant a whore or insisting that Rauh, at forty-three, was too old to play a character who is, for half the play, seven years older. But women also encountered hostility from each other.

Clearly the most serious conflict between women was that between Kenton and Fitzgerald, which developed into conflict between Fitzgerald and Glaspell. The most striking contrast between women's approaches to power lay in the markedly different managerial styles displayed by the two most influential executives: Kenton and Fitzgerald. Kenton relished power, enjoying even the conflicts. She was perceived by her allies as constant ("the only voice against alien gods"), by her adversaries as contentious ("a thorn in the side"). Fitzgerald, on the other hand, achieved her influential position through conventionally "feminine" behavior: nurturing. Influenced, perhaps, by anarchist philosophy as well as conventional gender expectations, Fitzgerald was reluctant to exert authority, and confrontations that stimulated Kenton confused and dismayed Fitzgerald. Of Provincetown's seven women executives, only Fitzgerald, who displayed the most traditionally feminine characteristics, who nurtured and "mothered" the company, had a lasting career in the theatre. Fitzgerald's role in both organizations deserves closer scrutiny—Kenton was hardly an impartial witness, and Fitzgerald herself felt misrepresented by Deutsch and Hanau. O'Neill and Macgowan, of course, were absolutely right to blame Kenton for the difficult transition (Kenton, who was fond of scientific metaphors, might have called it a "mutation") from Provincetown Players to Experimental Theatre. She had never wanted this group—too close in some ways, and too distant in others—to take over at 133 Macdougal. O'Neill was wrong, however, in assuming that the name of a building could hold no importance. For Kenton, but perhaps especially for Glaspell, "Provincetown" represented something very special indeed, a vision she had helped articulate to express a spiritual and geographic community she had helped create. For Fitzgerald, the "Provincetown idea" was applicable to any theatre that provided opportunities for artistic experimentation, and she refused to be excommunicated. Fitzgerald's persistence in self-identification as a Provincetown Player and Kenton's and Glaspell's equally persistent efforts to deny such identification are, for each of them, proof of a strong, personal commitment to the ideological and spiritual community that was the Provincetown Players.

Differences between and among the women dispel the romantic illusion of universal sisterhood even in so homogeneous a group as this. The possibility that racial prejudice poisoned relations between Bryant and Rauh, or Bryant and Ballantine, reminds us of the divisions among women that still plague efforts to unite in common cause. Despite their differences and the difficulties they encountered, Provincetown's women executives were instrumental in establishing and maintaining the artistic and administrative policies of this company, policies and practices that would provide extraordinary opportunities for women artists.

# 3

## *Writing Women*

Miss Glaspell has left the conventions of the stage behind—she has chosen a woman instead of a man to incarnate the restless audacious, creative spirit.

—Maida Castellun, review of *The Verge*

Among the fifty-one playwrights produced by the Provincetown Players were sixteen women who together wrote or cowrote thirty-five plays, over a third of the total number produced.[1] To demonstrate just how unusual the Provincetown Players were in welcoming women playwrights, consider the prevailing circumstances elsewhere. Only 17 of 135 plays produced on Broadway during the 1915–16 season were by women—a modest 12.5 percent of the total number produced.[2] But Broadway has always been notoriously inhospitable to women, and it might be generally assumed that women playwrights found little theatres more receptive. Published repertories from 1917, however, prove otherwise. Although many little theatres were founded and directed by women, they produced very few women dramatists. For example, only three of the Toy Theatre's forty productions and two of the Little Theatre of Philadelphia's forty-eight productions were by women. Of fifteen plays listed, the Vagabond Players of Baltimore produced only one play by a woman.[3] The Neighborhood Playhouse, whose artistic staff was entirely female, had a somewhat higher percentage, producing five plays by women of twenty-two plays listed.[4]

The rate of participation by women writers at Provincetown, however, is not consistent throughout the group's existence, but drops sharply in the company's final season from an average participation rate above 40 percent (from 1915 to 1920) to 25 percent (1921–22). Only two plays by women were produced in the Players' final season, both by Glaspell. The impressive overall degree of participation by women playwrights at Provincetown has been noted, as well as their puzzling disappearance by the last season.[5] A close investigation into the causes for either phenomenon, however, has not been attempted. Why was this company so welcoming to women writers? How and why did that welcome wear out?

The unusual opportunities for women writers at Provincetown stemmed in part from the group's decision to produce new plays by American authors only. Although the Players never formally expressed a desire to encourage *women* dramatists specifically, their ban on European drama increased the likelihood of a sexually integrated repertory because the European dramatists who formed the repertories of little theatres across the country were overwhelmingly male.[6] To what degree the female, as distinct from the male, founders of Provincetown influenced the group's all-American policy is unknown. As we have seen, however, a number of women were instrumental in formulating the group's artistic policies, and at least two of them, Boyce and Glaspell, had each completed a play by 1915. In fact, the rejection by the Washington Square Players of both these plays, *Constancy* and *Suppressed Desires,* helped precipitate the creation of the Provincetown Players.[7] We have also seen that the company's faithfulness to American playwrights throughout its history owed much to the intervention of women, particularly Glaspell and Edna Kenton.

Provincetown's method of play selection, which went through three developmental stages, was another probable factor in women's participation. Initially, the choice of plays was determined by a majority vote of a quorum of the active membership. Plays were read aloud—by their authors or any other active member—at membership meetings, discussed by the group, and then voted on. That roughly half of Provincetown's members were women and that a considerable number were feminists may explain why so many plays by women were accepted for production early on. When playreading and play selection fell largely into the hands of a committee, that committee was dominated by women. Because the women most closely involved in play selection (Rauh, Glaspell, and especially Kenton) were not just women but feminists, they had even stronger motivations for increasing opportunities for women. One might also expect these women to be especially welcoming to plays that treated issues they found personally compelling— that is, feminist issues.

Not only was there an unusually large number of plays by women in the Provincetown repertory, but there was also an unusually large number of plays that may be labeled feminist. Judith Barlow's recent survey of women's drama at Provincetown identifies the most universally shared feature as the presence of female protagonists.[8] Barlow has described these writers' perspectives as "particularly female (if not always feminist)."[9] The unmistakably critical attitude toward marriage, maternity, sexual stereotyping, and conventional gender roles found in the majority of the plays, however, suggests that feminist perspectives prevailed. Even by contemporary standards, the defiance of traditional gender roles is impressive. The protagonist of Boyce's *Winter's Night* rejects a marriage offer from her late husband's brother in order to start a dressmaking business; her rejected suitor commits suicide. Evelyn Scott's female protagonist in *Love* similarly drives her bourgeois husband to suicide by initiating a taboo relationship with her stepson. The protagonist of this play, Carroll Lamont, is the first of a frequently recurring character in Scott's writing, a woman who "demands the right to express her sexuality on equal terms with men . . . who resents her dependence on men and rejects her socially defined roles."[10] The story calls to mind both Racine's *Phaedre* and Ibsen's *Hedda Gabler;* in Scott's version, however, it is the husband, not the wife, who commits suicide. The heroine of Glaspell's *The Verge,* Claire Archer, metaphorically engaged in creating a new plant species, is actually seeking a radically different way to be human, especially woman. Claire is openly contemptuous of her husband and her conventional daughter, and she ends up strangling the man she loves because she senses doom in his promise to "keep her safe." In Glaspell's *Trifles,* a farm woman has strangled her abusive husband. In Alice Rostetter's comic *The Widow's Veil,* a young Irish matron's dream of widowhood is thwarted by her husband's untimely recovery. Rita Wellman's *Funiculi-Funicula* depicts the tragic consequences of maternal obligations for a woman "who was never intended to be a mother." Boyce's *The Two Sons* treats family tensions between a mother and her sons. The story of this play (two brothers in love with one woman), the characterizations of the two brothers (one sensitive and idealistic, one rough and cynical), and their conflicting attitudes toward women anticipate O'Neill's in *Beyond the Horizon,* produced four years later.[11] All three of Barnes's plays challenge sexual stereotyping: *Three from the Earth* features an enigmatic encounter between a serenely self-assured woman and the three rather oafish young

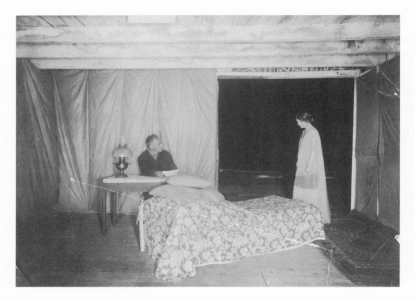

Neith Boyce and Hutchins Hapgood in their *Enemies.* The Wharf Theatre. Courtesy Yale Collection of American Literature, Beinecke Rare Book and Manuscript Library, Yale University.

*Left to right:* Clark Branyon, Susan Glaspell, Ida Rauh, Justus Sheffield, three unidentified women, and Norma Millay in Glaspell's *Woman's Honor.* 139 Macdougal Street. Courtesy Fales Library, Special Collections, New York University.

sons of her former lover; *An Irish Triangle* describes a peasant couple's unconventional domestic arrangement with the lord and lady of the manor; and *Kurzy of the Sea* portrays another cloddish Irish lad alternately tempted and taunted by a mer/barmaid.

Even in plays that offer the traditional embrace at curtain—Boyce and Hapgood's *Enemies* or Cook and Glaspell's *Suppressed Desires*—the reconciliation appears tenuous. Both these plays, cowritten by married partners, treat domestic conflict comically and end in an embrace. When women wrote independently of domestic conflict, the treatment was usually serious and the plays frequently concluded in death—the man's.[12] In lighter treatments of sexual conflicts by women, men are allowed to survive, but they are depicted as vacillating fools or oafs. Boyce's *Constancy*, Glaspell's *Bernice, Woman's Honor,* and *Chains of Dew,* and Barnes's *Three from the Earth* and *Kurzy of the Sea* all include such misophallic portrayals.

Women in these plays are heroic: a miner's wife spurns her husband for betraying his fellow workers in Mary Foster Barber's *The Squealer;* a young woman suffers imprisonment for actions on behalf of Indian (Hindu) revolutionaries in Glaspell's *Inheritors.* Women in these plays are loyal—to each other. The farm women suppress evidence that would convict their neighbor in *Trifles;* two reclusive women help each other to a reaffirmation of life in Glaspell's *The Outside;* a servant's lie saves her mistress from her fear of inherited insanity in Rita Creighton Smith's *The Rescue;* and the gift of a baby carriage from one immigrant woman to another is a poignant expression of women's shared dreams in Bosworth Crocker's *The Baby Carriage.*

If we consider, as many of the era's feminists did, peace as a prerequisite to women's equality, then Millay's poetic antiwar fable, *Aria da Capo,* and Rita Wellman's ironic treatment of anti-German hysteria, *Barbarians,* both qualify. Wellman's depiction of "three unprotected young women in a bombarded village, at once fearing and hoping for the worst," who find soldiers of the invading army "courteous, considerate [and] all but brotherly" subverts gender as well as ethnic stereotypes, and at least one writer has perceived a critique of heterosexual relations as latent discourse in Millay's antiwar fable.[13]

Clearly, plays by women at Provincetown overwhelmingly challenged conventional gender ideology. Like their creators, these female protagonists are rarely virtuous, nurturing, submissive, or self-sacrificing. They are women struggling to live exactly as they please, who put their per-

Norma Millay and Harrison Dowd in Edna St. Vincent Millay's *Aria da Capo* (rehearsal). 133 Macdougal Street. Courtesy Billy Rose Theatre Collection, New York Public Library for the Performing Arts, Astor, Lenox and Tilden Foundations.

sonal and professional needs ahead of those of their husbands and children, who dare to be selfish, perhaps the most gender-defying trait of all. Men, especially husbands, are *rarely* sympathetically portrayed; children are generally depicted as mistakes—when Seymore's mother gives a generous donation to the birth control cause in *Chains of Dew*, Glaspell targets husbands and children in one fell swoop. In only two plays by women do female characters make expressly self*less* choices: a woman sacrifices her chance for personal happiness to serve her family in Edna Ferber's *The Eldest*, and a woman sacrifices her life to save her husband's honor in Rita Wellman's *The String of the Samisen*. Wellman's play, based on an eighteenth-century Bushido legend, is romantic. Ferber's is bitter.

The inspiration for these plays lies firmly rooted in the personal lives of the playwrights as well as their Provincetown colleagues, and it is hardly surprising that such plays were welcomed. But Provincetown was committed to artistic as well as social revolution. Plays by women also reflected the company's aesthetic ideal of artistic experimentation.[14] Their plays frequently deviate from traditional structures, concentrating on mood or atmosphere, dialogue, and characterization rather than on linear and climactic action. Examples include Crocker's *The Baby Carriage,* Smith's *The Rescue,* Barnes's *Three from the Earth,* and Glaspell's *Bernice,* which explores the psychological motivations behind a dying woman's wish to present her death as a suicide. In both *Trifles* and *Bernice,* Glaspell employs the nontraditional device of an unseen protagonist. A number of their plays mix stylistic features, combining realistic dialogue, domestic interiors, and symbolic, expressionistic, or surreal undercurrents. Naturalistic dialogue prevails in plays like *The Squealer, The Baby Carriage,* and *The Eldest.* Barlow cited the caged bird in *Trifles* and flowering plants in *Winter's Night* as typical uses of symbolism in otherwise naturalistic plays.[15] The baby carriage and widow's veil in plays of those titles are additional examples. *The Verge* and *Three from the Earth* represent perhaps the most radical combination of realistic and symbolic elements. *Three from the Earth* provides a striking contrast between its realistic setting (Kate Morley's boudoir) and its nonrealistic treatment of character and dialogue. *The Verge* features contemporary, realistic characterizations; dialogue that is realistically frank (perhaps the first time New York audiences heard the word "whore" onstage), heavily symbolic (Claire enjoys a purely physical relationship with "Dick"), and inventive (perhaps the first use of "otherness" as a sense of identity defined by what it is *not*); and an expressionistic visualization. Two plays (Wellman's *The String of the Samisen* and Glaspell's *Inheritors,* which spans forty years) employ realistic, noncontemporary locations. Four plays employ abstract or fantastic settings: Louise Bryant's *The Game,* Mary Carolyn Davies's *The Slave with Two Faces,* and Edna Millay's *The Princess Marries the Page* and *Aria da Capo.* Although Provincetown plays by men also generally exhibited innovative aesthetics, some of the most daring experiments were by women, including Glaspell's linguistic innovations in *The Verge* ("she is groping after a new idiom")[16] and the proto-absurdism of Barnes's *Three from the Earth:* "We have come to believe a play must tell a complete story—just like a novel—and that is wrong and *Three From the Earth* proves it. . . . It calculates only to produce a certain mood. It cannot be called realism or

Mary Carolyn Davies's *The Slave with Two Faces* (*left to right*): Dorothy Upjohn, Blanche Hays, Hutchinson Collins, Otto Liveright, Alice Macdougal, and Ida Rauh. 139 Macdougal Street. Courtesy Billy Rose Theatre Collection, New York Public Library for the Performing Arts, Astor, Lenox and Tilden Foundations.

artificialism or even symbolism. It establishes a new form, a new technique for the theatre—one that is going to develop a great deal in the future."[17]

Although Provincetown established policies and practices favorable to women and feminist playwrights, the presence of plays by women also depended upon their acceptance by contemporary audiences. One way to assess audience response is by revivals. Because Provincetown audiences sometimes voted on which plays to revive, the plays chosen were almost certainly the season's most popular offerings.[18] Twelve of the thirty-five plays written by women were revived at least once, a slightly higher percentage than the number of revivals among male-authored plays (nineteen of sixty-two).[19] The Players also occasionally staged revivals, presumably without consulting audiences, when a promised play was not completed in time or for other practical reasons.

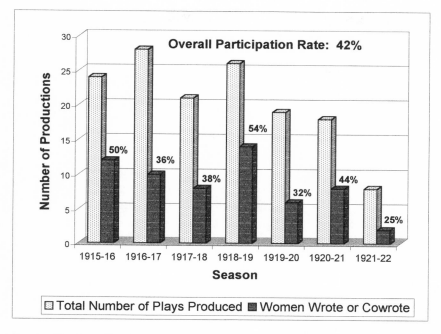

Graph 1. Number of Productions of Plays Written or Cowritten by Women

In April 1921, when director Jasper Deeter selected a repertory bill of four plays, three were by women.[20] In fact, the number of *productions,* as distinct from the number of plays, reveals that women's plays accounted for 42 percent of Provincetown's productions, 50 percent or more for two seasons. Thus, the participation of women playwrights at Province-town is even greater than previously realized (see graph 1).

In addition to the general public, reviewers also generally admired Provincetown's women playwrights. Although the Provincetown Play-ers initially declared themselves independent of critics, refusing to offer press tickets until the third season, a number of critics paid for the privi-lege of witnessing Provincetown's experiments. Glaspell, especially, earned early critical approval; throughout her Provincetown career, only O'Neill was considered her equal. In 1919, critic Gorham Munson pub-lished a lengthy evaluation of the Provincetown Players, citing Glas-pell's "satiric comedies of intellectuals" and O'Neill's "striking bits of sailor life" as most impressive. He then named eight Provincetown plays, including five by women, that "redeemed the depressing mediocrity of the past theatrical season."[21] Following Glaspell, Millay and Barnes shared second place in reputation among women writers, and both were included at least once in general surveys of Provincetown's best playwrights.[22] Individual plays by women that were especially praised include Millay's *Aria da Capo*, Rostetter's *The Widow's Veil*, Florence Kiper Frank's *Gee-Rusalem*, and Glaspell's *Suppressed Desires*, *Trifles*, and *Bernice*.[23]

Few plays by women were dismissed outright, but these included several from the first season: Heywood Broun did not like *Enemies* ("fearsome tedious talks between husband and wife"), *The Two Sons* ("a little experiment in decadence"),[24] or *Barbarians* ("a good enough story, but slight").[25] Despite Broun's dismissal of Wellman's antiwar satire as "slight," *Barbarians* was apparently a great favorite with the company: Kenton recalled it as "one of the timeliest, cleverest, little comedies we ever laid our hands on."[26] Although Broun was reputedly a feminist and cofounder, with his wife, Ruth Hale, of the Lucy Stone League, he may be exhibiting sexist bias in his dismissal as "tedious" a subject women at the time found crucially pertinent—marital relations—or his perception of Boyce's portrayal of conflicted mother/child relationships as "decadent." At least one woman in the company differed: "I think it is by far the best thing Neith has ever done."[27]

The general admiration of most of these plays by audiences, colleagues, and critics joined with the original artistic mission and methods of play selection by the Provincetown Players to encourage production by women writers. By the last season, however, women playwrights had nearly vanished. What happened? Judith Barlow offered several possible explanations for the decline: a shift from production of one-acts to full-length forms, the departure of Nina Moise and other women directors, and an organizational shift from consensus to hierarchy.[28] Although several factors, including those mentioned by Barlow, may be involved, they all converge in the structural transformation of the company that began in the 1919–20 season. Radical changes in operation, beginning during this season, directly affected the number and kind of plays produced. At that time, Cook and Glaspell were taking a sabbatical season in Cape Cod, leaving Ida Rauh and James Light to share general direction of the company. Because she was offered a job on Broadway, and because she was, apparently, feeling unwelcome ("out of it and unhappy"), Rauh departed in midseason, leaving Light in charge.

At Light's instigation, the Players produced their first European drama, *Last Masks* by Arthur Schnitzler, in March 1920.

When Cook and Glaspell returned in the fall of 1920, Light was sufficiently influential to be named codirector, with Cook, for the season. Perhaps to assert his power, but also to exploit the theatrical possibilities of O'Neill's latest effort, *The Emperor Jones*, Cook insisted that the company install a curved plaster cyclorama (*Kuppelhorizont*). With the installation of this scenic device, the first in America, the Players were able to achieve an illusion of great depth and to create such amazing lighting effects that audiences demanded encores. The suddenly increased technical possibilities brought Robert Edmond Jones back into the group (he had not actively participated in production since July 1915) and attracted newcomer Cleon Throckmorton, who would become the company's first permanent scenic designer and technical director.[29] Throckmorton's impressive use of the *Kuppelhorizont* in this production established a new emphasis on design and technology in Provincetown productions. Throckmorton, especially, sought plays in which the new technology could be used to advantage—that is, exterior settings.[30]

At about the same time, the Provincetown Players began to experience the intense changes wrought by sudden success. *The Emperor Jones*, which opened on 1 November 1920, created a sensation. The tiny theatre was mobbed, and one month later the play moved to Broadway, taking *Tickless Time* as curtain-raiser and over twenty actors with it. During the next two seasons, the Players moved three additional plays uptown, O'Neill's *Diff'rent* and *The Hairy Ape*, which enjoyed successful runs, and Cook's *The Spring*, which did not. These three plays required thirty-eight actors, nearly half the total number needed (eighty-one) for the previous season.

Thus, for the first time in the company's history, a play's Broadway potential entered the equation in play selection. Whereas Provincetown's subscription audiences had evidently supported plays that were artistically innovative and politically controversial, and were perhaps unusually sympathetic to plays with feminist themes, the wider appeal of such plays was doubtful. Then, as now, desire for commercial success discouraged risk taking, and so the nature of the plays selected was being subtly shifted.

The desire to produce full-lengths rather than one-acts was encouraged by the successful transfer to Broadway of O'Neill's longer plays.[31]

In the 1920–21 season, the Players produced only one bill of one-acts. Although the immediate, direct effect of this decision was the production of fewer new plays and hence fewer opportunities for any new playwrights, male or female, this decision may have especially discouraged submissions from women, whose time to write, as Barlow suggested, was already severely limited by professional and domestic responsibilities. The 1920–21 season included only two new plays by women, both full-length: Scott's *Love* and Glaspell's *Inheritors*. The following season, the Players' last, included only eight plays (five full-length and three one-acts); in this season, Glaspell was the only woman playwright represented.

The question of hierarchy versus consensus was addressed in the previous chapter, and we have seen that a number of women, in fact, facilitated this shift. Who holds power, however, is crucial. The power structure at Provincetown, already altered by the events of the 1919–20 sabbatical season, was transformed after the success of *The Emperor Jones*. Although O'Neill was already the company's most produced playwright, the double triumph of *The Emperor Jones* and *Beyond the Horizon*, which had opened on Broadway earlier that year, catapulted him into an unprecedented position.[32] From then on, he and his plays commanded the company's greatest attention. The large casts and technical demands of *The Emperor Jones* and *The Hairy Ape*, which opened in April 1921, drained the company's human and material resources. Plays unfortunate enough to be scheduled at roughly the same time as an O'Neill play, like Evelyn Scott's *Love*, which opened in February 1921, could easily be "lost in the shuffle."[33] During *Love*'s rehearsal and performance, most of the company were playing, or hoping to play, uptown, and "interest in the downtown stage had sagged."[34] Apparently, Scott left the dress rehearsal in tears and went straight into seclusion.[35]

The shifting of power relations brought other individuals to greater influence—all men. The technical achievement of *The Emperor Jones* brought greater prestige to designers in general and Throckmorton in particular. The installation of the *Kuppelhorizont*, which promoted plays with exterior sets that could take advantage of the new technology, was also a factor in the staging of fewer plays by women, as the great majority of these employed interior sets. Glaspell was canny in her conception of an expressionistic interior for *The Verge* that would still present an interesting challenge for Throckmorton: "The scene is a room in a tower, which starts to be round but doesn't complete the circle. The back is curved, then jagged lines break from that, and the front is a queer bulging window—in a curve that leans."[36] A clique of newly influential members, including Throckmorton, Deeter, Light, and Ellis, formed with O'Neill at the center. Moreover, the small but powerful outsider group, which included Robert Edmond Jones, Kenneth Macgowan, and producer-director Arthur Hopkins, began to intrude on Provincetown's operations. They were interested only in O'Neill, but their presence suffused the formerly amateur company with the aura of Broadway.[37] In December, O'Neill asked the company, apparently for the first time, for royalties.[38] The following season, Theodore Dreiser also received royalties for his *Hand of the Potter*.[39] Conflict between O'Neill's group and the older members intensified and resulted in further administrative changes. During the 1920–21 season the executive committee changed membership two times, from seven to ten to twelve members; most of the new members were male, including O'Neill, Throckmorton, Deeter, Ellis, and Light.[40] Rauh resigned, and Fitzgerald sided with the "new" group. By the spring of 1922, only Kenton remained to uphold the old ways. The decision to stop production for a year had already been made, the executive committee had reverted to five members (Glaspell, Kenton, Fitzgerald, Cook, and O'Neill), and the future of the Provincetown Players was extremely doubtful.[41]

At about the same time that power and influence began to shift within the company, plays by women, even the admired Glaspell, began to attract more negative and overtly biased criticism. Gender ideology revealed in early critical response to the works of O'Neill and Glaspell helps illuminate the biased criticism of her later plays. The simultaneous emergence of O'Neill and Glaspell inspired an effort by critics to gender their work appropriately—as if American drama could only be born by a mating of O'Neill's "masculine vigor" and Glaspell's "feminine intuition."[42] At the end of the Players' first season, O'Neill was lauded for "tense and heartfelt realism" and Glaspell for "sensitive feminine perceptions."[43] Later, Glaspell's plays received special recognition as "distinctively feminine in their social satire, keen observation, and trenchant dialogue."[44] She was also praised for her "intensely feminine minuteness of observation.[45] O'Neill's "familiar virtues," on the other hand, included writing plays that were "sharp and incisive" and "full of punch."[46] Despite his detection of a *hint* of femininity in O'Neill's dramaturgy, critic John Corbin labored to gender Glaspell and O'Neill appropriately:

> Is there any dramatist of the great white way who equals Susan Glaspell in subtle feminine intuition, in keen social satire? In her little unconventional tragedy of *Trifles* she disclosed a whole region of poignant feminine suffering. In *Suppressed Desires,* she threw a flood of genial ridicule upon the Village's pose of "freedom." Her talent is for genre painting at its most intimate—a talent which, except for the players, would never have been known to our theatre. . . .
>
> Mr. O'Neill has an almost feminine fineness in the divination of character; yet at his best he has a masculine vigor and raciness as intense as that of Kipling—Mr. O'Neill has done nothing finer and robuster than the portrait of the master whaler who wrecked his wife's reason and his own happiness at the bidding of his professional pride.[47]

Although Provincetown women had arguably been writing feminist plays all along (Glaspell's *Trifles* is now considered a feminist anthem), critics did not seem to notice for a while. By 1921, they did. Although a number of critics, as well as company members, considered Glaspell's *Inheritors* one of the company's best plays,[48] others objected to it as too political—a "batch of platitudinous fudge."[49] One writer objected to the protagonist of *Inheritors* (who goes to prison for her political convictions) as inappropriately heroic: "Martyrdom for an abstract principle represented in two natives of India is not the natural expression even of high-mindedness in a healthy young American of the gentler sex at twenty-one—it should claim its martyrs among its natural and fitting devotees; in the Professor Holden of this play, in Galsworthy's Stephen More or Ibsen's Dr. Stockman."[50] A letter from a company member suggests that *Inheritors* was too politically radical for wide approval: "Susan's play is great. . . . They have great hopes of uptown for it, but I doubt it, too anti."[51] Two reviews, one by Heterodite Maida Castellun and the other by Kenneth Macgowan, identified this play as an attack on postwar "reaction" (backlash).[52] That Glaspell's *Inheritors* was "too anti" to transfer was probably due to radical politics rather than radical aesthetics. *Inheritors* is not particularly experimental in form. O'Neill's

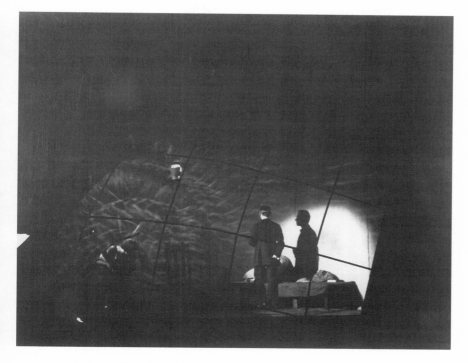

*The Verge,* by Susan Glaspell. 133 Macdougal Street. Courtesy Billy Rose Theatre Collection, New York Public Library for the Performing Arts, Astor, Lenox and Tilden Foundations.

most successful uptown transfers, after all, were rather daring experiments in expressionism.[53]

Even more passionate and controversial was the critical debate inspired by Glaspell's *The Verge,* which opened in the fall of 1921. *The Verge* apparently drew a loyal audience (Alexander Woollcott noted that "the faithful packed the little theatre to suffocation"),[54] but critical opinion was sharply divided. Some criticism focused on Glaspell's experimental aesthetics. Woollcott disparaged the writing as "miscellaneous, unselective, helplessly loquacious."[55] What Woollcott called "rubbishy language" another called "babble à la Gertrude Stein."[56] Critics who found the play incomprehensible used adjectives like "perplexing," "strange," "puzzling," "bizarre," "absurd," and "hazy" to describe it.[57]

Most negative criticism, however, centered on the play's radical feminist perspective and the behavior of its leading character. For Hutchins Hapgood, who was alarmed by the play's "half-mad feminism," *The Verge* was "a passionate expression of the feminism which rejected, with complete destructive desire, the world of man as opposed to that of woman."[58] Woollcott was similarly alarmed, insisting that its protagonist "provoke[d] combativeness in the onlooker" and that "the tormented and bewildering play—a study of an abnormal and neurotic woman—can be reviewed only by a neurologist or some woman who has journeyed near to the verge of which Miss Glaspell writes."[59] Five days later he revisited *The Verge,* presumably after being taken to task by Ruth Hale, among others: "Making fun of this groping play is a little like [shooting at a barn door]. . . . For a sympathetic and intelligent interpretation of the play the reader is hereby referred across the page to the letter from Ruth Hale. We greatly fear the average playgoer will be offended by Miss Glaspell's abject worship of the divinity of discontent."[60] Writers who were offended pronounced the play "unhealthy," "neurotic," "a queer study of eroticism," or "intolerable."[61] One reviewer condemned Claire as a "fraudulent female . . . an erotic, neurotic illtempered hussy."[62] In his summation of critical response, Macgowan scolded Glaspell for creating a character that "affrights so many."[63]

*The Verge* was an ideological litmus test. Among Heterodites, as dancer Elsie Dufour discovered, anything less than wholehearted support was sacrilege:

> It seemed to me, while these women were talking about *The Verge,* that I was in church, that they were worshiping at some holy shrine; their voices and their eyes were full of religious excitement. I was, I think, the only woman not under this spell. I tried at first to say a few things about the play that were in the line of ordinary dramatic criticism, which I thought had a reasonable basis; but when they all glared upon me, as if they thought I should be excommunicated, I spoke no further word.[64]

Feminist critics rallied around Glaspell. Ruth Hale specifically defended the play's central character: "I still believe that the woman made by Miss Glaspell and Miss Wycherly is as clear as glass, and that you had the key to her in any vagrant thought or intention of your own that might have involved you in any sort of clash with accepted physical or social habit."[65] Maida Castellun seemed to understand that Glaspell had offended so many because she violated gender ideology:

> Miss Glaspell has left the conventions of the stage behind. . . . [She] has chosen a woman instead of a man to incarnate the restless auda-cious, creative spirit that goes beyond the verge of human experience and social conventions.
>
> Claire is a superwoman. . . . Scorning established patterns in ideas, in social and family conventions . . . she allows her creative energies to range. . . . She brushes aside her "obligations" to husband and daughter . . . she is a female Lucifer—godlike in creation and de-struction.[66]

A feminist critic might wonder indeed why critics who applauded O'Neill's portrayal of a man who "wrecked reason . . . and . . . happi-ness at the bidding of his professional pride" were appalled by Glaspell's creation of a woman who did likewise. Many female characterizations by Provincetown's women playwrights challenged sexual stereotypes, but Glaspell's daughter-disdaining, lover-strangling "female Faust" an-nihilated them. And in creating her, Glaspell violated that crucially im-portant identity the critics had created for her—that sensitive woman with "fine feminine perceptions" to balance so nicely O'Neill's rugged masculinity. *The Verge* seriously jeopardized Glaspell's fitness to be the mother of American drama.

Glaspell's *Chains of Dew* may have irritated male Villagers by expos-ing the shallowness of men's commitment to social change. Broun complained that the leading male character was "an absolute prig and an idiot."[67] The ever sympathetic Castellun, however, identified this characterization as a significant theme: "showing up the male as your only true conservative in matters social and spiritual . . . as a social iconoclast the female of the species again proves more daring than the male."[68] *Chains* received both less and less favorable attention than Glaspell's other full-length works. Even staunch Glaspell advocate Ludwig Lewisohn found it "plainly inferior to both *Inheritors* and *The Verge*,"[69] and Woollcott, who had so ridiculed *The Verge* for its innova-tions, now complained that *Chains* was dated: "It has a good deal to do with bobbed hair—must have been written some years ago."[70]

Sexist criticism, which increased in virulence as feminist messages

became more overt, must have been especially discouraging for playwrights who regularly treated feminist themes. Although reviews lack
specific references to the female lead in Evelyn Scott's *Love,* Scott's depiction of an unabashedly erotic woman who drives her husband to suicide may explain her play's condemnation as "sordid" and the unusually
negative reviews received by Ida Rauh in the leading role. Castellun was
one of two writers who defended Scott's play.[71] But the significance of
criticism in explaining the decline in women's drama is also linked to
changes in the company's policies and procedures. Disregard of critical
reaction was related to their focus on experimentation and process,
rather than product, and their reliance on a small but faithful subscription audience. When they began to transfer productions to Broadway,
however, their priorities changed accordingly. Producers interested in a
hit cannot afford to ignore negative reviews. Therefore, critical dismissal
of women's plays during the first season may have had little effect on
women's contributions, but critical condemnation occurring in later
seasons probably did.

Changing attitudes toward publicity reflect the sweeping changes in
the company's modus operandi. These many shifts coalesced in 1922,
and their effects are clearly illustrated in the circumstances surrounding
the disastrous production of Glaspell's *Chains of Dew* in the spring of
1922. *Chains* was nearly canceled because Throckmorton was "mad to do
the [exotic and exterior] sets" for *Taboo* instead of the two realistic interiors required for *Chains of Dew:* "Interiors don't interest Throck
much."[72] Because it was scheduled during the run of *The Hairy Ape,*
finding personnel was difficult. Kenton had enormous problems finding
a director, eventually settling for Ralph Stewart, despite her misgivings:
"I just *felt* what Stewart would do in cuts . . . but he saved the day so let
it pass."[73] Finding a suitable cast was equally difficult: "We were man-
less. Everybody went uptown with *The [Hairy] Ape.*"[74] One male role
was cast two days before opening. Casting women was also a problem.
The actress cast as the mother, "a part that could make an actress," was
"adequate but no smash."[75] Stewart also made a puzzling choice for the
leading and much coveted role of Nora Powers. According to Kenton,
Stewart chose actress Marion Berry, who had just played the daughter in *The Verge,* because he was "wild about her innocence." Stewart
may have found innocence an attractive quality in a woman, but it

hardly seems appropriate for Glaspell's sophisticated protagonist, Powers (typically for Glaspell, the name is suggestive), head of the New York Birth Control League. Although Glaspell was relieved and grateful that Stewart had agreed to direct, she was clearly taken aback by the casting choices: "I saw there was nothing for me to do but get drunk, and so deaden the first pangs in the thought of Reese as Standish, Blanche as Dotty, and little Marion Berry as the on-to-herself Nora. Though I admit that last may work out. Little do our subscribers know how much finer is the comedy not being staged."[76] One reviewer's rather oxymoronic description of the character as "the intelligent and impertinent feather head" suggests a significant gap between the character as written and the character as performed.[77]

Stewart's cuts as well as his casting prompted frantically apologetic and defensive letters from Kenton: "Sue, my dear, I did what I could about cuts—all I could—which was precisely nothing! . . . Stewart was crazy with work and worry—and the day I sat in with him on cuts I should have had to be not only producer, actress, electrician and playwright, but AUTHOR, to have carried a thing. It had to be cut, and it had to be up to him."[78]

In the only version of *Chains of Dew* available today, Nora recruits her lover's wife, Dotty, as head of a midwestern chapter of the Birth Control League. Dotty, however, gives up her new position in order to devote herself to her husband. Kenton's letters indicate that Stewart made significant changes in the performed text regarding Dotty's recruitment:

[Stewart] could not—would not see Dotty as President of B[irth] C[ontrol] and so she wasn't. That is a day to remember. . . . It was what I had been afraid of with Stewart and why I broke my back trying to get some one else. . . . *You must believe* that I did everything in the world that I could. . . . But I had to pass on the thing that mattered so much to you. It was *impossible.* There was no time ever to try out things, what with the exits and exits of actors. And my entire lack of experience in the producing end made it impossible under the conditions to get feeling about the thing across. He doesn't even know that I tried to—If you had been here subtleties and ironies would have stayed in that went.

> I shall send you the acting script as soon as I can get Stewart's copy—if you have nerve enough to read it, do it—if not, Greece is surrounded by the sea—pitch it in from Sappho's cliff.[79]

Two weeks later, Kenton sent Glaspell the revised script, clearly anticipating a shocked reaction: "You may live through to the last act—what will happen then I know not."[80] Although Glaspell reassured Kenton that she was grateful to Stewart and generally pleased with the reviews, when the cut script arrived she could not bring herself to read it: "The script arrived, just as I was about to get on my mule to go up the mountain. There was room for it in the trunk that stayed behind, and as I am really fond of Ralph Stewart . . . I thought the script would do very well in the trunk till distance has dimmed all."[81] Glaspell, who never saw *Chains of Dew* in production, remained in Greece until after Cook's sudden death in January 1924.[82]

Glaspell wrote only three more plays, *The Comic Artist*, in collaboration with Norman Matson, *Alison's House*, which won the Pulitzer Prize in 1931 and *Springs Eternal* (1945). She served as director of the Midwest Play Bureau of the Federal Theatre Project from 1936 to 1938, then returned to writing fiction until her death in 1948. Despite the dissension marring the group's last seasons, Glaspell later recalled her Provincetown experiences as "the most exciting days she ever lived."[83] She was not the only woman playwright to look back fondly on her Provincetown years. Even the caustic Djuna Barnes published a sentimental recollection in 1929: "It was as good as suicide to write a one act play, have Norma Millay laugh at it, Charlie Ellis sit through it or hear Mary Blair connecting it with the Torah or Swedenborg, which ability was one of her charms. We used to sit on the most uncomfortable benches imaginable . . . glad to suffer partial paralysis of the upper leg and an entire stoppage of the spinal juices, just to hear Ida Rauh come out of the wings and say, 'Life, bring me a fresh rose!'"[84]

Between 1916 and 1926 at least twenty-five of the thirty-five Provincetown plays by women were published, making the works available across the country.[85] Nearly half were produced by little theatres, university theatres, or other amateur organizations throughout the next two decades. *Suppressed Desires, Trifles,* and *Aria da Capo* became little theatre staples. Four of Glaspell's plays (*Trifles, Woman's Honor, Inheritors,* and *The Verge*) had professional productions in America and London.[86] Despite the acceptance of their plays by these audiences, however, few of Provincetown's women playwrights enjoyed commercial success as playwrights, although most continued to work as writers. One of the playwrights who had a commercially successful career, Edna Ferber, is better known as a Pulitzer Prize–winning novelist, but she also won fame for Broadway comedies written in collaboration with George S. Kaufman. In 1918, Rita Wellman's play *The Gentile Wife* was produced on Broadway (directed by Arthur Hopkins), but she then turned to other literary forms, publishing a translation of Mussolini's diaries, biographies of Empress Eugenie and Queen Victoria, and a novel, *The House of Hate*. Millay, who won a Pulitzer Prize for poetry in 1923, published eleven volumes of poetry, six plays, and one opera libretto before her death in 1950. Barnes published a number of plays in little magazines in the 1920s; her *The Dove* was produced in New York in 1926, and her full-length *The Antiphon* was produced in Sweden in 1961. Barnes is better known, however, for her modernist novels *Nightwood* and *Ryder*. Florence Kiper Frank continued to write plays for amateur groups and to publish poetry. Mary Carolyn Davies published seven volumes of poetry and became president of the Northwest Poetry Society. Grace Potter, who became a psychoanalyst, published a full-length play, *I a Stranger*, in 1946. Alice Rostetter published *Which Is Witch or Mable and Maisie* in 1924. Alice Woods Ullman returned to novels and magazine writing. Evelyn Scott also became a respected novelist—too good for America, according to Alexander Berkman.[87] Neith Boyce published one more novel and, in 1923, a biography of her oldest son, who had died in the influenza epidemic of 1919.

That Provincetown's women playwrights were also feminists and that they generally wrote plays treating feminist themes is relevant both to their initial acceptance by this company and to their eventual disappearance. A female and largely feminist leadership was predictably eager to stage feminist plays by women. As there were several male Provincetowners, including Cook, Dell, and Deeter, who promoted plays by women, the decisive factor may be "feminist," as opposed to "female," leadership. That the presence of women and/or feminists in the play-selection process leads inevitably to the production of more plays by women is an assumption, to be sure, but one supported by the repertories of the Neighborhood Playhouse, the Provincetown Players, and the Experimental Theatre, the company formed by those whose power increased during the last two years of Provincetown's existence. In two important instances, women executives helped ensure productions of plays by women: in 1921, when Fitzgerald supported *Inheritors* over the objections of other influential company members; and in 1922, when Kenton insisted on producing *Chains of Dew*. What happened to Provincetown's women playwrights suggests that whether a hierarchy per se is advantageous for women depends on who has the power. The difference between the old and the new hierarchies, in relation to women playwrights, is strikingly illustrated by the total number of plays by women produced by the Experimental Theatre throughout its six-year history: two.[88]

Despite their failure to achieve fame and fortune on Broadway, Provincetown's women playwrights have earned a distinguished place in theatre history and women's history. They participated significantly in America's first important era of dramaturgical experimentation, pioneering structural and stylistic features for which there was not yet a suitable critical vocabulary. Women's plays helped build this company's reputation as an important source of new American drama. Subsequent publication and production of these plays expanded that reputation across the country and in Europe. Although rarely produced commercially, plays by Provincetown's women playwrights remain in the repertories of educational and noncommercial theatres.

The inadequate attention and misinterpretation accorded *Chains of Dew* reflected the results of the power shift from the old group to the new, especially the new power granted designers to influence play selection, the lack of adequate casts or sympathetic directors, and the general lack of interest in plays not likely to transfer uptown, which specifically included plays with radical political themes. Despite the turmoil surrounding this production, it seems now expressly fitting that the final production of the Provincetown Players was of a play by Susan Glaspell, and for that circumstance Edna Kenton is almost entirely responsible.

The experiences of Provincetown's women playwrights explicitly illustrate how gender bias works in dramatic criticism and theatrical production. It can be as overt as calling a female protagonist "abnormal" or as subtle as casting more conventionally "feminine" (i.e., young and innocent) performers in feminist roles—and in production, turning feminists into "feather heads." At Provincetown, even the de facto ban on plays with interior sets may have served to discourage women writers whose plays typically unfolded in domestic interiors. The result is the same: women's voices, perhaps especially feminist voices, are eventually silenced.

In all fairness, it must be said that the leaders of the new group— Eugene O'Neill, Kenneth Macgowan, and Robert Edmond Jones—did ask Glaspell to join the Experimental Theatre. Had she accepted, perhaps the ratio would have improved a bit, but the record as it stands suggests that, whereas women playwrights were regularly represented at Provincetown, they were exceptional at the Experimental Theatre. Despite the considerable attention awarded Provincetown's women playwrights during their brief but vital flourishing, no one seemed to notice their disappearance at the time. Five decades would pass, in fact, before the continued absence of women playwrights in American theatre would begin to receive serious attention.[89]

# 4

## *Performing Women*

I am looking for something simpler in the theater, something which is more natural.

—Ida Rauh, *New York Call*

As we have seen, Provincetown produced an unusually large number of plays that featured strong female protagonists. Aspiring actresses, re-membered by Djuna Barnes as the "girls who used to fight to get into the Provincetown casts,"[1] recognized the particularly desirable opportu-nities available. Roles in Glaspell's plays were especially coveted. In 1921, Jig Cook reported to Susan Glaspell that he had interviewed one hun-dred women for roles in her play *The Verge*.[2] Years later, Kirah Markham recalled her disappointment at not being cast in *The Verge*, as well as her gratitude for the opportunity to perform in *Trifles* ("the best-written play in which I ever appeared") and *Inheritors* ("I found myself en-grossed in becoming that woman, because Susan Glaspell wrote so well").[3] These unique opportunities for women—in both quantity and quality of roles—occurred at a critical time in the development of American performance.

During the last decade of the nineteenth century and the first two decades of the twentieth, American acting was still heavily influenced by declamatory, "grand and lofty" traditions, although a few pioneers, including James A. Herne and Minnie Maddern Fiske, had begun the move toward greater psychological truthfulness in acting.[4] During this transitional era, professional acting schools in America challenged the old, "imitative" method of performing, whereby experienced actors taught apprentices how roles should be played, in favor of new meth-ods that advocated "imagination, 'emotional memory,' feeling, instinct, spontaneity and sympathetic identification."[5] Although the Province-town Players did not explicitly articulate allegiance to any particular style of acting, their challenge to conventional dramaturgy effected a challenge to conventional acting as well: "'Why, it's like the Irish Players,' breathed someone in the audience when the curtain went down on Mary Heaton Vorse and George Cram Cook and Nancy Schoonma[k]er in *Winter's Night*. The Provincetown Players, like the Irish Players, are trying to get away from stage convention, to act naturally and simply, to be on the stage much as they are off the stage."[6]

The Provincetown Players became advocates of what may be called the "new acting" pioneered in Europe by the Moscow Art Theatre and the Irish Players of the Abbey Theatre. Cook and Glaspell had been especially impressed by the Irish Players, who toured America in 1911: "Quite possibly there would be no Provincetown Players had there not been Irish Players," wrote Glaspell. "What [Cook] saw done for Irish life he wanted for American life—no stage conventions in the way of projecting with the humility of true feeling."[7] Here she is talking about breaking conventions in acting as well as dramaturgy. Louis Sheaffer recorded O'Neill's enthusiasm:

> Eugene was scornful . . . of the critics who failed to realize that the Dubliners were pioneers of a new style of acting, honest, true, without the familiar tricks. "As a boy I saw so much of the old, ranting, artificial, romantic stage stuff that I always had a kind of contempt for the theatre. It was seeing the Irish Players for the first time that gave me a glimpse of my opportunity. . . . I thought then and I still think that they demonstrated the possibilities of naturalistic acting better than any other company."[8]

That modern American drama could not develop without a corresponding effort to develop modern American performance seems self-evident. Yet, although theatre historians have recognized the importance of the Provincetown Players in cultivating drama, they have generally overlooked its significance in developing performance, specifically in facilitating the transition from the "old, imitative" methods to the "new" methods seeking greater psychological truthfulness and individual imaginative creation. The abundant opportunities offered to Provincetown actresses allowed them to contribute significantly both to the overall success of the company and to the important new developments in American performance.

The company's original female membership had minimal acting experience and no aspirations for theatrical careers. Some did have amateur experience, in school or in the dramatic branch of the Liberal Club, and a few had appeared in the first season of the Washington Square Players. Undeterred by their lack of training, writers like Glaspell, Boyce, Bryant, and Vorse enthusiastically acted in each other's plays or in their own. At first, casting was a casual affair between the playwright and a small pool of willing volunteers. Eleven of the company's thirteen female charter members acted at least one role during the group's two summer seasons.[9] When the company organized formally and moved to Greenwich Village in the fall of 1916, casting became less casual and the pool widened. Only four of the female charter members performed in New York.[10] Playwrights theoretically had the final word on casting throughout the company's history, but important active members, directors, and the executive committee generally influenced decisions. Although committed to noncommercial goals, the Players progressively sought greater proficiency in performance. By the fall of 1917 they had instituted open casting calls; by 1919 they had begun to pay performers.[11] Of the many women who performed for the company, ten were especially influential, as judged by the extent of their participation, the acclaim awarded them by critics and colleagues, or both.

One of the first Provincetown actresses to attract attention was Mary Pyne, who performed eight roles for the Players from 1916 until 1919. Raised in poverty, Pyne had aspired to act while she worked as a cashier, dance-hall instructor, and waitress. In 1915 she married "hobo poet" Harry Kemp and became part of the Greenwich Village/Provincetown community. By all accounts, Pyne was exquisitely beautiful. Of the many rapturous descriptions of her ethereal loveliness, Lawrence Langner's is typical: "Mary had titian red hair, gray-blue eyes and the kind of creamy skin and red lips found in paintings by Henna. She combined the charm of Mimi in La Bohème with the spiritual beauty of a Della Robbia Madonna."[12] Despite her beauty, Pyne was cast as the shrewish wife in O'Neill's *Before Breakfast* in December 1916. Apparently pursuing Provincetown's naturalistic approach to acting, Pyne ran afoul of the playwright's father, veteran stage star James O'Neill, one of America's most celebrated practitioners of the "old school." O'Neill Sr. did not approve of Pyne's diction and gestures and tried to show her "how acting was done."[13] Happily, the younger O'Neill allowed Pyne to ignore

Mary Pyne. Courtesy Papers of Djuna Barnes, Special Collections, University of Maryland Libraries.

his father's advice, and the Players, who had "no wish to revive the histrionic technique of a bygone era," were thrilled by Pyne's "fine performance."[14] Pyne evidently impressed other members of the Greenwich Village community with this performance as well. Nani Bailey informed John Reed that "Mary Pyne certainly did a fine piece of work for Gene in *Before Breakfast* and maybe will land a job with [Frank] Conroy in his new theatre [Greenwich Village Theatre]."[15] Langner recalled the performance as "a moving success" and considered Pyne "one of the most promising young actresses of the Provincetown Players."[16] For Hutchins Hapgood, this was Pyne's most creative performance: "She showed one of the most characteristic qualities of an actress in that she seemed to render another woman's personality, to which she had no resemblance—a pure act of imaginative creation."[17]

The Players voted Pyne to active membership in January 1917 and offered her five roles in the next three bills.[18] Although only one of these performances was reviewed (the critic remarked that Pyne was "seen to advantage" in her husband's *The Prodigal Son*),[19] her performances were obviously esteemed by the company's active membership. In March 1917 they voted that "a *good* part be found for Mary Pyne and that the [executive] committee have power if necessary to change the bill in order to accomplish this."[20] Apparently the "good part" was that of Mabel, Pyne's next role, in a revival of Glaspell and Cook's *Suppressed Desires.*[21]

Pyne's Provincetown successes attracted the attention of commercial producers, including America's foremost theatrical entrepreneur, David Belasco. Concerned that Belasco's interest might be personal as well as professional, Pyne declined his offer to groom her for Broadway stardom.[22] She did accept, however, an offer from Frank Conroy of the Greenwich Village Theatre and appeared there in *Karen,* which opened in January 1918 and ran for eighty performances, and again in *Pan and the Young Shepherd,* which opened in March 1918 and ran for thirty-two performances.[23] In January 1919 Pyne returned to the Provincetown Players in one of her most memorable roles, Katy MacManus, the charming young wife who would be widowed, in Alice Rostetter's *The Widow's Veil.* Several reviewers praised Pyne's performance in this play.[24] One critic nominated Pyne, along with Rostetter and Edna St. Vincent Millay, as the three best actors on the bill.[25] Pyne's promising career was halted when she suddenly, tragically contracted tuberculosis. She died at Saranac Lake Sanatorium in November 1919, at the age of twenty-six. Djuna Barnes, who tried to claim Pyne's body, declared that she would never get over the loss, and Kemp tried to contact Pyne in the spirit world through his second wife, who was a medium.[26]

Although no one ever completely replaced Pyne on the Provincetown stage or in the hearts of the Players, another ethereal ingenue had appeared in the fall of 1917 to join Pyne as one of the beautiful and gifted young actresses on Macdougal Street. The newcomer was Edna St. Vincent Millay. Best known to Provincetown historians as the author of *Aria da Capo,* Millay came to the company as an actress. Like Pyne, Millay sought a professional career as an actress. Before her Provincetown debut she had earned considerable experience in musical and dramatic performances at Vassar, winning the admiration of local dramatic critics and the adoration of an undergraduate fan club, which sent flowers whenever she appeared in a play.[27] After graduation in 1917 Millay moved to Greenwich Village, armed with letters of introduction to theatrical managers from actress Edith Wynne Mathison.

Although frankly seeking professional employment ("I have a perfect passion for earning money"),[28] Millay attended an open call for the

Provincetown Players just a few months after her arrival in Greenwich Village. Her reading for Floyd Dell's *An Angel Intrudes* won her the role: "She looked her frivolous part to perfection, and read the lines so winningly that she was at once engaged," Dell recalled.[29] Millay's sister Norma, who lived with Millay in the Village, suggested that Millay was willing to forego remuneration for publicity: "Vincent has a part in a one act play with the Provincetown Players and we are so very pleased. She won't get anything but notoriety but quite a bit of that however. They produce their own plays and have quite a name around town."[30] Norma also reported that the Players, who had immediately voted Millay into active membership, were "wild about our sister."[31] Villagers recalled Millay's performance in *The Angel Intrudes* as "delicious."[32] Dell, hopelessly smitten, cast her in his next play, *Sweet and Twenty*.

Millay possessed a number of natural gifts, including a striking physical presence and rare charm. As Lawrence Langner recalled, "the club rooms became brighter for the presence of an exquisitely delicate, elfin-like girl, who shed a radiance all around her."[33] Director Nina Moise likewise remembered Millay's "great enchantment."[34] Floyd Dell was especially enraptured by her voice: "Her reciting voice had a loveliness that was sometimes heartbreakingly poignant. I fell in love with her voice at once."[35] Another gift Millay possessed, or skill she developed, was versatility, for which she won critical praise.[36] Dell elaborated:

> [She exhibited] a startling variety of appearances. When reading poetry a fragile little girl with an apple blossom face. When she is picnicking in the country she will be, with her snub nose, freckles, carroty hair, and boyish grin, an Irish "newsy." When she is meeting the bourgeoisie in its lairs, she is likely to be a highly artificial and very affected young lady with an exaggerated Vassar accent and abominably overdone manners . . . a New England nun; a chorus girl on a holiday; the Botticelli Venus . . . she is all of these and more.[37]

Millay's versatility revealed itself in wide-ranging characterizations. Immediately following a "charming" portrayal of the willful princess in her own *The Princess Marries the Page*,[38] she "assumed an almost unbelievable plainness as the protesting [maid] Annie"[39] in Cook and Glaspell's *Tickless Time,* and in January 1919 she transformed herself into a Japanese woman for her role in Rita Wellman's romantic tragedy *The String of the Samisen:* "I can sing a Japanese song now, for all the world as if I had been born in Nikko, and my eyes are slowly beginning to turn up at the corners . . . soon I shall look like a wood blocked outomaro, with the colors put on a little bit wrong, that's all."[40] Later that season, critics praised Millay's "sterling performance" as an "indescribably attractive peasant girl" in Harold Chapin's comedy *The Philosopher of Butterbiggins.*[41] Millay didn't even have to be seen to win critical praise. Three reviewers of O'Neill's *The Moon of the Caribbees* applauded the "effective offstage crooning" supplied by Millay, her mother, and her two sisters.[42]

Millay, too, attracted favorable attention from other theatrical producers,[43] including Edward Goodman of the Washington Square Players, who cast her as the female lead in *Enter the Hero* in 1918, and Lawrence Langner of the Theatre Guild, who cast her in their premiere production of the Spanish commedia *Bonds of Interest* in May 1919.[44] Unfortunately, the Washington Square Players' production was canceled before opening, and the Theatre Guild's presentation was not successful. That a professional career in acting eluded Millay baffled writer Allen Churchill, who found it "hard to fathom" that "anyone as talented as Millay never gained a foothold on Broadway."[45] Perhaps Millay, who was ambitious and "passionate" to earn money, was lured away by more forthcoming literary awards. Her first volume of poetry, *A Few Figs from Thistles,* was published in 1920, and the next year *Vanity Fair* sent her to Paris as a correspondent. In addition to her own notable appearances in seven plays, Millay introduced to the company her entire family: her mother, Cora, who performed in *From Portland to Dover;* her sister Kathleen, who performed in *Three Travelers Watch a Sunrise;* and, especially, her sister Norma, who performed in thirteen Provincetown productions from 1918 to 1921.[46]

Millay introduced Norma—whom she called "Hunk" or "old blonde plumblossom"—to the Provincetown Players during rehearsals for *An Angel Intrudes.*[47] The Players were quick to welcome Millay's younger sister, who had also been active in drama and music at Vassar and was considered even more conventionally beautiful. Everyone not in love with Millay fell in love with Norma, including Provincetown actor Charles Ellis, whom she married in 1921. Norma specialized in comic leads and ingenues, including the mer/barmaid in Djuna Barnes's *Kurzy of the Sea* and Columbine in Edna Millay's *Aria da Capo.*[48] Norma and the Provincetown Players obviously had a mutually beneficial relationship. The frequency of her appearances suggests that the Players held her in high regard. Critical reviews are sparse but favorable; in his otherwise unfavorable review of Winthrop Parkhurst's *Getting Unmarried,* Kenneth Macgowan observed that "Norma Millay's good acting—quite as charming and capable as half a dozen leading Broadway women, doesn't save it."[49] As a member of the cast of *Tickless Time,* curtain-raiser to *The Emperor Jones,* Norma was one of the first Provincetowners to receive a salary and to perform on Broadway. She invested her weekly salary of fifteen dollars in the production and tripled her capital.[50]

Norma was one of the few Provincetown actors who made the transition from Provincetown to the professional theatre. While performing at Provincetown, Norma was wooed by commercial managers, including vaudeville producer Tom Shea, and she began to work professionally as an actress and singer in the 1920s. Companies she worked for included the Experimental Theatre, the Cherry Lane Theatre, the Intimate Opera Company, and the Studio Theatre, where she acted in Barnes's *The Dove* in 1926.[51]

Another young actress who appeared regularly with the Players was Blanche Hays, who also served as costume supervisor for the last two seasons. Hays, who had performed with the Washington Square Players in their 1916–17 season, made her first Provincetown appearance in January 1918. Between 1918 and 1922 she appeared in thirteen Provincetown productions in a variety of supporting roles. As with Norma Millay, the number of roles entrusted to her implies her value to the company, and reviews of her performances, though sketchy, suggest convincing and imaginative creation. She was particularly commended for her truthful depiction of an elderly pioneer woman in Susan Glaspell's *Inheritors* and for her rendering of an Irish peasant girl, one of her rare leading roles, in Barnes's *An Irish Triangle.*[52] Of this performance, Heywood Broun observed that "Blanche Hays sustains a difficult role with a great deal of charm and skill. It is altogether a first class performance."[53] Hays remained active with the Players until the company's dissolution in 1922.

For slightly older supporting characters, particularly in comic roles, the Players discovered Alice Rostetter. A high school teacher with no previous acting experience, Rostetter made a sensational debut as the morbidly generous neighbor in her own *The Widow's Veil.* The play itself was enthusiastically praised, but the critics universally agreed with Heywood Broun that Rostetter's "clever acting vastly embellished" the evening. Broun devoted most of his review to the performance. After declaring both Rostetter and her costar, Mary Pyne, "all that the most exacting critic could require," he continued: "Alice Rostetter gave one of the best character performances we ever saw in our life. We've consulted the local authorities to find out who this remarkable person might be and learned that it was the first time Miss Rostetter had ever acted."[54] During the next three seasons, Rostetter performed similar roles in six plays, including Mrs. Rooney in Bosworth Crocker's *The Baby Carriage,* The Motherly One in the revival of Glaspell's *Woman's Honor,* Mrs. Stubbs in the revival of Glaspell and Cook's *Tickless Time,* Fanny in Lawrence Vail's *What D'You Want,* and Annie Mulligan in Lawrence Langner's *Pie.*[55] Rostetter performed her last role for the Players in Eugene O'Neill's *Diff'rent* in December 1920. In 1925 she appeared in the Experimental Theatre's production of *A Dream Play.*[56]

One of the Players' most influential actresses was Susan Glaspell. Beginning in the summer of 1915, Glaspell enacted seven roles, always in her own plays.[57] Responses clearly establish her commitment to a naturalistic performance style, one especially esteemed by her Provincetown colleagues. Nina Moise, who directed Glaspell in several plays, considered her "a fine actress—a very interesting actress and a joy to work with [who] interfered very little with direction—hers was a very real kind of acting, not professional."[58] Provincetown designer William Zorach agreed that Glaspell was "a natural actress"[59] and uniquely gifted: "Susan Glaspell was a marvelous actress. Acting played a minor part in her life, but she had that rare power and quality inherent in great actresses. She had only to be on the stage and the play and the audience came alive."[60] Edna Kenton's appraisal is further corroboration: "Susan was the instinctive actress, delightfully natural, and in her own plays particularly, always thoroughly good. Knowing her own particular quality of irony to its last twist, she was able to express it as few others could."[61]

Critical evaluation is scanty, but it generally affirmed Glaspell's aptitude for convincing portrayal while lamenting a lack of "technique." Reviewing *The People,* Heywood Broun noted that Glaspell "plays with depth and spirit."[62] Of her supporting role in *Bernice,* he asserted that "Glaspell is not so technically adept [as actress Ida Rauh], but she plays with convincing spirit and feeling."[63] Another writer who reviewed this production declared Glaspell's performance an "extraordinary success—not because she is really much of an actress, but because the role happened to fit her so well. In appearance, mental makeup, and manner, Susan Glaspell is so very much of New England as to seem quite strange in the Village at times."[64] This writer may have delivered a more favorable appraisal than intended. Glaspell was in fact from Iowa; that she so convincingly portrayed the "appearance, mental makeup, and manner" of a New Englander suggests that her "artless" naturalism, her presumed technical ineptitude, may have resulted from conscious effort. The most revealing assessment of Glaspell as an actress came from Jacques Copeau, who saw the Provincetown Players' production of *The People* in the spring of 1917. Although Copeau accused the cast of technical deficiency in general ("They do not know how to stand on stage, nor how to enter or go off"), he recognized and admired in Glaspell's performance the rejection of existing "technique": "Mrs. Glaspell momentarily, in the midst of all this disorder, touched me to the core by the simplicity of her attitude, the pure quality of her person, the inimitable feeling in a nuance of her intonation. Never have I so well understood as at certain moments of this presentation how important it is to reject today's theatrical technique, even at the price of a long period of renewed trial and error."[65] Copeau reiterated these impressions, without identifying the actress, in a subsequent speech to the Washington Square Players, insisting that "the actor become a human being again, and all the great changes in the theatre will follow from that."[66] Copeau's perspective may be illuminated by noting that he had previously, on this trip, dismissed Broadway stars Arnold Daly and John Barrymore, unquestionably masters of existing theatrical technique, as an "imbecile" and a "ham," respectively.[67]

Although they do not match Pyne, Edna and Norma Millay, Hays, Rostetter, and Glaspell in number of performances, three Provincetown actresses deserve recognition for especially memorable ones: Mary Blair in O'Neill's *Diff'rent*, Ann Harding in Glaspell's *Inheritors*, and Margaret Wycherly in Glaspell's *The Verge*. Before appearing in *Diff'rent*, Blair had performed small roles in three Theatre Guild productions, including *Bonds of Interest* (with Edna Millay) and *Power of Darkness* (with Ida Rauh, Helen Westley, and Djuna Barnes). Casting twenty-five-year-old Blair, with only three bit parts to her credit, in the difficult role of Emma Crosby, who ages thirty years between acts, was a calculated risk that apparently paid off. Both play and performer received considerable critical attention and eventually moved to Broadway. Admiring critics pronounced Blair's portrayal "splendid," "superb," or "excellent."[68] Even the most negative reviewers agreed that Blair's performance was a remarkable achievement given the difficulty of the role. One writer observed that she "deserves a dramatic *croix de guerre*."[69] Another elaborated: "Even the extraordinarily difficult part of the girl, who must range from 16 to 46 and from maidenly modesty to a pitiful spectacle of unashamed pursuit, is not too much for Mary Blair. Perhaps it is a part which no one woman can completely compass; but Miss Blair does surprisingly well with it."[70]

As with Glaspell, Blair's naturalistic style was perceived as technical deficiency—one critic commented that the entire cast lacked "professional" skills.[71] Kenneth Macgowan's recollection of this performance four decades later suggests that Blair was considerably ahead of her time: "She had a beat generation quality, intensity and sincerity, didn't have technical ability, but she had a quality."[72] Ironically, Blair's sincerity may have cost her a Broadway role the following season. Although Blair played Mildred Douglas in O'Neill's *The Hairy Ape* on Macdougal Street, director Arthur Hopkins replaced her when the play moved uptown. According to James Light, Hopkins thought Mary was "too real. He wanted the rich girl to be a shell, a prototype, not a real person."[73] Blair enjoyed a successful career as a professional actress until the mid-1930s, winning special acclaim as an interpreter of O'Neill. Among the theatres she worked for was the Experimental Theatre, where she appeared in *Spook Sonata, Fashion, All God's Chillun Got Wings, The Crime in the Whistler Room, Patience, East Lynne,* and revivals of *Before Breakfast* and *Diff'rent.*[74] She developed tuberculosis in 1935 and died, after years of illness, in 1947.

Ann Harding created a sensation as Madeline Morton in Susan Glaspell's *Inheritors.* When the completely inexperienced nineteen-year-old Harding auditioned, director Jasper Deeter thought "she might do for one of the giggly girls," but Glaspell recognized in Harding exactly the quality desired: "She was natural."[75] Critical response validated Glaspell's judgment. For Ludwig Lewisohn, "Miss Ann Harding's impersonation of Madeline has freshness and sincerity, a cool charm and a beautiful gift of aspiration."[76] Deutsch and Hanau reported general

Ann Harding. Courtesy Billy Rose Theatre Collection, New York Public Library for the Performing Arts, Astor, Lenox and Tilden Foundations.

critical reaction: "A new actress of startling beauty and sincerity swept the whole thing along on a wave of emotional conviction. Ann Harding and the wave did much to heighten the reaction to *Inheritors.* The reviewers agreed . . . that, as its heroine, Ann Harding was superb. The Provincetown, so rich in discoveries, had made one of its rarest finds."[77] After *Inheritors'* four-week run, Harding was swept up immediately by commercial producers and enjoyed a long professional career in theatre and film.

One of the most highly praised individual performances by a Provincetown actress was Margaret Wycherly's portrayal of Claire Archer in Susan Glaspell's *The Verge,* which opened in the fall of 1921. A veteran stage actress, Wycherly had studied at the American Academy of Dramatic Art, making her professional debut in 1898 at the age of fourteen. It was a coup for the Provincetown Players to feature a performer of Wycherly's reputation; she had been so impressed by *Bernice* that

she asked Glaspell to write a strong leading role for her.[78] Despite
the critical scorn heaped upon the character she played, Wycherly's performance was praised as "magnificent," "radiant," "sympathetic," "extraordinary," "moving," "uncommonly understanding," and "the very
embodiment of Claire Archer."[79] Maida Castellun offered one of the
more thoughtful analyses: "Margaret Wycherly transcends herself. . . .
an actress who has always scorned the patterns of the stage, lends her
intelligence, her sensitive intuitions, her poetic beauty and her artistic
sincerity to make Claire live, and transcends anything she has done before. . . . the signs of genius on the verge of madness are delicately
indicated and the final scene of madness is relentless in its truth."[80]
"Scorn[ing] the patterns of the stage" in this instance may refer to rejection of traditional methods of performing, which Wycherly would
have learned at the American Academy of Dramatic Art, founded by
Franklin Sargent in 1884. Sargent, who represented the new movement in American acting, aimed "to develop the originality of the student, not to impose certain fixed conceptions of character."[81] Although
Wycherly directed two plays for the Provincetown Players, *The Verge*
marked her only appearance with the company as an actress. She enjoyed a tremendously successful career onstage and in film, making her
last appearance onstage as the Dowager Duchess of York in *Richard III*
in 1953.

As valuable as are the consistent and reliable contributions of recurring performers like Glaspell, Hays, Rostetter, Edna and Norma Millay,
and Pyne, or the infrequent but exceptional achievements of performers
like Wycherly, Harding, and Blair, none was more influential in promoting the new methods of acting than the company's most prolific
performer, Ida Rauh. Called "the Duse of Macdougal Street," an "experimental Bernhardt," a genius, and a star, Rauh performed twenty-six
roles throughout her Provincetown career (1915 to 1921)—twice as many
as any other woman in the company, and eight more than any other
performer, male or female, during the same period.[82]

As an actor, Rauh possessed several natural attributes. According to
contemporaries, she displayed the grace of a panther,[83] the bearing of a
lioness,[84] the head of an Old Testament heroine,[85] a strong and fascinat-
ing face,[86] and the voice of a viola.[87] Before helping to found Provincetown, Rauh had participated in Floyd Dell's "communal rituals"[88] at the
Liberal Club and had performed with the Washington Square Players.

Margaret Wycherly. Courtesy
Schlesinger Library, Radcliffe
Institute, Harvard University.

In 1920, Rauh articulated her rejection of "old-fashioned" acting in favor of the new methods:

> I am looking for something simpler in the theater, something which is more natural. In the role of Anisja, I have wanted to eliminate the "theatricals" and make it simple. . . . If I take the part of a peasant woman, I want to talk and act like one. All the old-fashioned theatrical tricks should have no place in it. What peasant woman says "cawn't" and "mawster"? Yet the treatment of the stage is unreal today. It continues to use those old feelings and methods which to other people do not mean much.[89]

Rauh developed a prolific and varied acting career at Provincetown. Her performances during the two summer seasons evidently established her as one of the group's most valuable actors.[90] She appeared in seven of the twenty new plays produced during the company's first New York

season and in eight productions during the second.[91] Although critical
response is scanty during these early seasons, Rauh was encouraged by
the response from colleagues and audiences: "The theatre has been a joy
to me, and it seems as if I had made good. At least I have heard many
fine things about my acting."[92] Rauh made five appearances during the
third season.[93] During the Players' next three seasons, however, she appeared in only three productions: Barnes's *Three from the Earth*, Evelyn
Scott's *Love*, and Glaspell's *Suppressed Desires*.[94] The striking decrease in
the number of roles is partially explained by the steadily decreasing
number of productions,[95] but it is explained as well by Rauh's increased
involvement in stage direction,[96] her appearance with another company
in January 1920, the increasing dissension among company members
regarding reorganization, and her deteriorating relationships with other
influential company members, most notably O'Neill. Her inclusion in
the Broadway *Suppressed Desires/The Emperor Jones* production in the
spring and summer of 1921, despite her differences with O'Neill and
others, suggests that she still exerted considerable influence within the
company.

Rauh's performances earned, by Provincetown standards, considerable critical attention. Kenneth Macgowan commended the "truth of
the acting" in *Cocaine*.[97] By the fall of 1918, Rauh's name had been linked
with two of the world's greatest actresses. jane heap dubbed her the
"Duse of Macdougal Street,"[98] and *Current Opinion* hailed her as "an
experimental Bernhardt" who "brings keen intelligence to the interpretation of her parts."[99] Gorham Munson characterized Rauh as "an emotional actress particularly strong in tragic roles, at least akin to the
great."[100] Heywood Broun became one of Rauh's strongest supporters,
commending her performances in *The Athenian Women, Where the Cross
Is Made, The Squealer,* and *Bernice*.[101] Rauh's portrayal of the female lead
in Barnes's *Three from the Earth* won special praise. One writer con-
gratulated her for making the mystifying play "say something."[102] Another featured Rauh's latest achievement in an article that also indicated
interest from commercial producers: "The famous star of the Provincetown Players, whom Broadway managers have not yet been able to lure
from Greenwich Village . . . has achieved the hit of her career [in *Three
from the Earth*]. Critics say she shows the quality of Bernhardt in her
interpretation of the character."[103] Glaspell's full-length drama *Bernice*
brought Rauh her most critically acclaimed role: the intuitive and com-

passionate Margaret Pierce. Reviews in the *Baltimore Sun, New York Daily Herald, New York Daily Times,* and *New York Tribune* applauded her performance.[104] Broun was most effusive, paying tribute within his review to her past accomplishments as well: "Miss Rauh's performance was magnificent. This was hardly accident, for Miss Rauh has given enough first class performances to convince us that she is a splendid player in emotional roles; more particularly in roles in which the emotion is designed to smoulder."[105] A few weeks later Broun included Rauh in his list of the season's twelve best actresses, a list that also included Minnie Maddern Fiske and Helen Hayes: "Miss Rauh has not been seen on Broadway. All her experience this season has been at the little Provincetown theatre. She belongs in the list because of a superb performance which she gave in Susan Glaspell's inspiring *Bernice.* Miss Rauh can hold a role under the tightest rein throughout an evening and yet convince everybody in an audience that something is smouldering underneath the repression."[106] In May, an article featuring Rauh declared that "the only acting of genius New York has seen for many seasons is that being done by Ida Rauh, the star of the Provincetown Players."[107]

Rauh received unfavorable reviews in only two instances, for her portrayals of Fanny in Wilbur Daniel Steele's farce *Not Smart* and of Carroll Lamont in Scott's melodrama *Love. Not Smart* appeared on the same bill as *The Squealer,* in which Rauh also assumed a leading role. As one writer commented, "Ida Rauh displayed a very emotional power [in *The Squealer*]. Her technique however, seemed not very firm—her limitations obvious in comedy."[108] Heywood Broun concurred: "Ida Rauh, one of the best players of the Provincetown group, is less effective in farce than in more substantial drama. She gives a sincere, strong and shrewdly modulated performance in *The Squealer.*"[109] Rauh's appearance in *Love* in the spring of 1921 was her least successful; play and cast were overwhelmingly panned. Edwin Bjorkman's notice is typical: "Miss Rauh has undertaken an impossible task and the handicap proves too heavy for a gift so largely based on temperament."[110] Apparently Rauh, like so many of her sister actresses at Provincetown, was generally regarded by critics as emotionally truthful yet technically deficient. In fact, Rauh may have been at least partially responsible for the prevalence of the "new acting" at Provincetown, as her influence on acting at Provincetown went beyond her own portrayals. As a member of the executive committee and a director, she helped cast and coach actors. Apparently Rauh offered criticism even when others were directing. As Kirah Markham rather resentfully recalled, "When I was cast in a play Ida Rauh quarreled with everything I did. Jig had to come to my rescue."[111]

Rauh did not make the transition from Provincetown to a professional career, and whether she ever wanted to is difficult to determine. While associated with the Provincetown Players, she made two outside professional appearances: the Greenwich Avenue Theatre's production of *Woman's Honor* in the fall of 1918 and the Theatre Guild's production of *Power of Darkness* in January 1920. In 1924, Rauh tried to interest investors in a play about Mary Wollstonecraft, with herself in the lead, but the project never materialized. One reason may have been resistance from her lover, Andrew Dasburg, who was reportedly "furious" that Rauh intended to return to the stage.[112] She did not seriously pursue an acting career after that, even declining a role written for her by D. H. Lawrence.

The experiences of these actresses indicate an extraordinarily beneficial relationship between Provincetown's women writers and actresses. Of the eighty-four plays in which the actresses performed, more than half (forty-six) were written or cowritten by women. Although Mary Blair's greatest success was in a play by Eugene O'Neill, most actresses received notable triumphs in roles written by women: Pyne and Rostetter in Rostetter's *The Widow's Veil,* Hays in Barnes's *An Irish Triangle* and Glaspell's *Inheritors,* Glaspell in all her own plays, especially *The People,* Harding in Glaspell's *Inheritors,* Wycherly in Glaspell's *The Verge,* and Rauh in Glaspell's *Bernice* and Barnes's *Three from the Earth.* The creative and convincing interpretations of Provincetown's actresses illuminated complex new plays. The esteem granted Susan Glaspell, the writer, was due in no small part to Susan Glaspell, the actress. Similarly, the recognition awarded male dramatists like O'Neill and Dell depended, at least in part, on the sensitive and effective portrayals of actresses like Pyne, Millay, and Blair.

That the Provincetown Players acquired "quite a name around town," then, depended not only on plays, but also on notable performances. The performances of Pyne, Glaspell, and Rauh during the first New York season brought publicity and prestige, from individuals as influential as David Belasco and Jacques Copeau, to an experimental theatre company that was, at that time, obscure. The remarkable degree of favorable publicity that Rauh continually enjoyed must certainly have enhanced the company's reputation. Wycherly's "star" turn also enhanced the company's prestige, and her appearance is entirely due to Glaspell. Future careers of some of these actresses suggest continuity between the Provincetown actresses and the Experimental Theatre; Mary Blair, Norma Millay and Alice Rostetter, as well as a number of Provincetown actresses not profiled in this chapter, worked later for that organization.[113]

While the successful performances of Provincetown's actresses most certainly helped bring fame to the company, the actresses also won recognition for themselves. Most (Pyne, Edna Millay, Norma Millay, Blair, Harding, and perhaps Rauh) had professional ambitions, and all received professional offers after Provincetown debuts. Three (Blair, Harding, and Norma Millay) went immediately to professional careers. Mary Pyne would doubtless have had a professional career had she lived. Edna Millay seemed headed for an acting career when, perhaps, the literary world offered more immediate rewards. That Glaspell limited her acting career to Provincetown suggests a commitment to the company rather than to an individual career, and that she appeared only in her own plays suggests a stronger commitment to playwriting than to acting. That Rauh, despite an extraordinary amount of favorable critical attention, did not make a serious attempt to act professionally after 1922 suggests that she, too, may have been more interested in the company than in an individual career.

Although each of these actresses possessed individual attributes, they shared a commitment to the "new school" of acting, rejecting conventional performing methods (what Rauh called "old-fashioned theatrical tricks") in favor of simple, sincere, and individually unique characterizations. It is impossible to know for certain precisely what the critics meant by "technical" and "professional" skills, but evidence suggests that what critics were calling "professional techniques," actors like Glaspell and Rauh considered "old-fashioned tricks." What contemporary critics perceived as artless inability to master technique seems here revealed as a conscious attempt to experiment with a new style of acting, to find new techniques and methods more suitable to the new types of plays and characters being created. Pyne's convincing creations, Edna Millay's transformative use of her own chameleon personality, Glaspell's "very real kind of acting," Blair's "too real" impersonations, Rauh's "something simpler," and Wycherly's "embodiment" all suggest the "sympathetic identification" called for by the new theories of performance.

Provincetown's actresses, no less than its playwrights, were ahead of their time in pioneering new styles. Jacques Copeau recognized Glaspell as a trailblazer in this effort. Kenneth Macgowan's description of Mary Blair's performance in *Diff'rent* ("beat generation quality, intensity and sincerity") links her to the quintessentially American "Method" of acting made famous by the likes of James Dean and Marlon Brando in the 1940s and 1950s. From Mary Pyne's rejection of James O'Neill's histrionic tutelage in the fall of 1916 to Margaret Wycherly's "scorning the patterns of the stage" five years later, Provincetown's leading actresses were in the vanguard of American performers who valued emotional truthfulness and original, imaginative creation over mechanical proficiency and imitative re-creation.

In chapter 3, I suggested a relationship between performance and feminist expression—that casting actresses who exhibit conventionally "feminine" attributes may alter the perception of a character written as feminist. For Glaspell, Barnes, Scott, and other feminist playwrights, to have their strong female protagonists played by women like Ida Rauh and Margaret Wycherly, who were in fact strong women passionately committed to feminism, must have reinforced the feminist impact of these productions.

# 5

## Staging Women

They didn't want me, I wasn't one of them, but they needed me.
—Nina Moise, interview with George Voellmer

Stage direction in American theatre, as well as performance, was in transition at the time of Provincetown's creation. At the turn of the century, directorial functions (script interpretation, casting, staging) were typically assumed by leading actors, producers, or playwrights, who performed those duties in combination with other major responsibilities. The term "director" was rarely employed; "producer" generally served to mean anyone who assumed producing or directing responsibilities. Contemporary theatre critics seemed unaware of the specific contributions of directors, gave scant attention to directorial functions, and rarely credited directors by name.[1] The second decade of the twentieth century brought a significant increase in the importance of the stage director and increased reliance on the specialist.[2]

Given their original mission to "encourage American playwrights," it is not surprising that the Provincetown Players initially stipulated that playwrights should direct their own plays "without hindrance, according to [their] own ideas . . . select [their] own cast[s], see to it that they are rehearsed, and generally direct [the] production."[3] The Players' president, Jig Cook, was authorized to assist the writer in these tasks; the active membership made casting suggestions, and any active member was entitled to attend rehearsals and offer suggestions.[4] In proposing a playwright/director, the Players adopted a practice common in the commercial theatre, where many well-known theatre artists (e.g., David Belasco, Rachel Crothers, and George M. Cohan) combined the two roles. In proposing widespread collaborative "assistance," a practice all but unheard of in the commercial theatre, the Players invited chaos.

The group's writers, who had no directing experience, were apparently unable or unwilling to exercise final authority within this collaborative framework (what Edna Kenton called "the synthetic process").[5] Even before the company moved to New York, Eugene O'Neill, Susan Glaspell, and Louise Bryant sought help in staging their plays.[6] During the company's first New York season, rehearsals degenerated into debates between playwrights who were "insisting on rhythms" and actors who "argued crosses until they were stepped on or pushed aside to get them out of the way."[7] The Provincetown Players were, in fact, quick to recognize that directing requires special skills not necessarily possessed by even the most talented writers and actors. Abandoning constitutional stipulations, they began to designate individuals to assume control of most plays and to actively seek outside directors.[8] In March 1917 they created a new salaried position of "producing director" to oversee stage direction of all productions.[9]

In their early recognition of the director as specialist, the Provincetown Players once more placed themselves in the forefront of modern theatre practice. The degree of autonomy given directors almost certainly varied throughout the company's history and depended on a number of circumstances. For the most part, collaboration seems to have given way to individual control with time. Casting probably remained the most ambiguous area; as late as 1921, the company as a group—particularly the executive committee—still advised in this area. Although Provincetown directors remained subject to advice from playwrights and other influential company members, they generally functioned as modern directors do: they interpreted plays for scenic and performing possibilities, cast actors and coached them in their roles, and blocked stage movement. Taking into consideration the collaborative nature of the theatre and even allowing that the Provincetown Players were more collaborative than most, Provincetown directors still significantly affected the success or failure of the plays they staged.

It is hardly surprising that a company offering so many plays by and about women should also offer unusual opportunities to women directors. Compared to their commercial counterparts, Provincetown's women directors enjoyed an extraordinarily high level of participation. In an era when women directed less than 5 percent of the plays on Broadway, women directed 46 percent of the plays produced by the Provincetown Players.[10] Of the eighty-nine Provincetown Players productions for which directing credit can be reasonably established, thirty-six were directed by women. Women shared directing credit with men for an additional five productions.[11]

Provincetown's women directors were not only prolific, they were influential, especially in facilitating the important shift from "synthetic" collaboration to specialization. A recent study has traced a common developmental pattern among women directors throughout the twentieth century. This pattern moves chronologically from the actress/director to the playwright/director to the specialist. Actress/directors (exemplified by Minnie Maddern Fiske, Mary Shaw, and Olga Nethersole) began directing around the turn of the century and generally performed the leading role in plays they directed. Playwright/directors (exemplified by Rachel Crothers and Edith Ellis) emerged around 1910 and generally directed their own plays. The woman director as specialist was a rarity until the 1930s.[12] Two studies have cited Agnes Morgan, company director for the Neighborhood Playhouse from 1915 to 1927, as a pioneer of this type.[13]

The first woman credited with directing at Provincetown, however, fit none of the traditional patterns. Marguerite Zorach and her husband, William Zorach, directed and designed Louise Bryant's *The Game* in the summer of 1916, and they are the only directors credited in production records for the season.[14] Although they had no specific theatrical experience, the Zorachs had strong opinions about what theatre should be, and their staging reflected their preference for symbolic, rather than illusionistic, presentation: "*The Game* is an attempt to synthesize decoration, costume, speech and action into one mood. Starting from the idea that the play is symbolic of rather than representative of life, the Zorachs have designed the decoration to suggest rather than to portray; the speech and action of the players being used as the plastic element in the whole unified convention."[15] *The Game* was one of the most memorable of the Players' early productions and the only one noted primarily for its presentation rather than its text: "*The Game*, a simple and not particularly brilliant morality play, was enhanced by the colorful mounting which William and Marguerite Zorach gave it, and by the fact that it was played in a stylized fashion."[16] Although she designed again for the company, individually and in collaboration with her husband, Marguerite Zorach did not direct again, possibly because she had little interest in realism, a style favored by most Provincetown play-wrights and actors.[17]

Like Zorach, Provincetown's next two women directors shared di-recting credit with their husbands: playwright Neith Boyce, who co-wrote and codirected *Enemies* with her husband, Hutchins Hapgood, and Alice Hall, who codirected her husband's play for children, *Mother Carey's Chickens*, in 1916. Deutsch and Hanau labeled *Enemies* "[one] of the more effective productions,"[18] and the Halls' fanciful production was very popular with the Provincetown crowd. *Mother Carey's Chickens* started as a Montessorian attempt to provide a creative outlet for the children (and keep them out of their parents' hair), but it became one of the Players' more ambitious projects, featuring elaborate costumes, special props, songs, and dances, as well as a huge cast of pirates, mer-maids, seagulls, and storm petrels (locally known as "mother carey's chickens"). The cast, which the Halls "drilled for weeks," included the three Hall daughters, the four Hapgood children, Nilla and Harl Cook, and Ellen and Heaton Vorse. Francis Hall became the first Province-town performer to receive a salary; her harried parents promised her a quarter if she would remember to wag her mermaid's tail.[19]

According to Louise Bryant, Sophie Treadwell, a member of the newly formed producing committee, became the first woman to assume individual control of a production (John Mosher's *Sauce for the Em-peror*).[20] Although Treadwell later became a successful playwright, she did not write for the Players. She directed her own *Lone Valley* on Broadway in 1933 to generally poor reviews.[21] Despite a number of suc-cessful productions, including three of the four directed or codirected by women, it became increasingly clear to the Players throughout the fall of 1916 that their "synthetic process" of directing was disastrous. In De-cember 1916, just before Nina Moise's association with the Province-town Players began, the company was struggling for survival. Conflicts caused by erratic artistic temperaments were compounded by lack of professional discipline: "The Provincetown Players are going along their thorny path. . . . They're hurrying on their play of Neith's—*The Two Sons*—for the third bill with only a week of rehearsal. I don't know if they've begun rehearsal for the fourth bill at all. . . . Everyone has a grouch, or is drunk. Some are both drunk and grouchy."[22] Although the Players decided to close their chaotically collaborative rehearsals in an attempt to avoid conflict, the atmosphere became increasingly one of depression, dissension, and discouragement. Even the indefatigable Cook feared that the Players might not survive their first season.[23] It was at this time, and under these circumstances, that Provincetown's most prolific and influential director, Nina Moise, appeared.

Although she performed a few roles,[24] Moise came to the company as a director, was always primarily a director, and was largely responsible for the shift in the company's directing methods from collectivism to specialization. Following an unsuccessful stock engagement, Moise visited her friend Margaret Swain in New York. Moise was seeking acting work, but Swain, who had just codesigned *Fog* for the Players, told her that the company needed directors. Moise, who had some directing experience, promptly met with Jig Cook and accompanied him to a rehearsal of David Pinski's *A Dollar*. After Moise made a few blocking suggestions, Cook invited her to direct the play.[25] She ultimately directed the entire bill, which included Neith Boyce's *Winter's Night* and Kenneth MacNichol's *Pan*. In quick succession, the Players elected Moise to active membership, made her chair of the producing committee, and, at the end of the first season, created and offered to her the position of producing director, one of four salaried positions within the company.[26] From her first assignment in January 1917 until her departure in May 1918, Moise directed seventeen plays and codirected three. Despite her brief tenure, Moise directed more productions than anyone else—male or female—throughout the company's existence.

Although Moise was young (twenty-seven), her training, experience, and personality enabled her to quickly win the confidence and respect of the Players. After receiving a degree in history from Stanford University in 1912, Moise had completed a rigorous training program at the Cumnock School of Oratory in Los Angeles. The Cumnock School curriculum included literary interpretation, oratory, and physical culture,[27] a background that particularly equipped her to direct for a theatre dedicated to the development of new dramatists. Moise's experience in stock had accustomed her to the one-act form, a fast-paced schedule, and a versatile repertory.[28] This experience doubtless aided her ability to get Provincetown's widely diverse plays up quickly and effectively.[29]

Moise's skill and tact in working with new playwrights is indicated by her successful collaboration with the company's leading writers. She worked amicably with Floyd Dell, who had disagreed violently with

David Pinski's *A Dollar* in rehearsal. 139 Macdougal Street. Presumably Pinski is standing house left and Moise seems to be giving stage directions at house right. Courtesy Brown Brothers, Sterling, Pennsylvania.

director Duncan Macdougal and Cook during the staging of one of his plays.[30] Dell, who remembered Moise as "so competent and friendly,"[31] had resigned in March 1917 but returned to the company shortly after Moise's appointment as company director. Although she codirected with Dell his *The Angel Intrudes* in December 1917, Moise alone directed Dell's *Sweet and Twenty* in January 1918, indicating his increased confidence in her direction. Moise collaborated successfully with Glaspell, directing all of her plays that were produced during Moise's tenure.

Perhaps most significant was Moise's ability to work effectively with O'Neill and to interpret his plays to his satisfaction. Although he insisted on deference to his wishes in production, O'Neill hated to attend rehearsals or even performances of his plays: "When I finish writing a play, I'm through with it."[32] As Moise explained, "Gene was concerned with plays, not theatre."[33] The only solution to O'Neill's dilemma was to find a director he trusted. He had not been happy with any of his options at Provincetown, however, until Moise arrived. Even Cook, an ardent believer in O'Neill's talent, did not arouse confidence: "O'Neill respected [Cook's] dedication and idealism . . . but he also would become impatient with his strain of impracticality, his vague yearnings and hopelessly fanciful ideas."[34] Moise, on the other hand, earned O'Neill's absolute trust: "You know my work and understand the spirit underlying it as few people do," he wrote in April 1918. "I have complete confidence in your direction."[35] O'Neill further demonstrated his faith in Moise by asking her to look in on a rehearsal of the Washington Square Players' production of *Ile*, which she had directed previously for Provincetown. A subsequent letter indicated that Moise agreed: "Many thanks for your kindness in regard to *Ile*. It takes a load off my mind. I trust not producers—oh—ah—but of course—save one."[36]

O'Neill apparently relied on Moise to elicit good performances: "*Make them act!*"[37] According to James Light, Moise did this: "She taught us acting."[38] Critical responses to the acting in Moise's productions suggest her skill in coaching: Heywood Broun admired all the performances in Glaspell's *The People*.[39] The *Brooklyn Globe*'s reviewer pronounced the "acting, staging, and atmosphere" of O'Neill's *Ile* "quite admirable,"[40] and the performances of Moise's production of O'Neill's *The Rope* earned praise from several critics.[41] In none of the reviews, however, was Moise's name given. Although we know very little about the methods she employed to draw effective performances from her casts, Alfred Kreymborg's report of one of her rehearsals for *The Long Voyage Home* reveals her method of prodding performers toward an appropriately vigorous approach to O'Neill's play:

A rehearsal was under full steam. . . . [The actors] were roaring and cursing in the raciest language of the sea, cuffing and mauling one another and finally turning on one of their number and sandbagging him senseless. . . . The actors, noisy and ponderous, reveled in their respective parts and resembled a football scrimmage at its most delirious height. . . . Suddenly he heard someone in the surrounding darkness roar instructions to the actors. "Where do you think you are—at a tea-party?" The voice called derisively, and the company repeated the scene with redoubled pandemonium. When the house lights went up, Zorach pointed out that the voice belonged to a stocky woman, the stage director, Nina Moise.[42]

Moise directed five of Provincetown's leading actresses (Mary Pyne, Glaspell, Edna Millay, Norma Millay, and Ida Rauh) in a total of sixteen productions, and surely she deserves some share of their successes. It was under Moise's direction that Glaspell received her notable praise from Jacques Copeau. Moise may also be at least partially responsible for the prevalence of naturalistic performance at Provincetown. She preferred realistic works, admitting in later years that she had had difficulty understanding Maxwell Bodenheim's poetic fantasy, *The Gentle Furniture Shop*.[43] Further evidence of Moise's proficiency as an acting coach comes from her later career as a dialogue director in charge of diction, deportment, and decorum of Paramount's players at Paramount Pictures (1931 to 1935).[44]

In addition to collaborating with playwrights and coaching actors, Moise orchestrated movement (blocking) for the Provincetown Players' stage, which measured only ten by twelve feet.[45] Kenton applauded Moise's skill in maneuvering actors on the Players' tiny stage, noting that Lawrence Langner and Philip Moeller of the Washington Square Players reacted with stunned appreciation to the first plays directed by Moise, "so much improvement in mere mechanics of movement did they show." In fact, Langner and Moeller hired Moise immediately to direct productions of the Washington Square Players School, a job she took on in addition to her Provincetown duties.[46]

Moise's staging of Cook's full-length drama *The Athenian Women* perhaps most clearly demonstrated her mastery of physical staging: "Nina worked out the difficult technique of grouping thirty-three amateur actors without crowding," wrote Kenton. "At no moment of the play did the little stage seem cluttered or over-filled. It was a real triumph in production against staggering physical odds."[47] Part of Moise's method included the use of various levels and the addition of three broad, shallow steps leading from the stage into the audience. Heywood Broun's review acknowledged the success of her strategies—without, however, identifying the director by name: "The Provincetown Players have succeeded in putting on a three-act play, with 30 speaking parts and a few slavewomen, bowmen and messengers, on their 12 foot stage. . . . [F]or the most part, the producer has done extraordinarily well. The

Jig Cook's *The Athenian Women*, directed by Nina Moise; Cook and Ida Rauh are stage right, other actors are unidentified. 139 Macdougal Street. Courtesy Billy Rose Theatre Collection, New York Public Library for the Performing Arts, Astor, Lenox and Tilden Foundations.

production may serve as an example of what may be accomplished when taste is substituted for money in the mounting of a play."[48] And in a newspaper article published in April 1918, Kenton confirmed Moise's contribution to improved staging: "They have a producer [director] to whom goes a larger share of their technical success than most of them know."[49]

Although the erratic and undisciplined Players obviously benefited from Moise's formal training and practical experience, any account of her success must credit her personal, as well as professional, attributes. In a letter written after her departure, O'Neill affirmed Moise's personality as crucial to her Provincetown success: "We—meaning the P.P.— and I especially have missed your 'pep' very much this year. . . . They put on *The Moon* on their second bill, and what with the small stage, the large cast—and the difficult set, well—just use your imagination!

The director—I forget his name—couldn't do anything under such conditions, and *didn't have personality enough to overcome them* [emphasis added]. So hasten East!"[50] Moise's "mid-Victorian" values, like her professional experiences, contrasted sharply with those of her bohemian colleagues at Provincetown: "Climbing through ash cans to keep an appointment was a new experience for me."[51] In contrast to Provincetown's brilliant, beautiful, and radical women, Moise was "a dark and trimly plump girl with a keen kind face"[52] who was a little wary of the sophisticated Provincetowners. Years later Moise ruefully remembered making "a great mistake" by calling Susan Glaspell "Mrs. Cook."[53] Clearly considering herself an outsider, Moise attributed her acceptance by the Players to her professional abilities: "They didn't want me, I wasn't one of them, but they needed me."[54] In fact, it was probably Moise's difference in background and temperament that allowed her to mediate the "poisonous rowing" among the volatile personalities at Provincetown and to instill confidence where there had been discord. Kenton, who typically championed strong leadership, looked on Moise's arrival as a godsend, just the "velvet-gloved tyrant" Kenton had longed for. Referring to the chaotic spring of 1917, Kenton described a patient Moise "standing by with folded hands when temperamental actors and playwrights got kinks in their psychology."[55] James Light similarly remembered Moise as "sturdy, cheerful, firm," a "maternal-looking" woman who "kept quiet order."[56]

It must have been quite a blow to both Provincetown and the Washington Square Players when Moise suddenly decided to return to California in May 1918, and the reasons for her departure are still unexplained. According to Moise, she left to see her family and to take a job with the Red Cross. One interviewer, however, has speculated that her complicated relationship with O'Neill, described by Moise as "close" but not an "affair," caused her sudden departure.[57] According to Moise, O'Neill once asked her to marry him. She did not take the proposal seriously, although "he didn't seem to be joking—at the moment, I think he was just a very lonely man who needed somebody."[58] Although strongly attracted, Moise claimed she resisted a sexual relationship. She knew there were other women in his life at the time, including Louise Bryant and Agnes Boulton, whom he married in April 1918.[59]

Moise continued to make notable contributions to the American theatre in California. In 1921 she became company director of the Santa

Barbara Community Arts Players, receiving in 1922 a $135,000 fund to remodel a 631-seat theatre, the Lobero, and install a German lighting system. She served as company director until 1925, staging at least nine full-length plays, including *Liliom, Miss Lulu Bett,* and *You Never Can Tell.*[60] At Santa Barbara, Moise engaged two former Provincetown colleagues, actress Edna James and designer Ira Remsen.[61] In 1925, Sheldon Cheney listed Moise, along with Irving Pichel, Raymond O'Neil, Sam Hume, Frederic McConnell, and Gilmor Brown, as among the best of the artist/directors who had chosen to work outside the "regular" theatres.[62] In the 1930s Moise worked for Paramount, not only as dialogue director but also as associate director to Cecil B. DeMille on the films *This Day and Age* and *Cradle Song.*[63] In 1941, official documents recorded her occupation as "dramatic coach."[64] She died in California in 1968. Although she left the Players for a larger and much more generously endowed theatre, Moise later told Kenton that her association with the Provincetown Players was the most meaningful of her life: "I still love the thought of those old days . . . maybe it is better in retrospect than it actually was, but time has cast a shadow over the memory of the difficulties we had, and I only seem to remember the vitality and young enthusiasm of it all. Nothing since has really been as good."[65]

Moise's tenure was brief, but she had made a lasting impression. Although playwrights continued to direct, or codirect, throughout the company's history, they did so with a clearer understanding of directorial responsibilities. Leading actors also took on the director's role, but they rarely combined the two responsibilities. Following Boyce, four other women playwrights exercised their constitutional right to direct. Like their counterparts in the commercial theatre, Edna Millay, Susan Glaspell, Grace Potter, and Rita Wellman all directed or codirected their own works. Glaspell and Millay directed twice, the others only once. Both Glaspell and Potter shared directing credit (Glaspell with Cook and Moise, Potter with Moise). Two playwright/directors assumed individual control of their plays: Millay directed both *The Princess Marries the Page* and *Aria da Capo,* and Wellman directed her *The Rib-Person.*

Millay was the only playwright/director with previous acting and directing experience.[66] According to a colleague, directing her own work was particularly appealing to her.[67] At Provincetown she cast herself in *The Princess Marries the Page* and her sister Norma in *Aria da Capo.*

Critical evaluation is scanty, but what evidence there is suggests that the playwright/directors handled the responsibility capably. *Aria da Capo,* especially, was considered a "double triumph" for Millay.[68] Deutsch and Hanau attributed its success to the "excellence of the production" as well as to the text.[69] One reviewer considered Provincetown's production of *Woman's Honor,* codirected by Glaspell and Moise, superior to the production of that play by the Greenwich Village Theatre.[70] None of the playwright/directors staged anyone else's work, and none pursued directing professionally, although Millay also directed her own work for the Other Players, a subsidiary group of Provincetowners who staged three poetic fantasies (two by Kreymborg, one by Millay) and a dance piece in March 1918. Because they directed only their own plays, Provincetown's women playwright/directors may have been more interested in ensuring faithful interpretation of their plays than in directing for its own sake.

Although a number of women who directed for Provincetown had considerable acting experience, or were primarily actresses, the term "actress/director" is only applicable in a few circumstances. Most actresses who directed for Provincetown did not act and direct simultaneously; two of them (Enright and Westley) never acted for Provincetown at all, and all are most accurately described as specialists. Margaret Wycherly, who directed Pendleton King's *Cocaine* in March 1917 and Norman C. Lindau's *A Little Act of Justice* in January 1922, is one of the few Provincetown directors to receive specific critical evaluation. The play, cast (including Rauh), and production of *Cocaine* received favorable comments.[71] One reviewer described the staging of *A Little Act of Justice* as "skillful," and another mentioned the "strikingly effective groupings" for this five-character comedy.[72] Wycherly was Kenton's first choice to direct Glaspell's *Chains of Dew* in the spring of 1922, but she was unavailable. Kenton clearly believed that Wycherly would have been a much more sensitive interpreter of Glaspell's script than its actual director, Ralph Stewart: "Margaret Wycherly could feel where things dropped out—what was you and what wasn't."[73] For the rest of her career, Wycherly worked primarily as an actress; she did, however, direct two plays on Broadway in the 1920s, playing the leading role in one.[74]

Florence Enright, who directed Florence Kiper Frank's *Gee-Rusalem* in November 1918 and Lawrence Vail's *What D'You Want* in December

1920, was a veteran performer who appeared regularly with the Washington Square Players, the Theatre Guild, and on Broadway. Her own acting skills apparently allowed her to cast and coach actors successfully. *What D'You Want* was chosen as a curtain-raiser to the Broadway production of O'Neill's *Diff'rent* in January 1921. *Gee-Rusalem* was also well received and its cast commended.[75] Norma Millay, who appeared in *Gee-Rusalem* and many other Provincetown plays, credited Enright with teaching her how to act in a nonrealistic, "staccato" style.[76] Further corroboration of Enright's skill in actor-coaching comes from her subsequent career as a drama coach and dialogue director for several major film studios in the 1930s. Her students included Katharine Cornell, Virginia Mayo, and Jane Russell.

Helen Westley, a leading actress and playreader for the Washington Square Players and the Theatre Guild, directed two plays by Djuna Barnes. As directing these plays marked her only association with the Provincetown Players, she may have done so as a personal favor to Barnes, who was a close friend. Westley, who, like Wycherly, had attended the American Academy of Dramatic Art,[77] was apparently also able to elicit convincing performances from her actors. Reviewers praised both Blanche Hays and Norma Millay, who played the leads in *An Irish Triangle* and *Kurzy of the Sea,* respectively.[78] Reading plays for the Theatre Guild may have given Westley skill and experience that helped her interpret new plays. Lawrence Langner recalled her "simple, direct enthusiasm for the greatest plays, her incisive mind, her disregard for appearances, her dislike of mediocrity, and her unwillingness to sacrifice art for money."[79] Westley later enjoyed a long career as an actress onstage and in film. Only two of Provincetown's actress/directors assumed the dual functions of acting and directing. Marjory Lacey-Baker had given impressive performances in *The Athenian Women,* the first production of *Woman's Honor,* and the Other Players' bill before directing the revival of *Woman's Honor,* in which she repeated her role as The Shielded One.

The company's leading actress, Ida Rauh, was also one of its most influential directors. She directed five productions in 1918 and 1919, performing in two of them. Rauh had been one of the first to promote specialized stage direction, and she apparently exerted her influence on staging even without formal authorization. During rehearsals for Floyd Dell's *A Long Time Ago* in the fall of 1916, Louise Bryant reported that director Duncan Macdougal wanted to stage the play "his way . . . not Ida's or Teddy's [E. J. Ballantine]."[80] A letter from Cook to Glaspell in October 1918 indicated that Rauh and Ballantine were overseeing rehearsals in Cook's absence.[81] Later that fall, Rauh directed her first play, O'Neill's *Where the Cross Is Made.* Evidently O'Neill did not want Rauh to direct his play: "Although O'Neill did not care much for the arrangement he tried not to be too disagreeable at first."[82] The play presented several staging difficulties: seven characters, exits through the ceiling, and the appearance of three ghosts onstage. The greatest challenge, however, arose from Rauh's conflict with O'Neill during a rehearsal period Kenton remembered as "one prolonged argument."[83] The major source of conflict concerned the presence of ghosts onstage: "Ida Rauh went right to the point and without too much tact,"[84] insisting that the audience would simply laugh. O'Neill refused to cut the ghosts, reminding Rauh of his prerogative to have his play directed "his own way, without hindrance."[85] The conflict accelerated; sides were taken. Many members of the company agreed with Rauh and urged O'Neill to follow her advice. O'Neill, however, was adamant. The ghosts stayed. Even though he got his way, "the struggle rasped his nerves."[86] Conflict between O'Neill and Rauh was heightened by the fact that she played a significant role in the production. Although Heywood Broun admired her "telling"[87] performance, O'Neill complained that the dual responsibility was "a bad handicap" and that her direction was "punk."[88]

Given his reaction to the directing of *Where the Cross Is Made,* O'Neill could not have wished for Rauh to direct *The Dreamy Kid* the following season. That she did so may suggest that few individuals were willing or available to undertake the task, but it may also indicate Rauh's general influence within the company. In casting *The Dreamy Kid,* Rauh was the first and only Provincetown director to entirely reject blackface performance in plays with nonwhite characters.[89] Instead, Rauh went to "the YMCA, the library, the churches, and everywhere else in Harlem," eventually acquiring an entirely African-American cast.[90] Although a few critics labeled the performances "amateurish," their support of Rauh's break with tradition was strong. As one writer observed, Rauh's casting "illumine[d] in a great many ways the psychological values of the piece."[91] Rauh's leading man, Harold Simmelkjaer, apparently unknown in 1919, appeared on Broadway in 1922.[92] Despite alienating O'Neill and James Light, another who did not like her direction,[93] Rauh directed three other plays for Provincetown: Rita Creighton Smith's *The Rescue* (in which she also performed a leading role), Winthrop Parkhurst's *Getting Unmarried* (featuring Norma Millay), and Bosworth Crocker's *The Baby Carriage* (featuring Alice Rostetter). Although Rauh directed five plays for the Players, her name is mentioned in only one newspaper review, for *The Dreamy Kid.*[94]

Rauh once described the director's role as "to suggest and coach the actors in interpretation,"[95] and a declaration from Norma Millay that she was "learning a lot" during rehearsals for *Getting Unmarried* implies that Rauh was a capable coach.[96] A letter from Glaspell to the Federal Theatre Project on Rauh's behalf indicated that Rauh was directing in Provincetown in 1938 and that she was skilled in textual interpretation as well as actor-coaching:

> There is no one whose feeling about theatre I find more stimulating, and with whom I myself would rather work. Whether in studying a play and proposing its revision, in direction, or in the creative ideas that keep the theatre a living thing I think she has the personality— the originality and enthusiasm that you would welcome in our Federal Theatre. I saw her work in direction up here [Provincetown] this summer and felt anew she had much to give. She has had a great deal to do in developing young playwrights [such] as Lynn Riggs and George O'Neil, who feel they owe her a very great deal, and she has an instinct for acting and directing that would be good in any teaching or coaching capacity.[97]

Lynn Riggs's biographer has strongly confirmed Rauh's ability to collaborate productively with new playwrights: "Most influential, however, among Riggs's Santa Fe friends was the actress and sculptor Ida Rauh Eastman. . . . It was she who challenged him to put his dramatic talents to use, producing his second one-act play, *Knives from Syria;* and she organized and directed the Santa Fe Players in its production [in 1925]."[98] Riggs, who dedicated two published volumes of plays to Rauh (in 1928 and 1936), frequently sought her advice: "I'm stuck in the second act again. It just won't go. Maybe I need a helping hand—yours."[99] In addition to organizing the Santa Fe Players, Rauh cofounded the

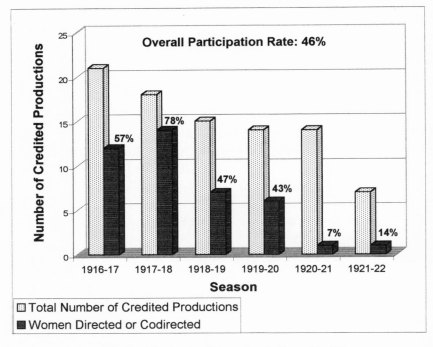

Graph 2. Number of Credited Productions Directed or Codirected by Women

Workers Drama League in 1926 and directed *Murder Sails at Midnight* on Broadway in 1937.[100] In Santa Fe she worked with a former Provincetown colleague, Margaret Nordfeldt.

One other woman received directing credit at Provincetown, Elsie Chapin, who directed her brother Harold Chapin's *The Philosopher of Butterbiggins* in 1919.[101] There is scant evidence from which to gauge Chapin's ability, but the play and cast, especially Edna Millay, were favorably reviewed.[102] After Moise's departure, the percentage of woman-directed plays at Provincetown dropped significantly, from a high in the 1917–18 season of 78 percent to lows of 7 percent in the 1920–21 season and 14 percent in the 1921–22 season (see graph 2). Rauh's diminished participation after the fall of 1919 also contributed to the decline. That other women did not emerge to take their place, allowing the participation percentages of Provincetown's women directors to drop closer to those of women directors in the commercial theatre, may be due to the company's association with Broadway that began in 1920. Throughout the twentieth century, women directors of any type have been vastly underrepresented in the commercial theatre.[103] In 1920, for example, women directed 3.6 percent of all plays produced on Broadway; in 1940, 6.4 percent; in 1970, 6.3 percent; and in 1990, 7.7 percent.[104]

In assuming the role of stage director—as a specially trained or qualified artist of equal or perhaps greater importance than the actor or dramatist—these women directly challenged two of the fundamental tenets of the Provincetown Players: the preeminence of the playwright and the feasibility of group collaboration. Although Moise may have been primarily responsible for securing a policy of individual control, others also exercised it, significantly altering the power structure of the company. Rauh's conflicts with O'Neill, in particular, illuminate the tensions that existed between playwrights and directors and suggest that playwrights, even the most powerful ones, did not necessarily always have the last word. As earlier studies have established Agnes Morgan as a pioneer among women specialist/directors, Provincetown's women specialists, Morgan's contemporaries, must be considered pioneers as well. Nina Moise, in particular, deserves recognition as a trailblazing woman director.

In assuming the dual functions of design and direction, Marguerite Zorach pioneered the new directorial model of designer/director, still relatively rare in American theatre practice.[105] Ida Rauh made a singularly influential contribution to American theatre history in her casting of *The Dreamy Kid*. In 1929, James Weldon Johnson called the Provincetown Players the "initial and greatest force in opening up the way for the Negro on the dramatic stage."[106] If his judgment is accurate, Rauh's role in that achievement deserves acknowledgment.

The experiences of Moise and Rauh reveal the influence of personality in directing and, specifically, collaborating with important male artists. The difference in personal style between Moise and Rauh parallels that between Fitzgerald and Kenton discussed in chapter 2 and provides further insight into the relationship between gender and power at Provincetown. The "maternal-looking" Moise, who exhibited traditionally feminine characteristics of tact, sympathy, and patience, encountered much less opposition than the forthright and unyielding Rauh. It was Moise, and not Rauh, who had a long-lasting career as a professional director.

In the early years, at least, the Provincetown Players provided rare opportunities for young and inexperienced directors, opportunities especially uncommon for women. Although some women directors at Provincetown, especially Moise, came to the company with valuable skills or training, the company afforded them exceptional opportunities to develop those skills. However, while similarly inexperienced actresses were successfully launched into professional careers from Provincetown's stage, even after only one performance, women directors did not make comparable transitions. That only two of the fourteen women, Enright and Moise, enjoyed sustained careers reflects the continued resistance to women directors in the commercial theatre.[107] Comparable studies of noncommercial companies do not exist, but the Experimental Theatre, for example, engaged only one female director during its existence.[108]

That the achievements of Provincetown's women directors had so little impact may also stem from the failure of contemporary newspaper critics to credit directors. Provincetown's women directors may have failed to establish directing careers or to become models for other women because almost nobody knew what they were doing. Those who did work subsequently (Moise, Enright, and Rauh) worked primarily in the West, outside the most visible arena for theatre practice in America: New York. Failure to establish subsequent directing careers, however, may also imply that these women were more interested in directing for this particular company than in having individual theatrical careers.

This investigation of women directors is further confirmation of a mutually interdependent network of women artists at Provincetown. Designer Margaret Swain introduced Moise to the company; Djuna Barnes probably brought in Helen Westley. Edna Kenton clearly championed Moise's authority. The bonds formed by these women survived the company's demise, as indicated by Moise's recruitment of Edna James in Santa Barbara, Rauh's working with Nordfeldt in Santa Fe, and Glaspell's efforts to bring Rauh into the Federal Theatre Project. As playwrights, producing committee members, or executive committee members, women frequently chose women directors, who in turn staged faithful interpretations of women's plays and helped coach actresses to successful performances. That Provincetown's women directors experienced a significant drop in participation at the same time as women playwrights is hardly coincidental. Moise's departure was voluntary, to be sure, but it was well before the company became commercially viable. Even though we know of at least one instance after 1920 when a male director was the company's second choice,[109] the disappearance of women directors and women playwrights just as the company's economic stakes rose supports the conclusion of previous studies that positions of power, prestige, and money are reserved for men: "If the job is lowly, the organization experimental or community-oriented, or the artistic skill new, women are likely to be found doing the work. Once the job becomes an executive or top administrative one or the organization successful . . . or the skill formalized into a profession, women's role seems to diminish."[110]

# 6

# *Designing Women*

I did my best for the little theatre that I loved.
—Blanche Hays, letter to Edna Kenton

Although their constitution did not specifically address methods of designing (who would do it and how), the Provincetown Players recognized scenic and costume designers as individual artists. In the printed announcement for their first New York season, the Players reiterated their primary objective to encourage the development of native drama, adding: "Equally it is to afford an opportunity for actors, producers, scenic and costume designers to experiment with a stage of extremely simple resources."[1] The Players seemed to have a greater appreciation for scenic designers as specialists than they did for stage directors. Only one Provincetown playwright, Floyd Dell, designed his own plays, and there is no record of the active membership attending dress rehearsals to critique sets or costumes. Apparently, playwrights recruited scenic designers from among the group's most likely candidates, usually painters. In the fall of 1916, the company established a ten-member scenic committee headed by Brör Nordfeldt. The membership included three women, Marguerite Zorach, Alice Hall, and Margaret Swain. The precise duties of this committee are unclear, but eight of the ten members, including two of the women, designed sets. In February 1917, Don Corley assumed leadership of the committee; there is no mention of it in the records thereafter.[2]

Although specific budgets for Provincetown sets are rare, general comments reflect escalating production costs after 1920. Edna Kenton recorded the cost of the *Lima Beans* set, designed by Marguerite and William Zorach in 1916, as $13.85 and the set for *Love*, designed by Don Corley in 1921, as $1,500.00, adding that *Love*'s set "wasn't worth it."[3]

Although there is no record of salaries for scenic designers, doubtless Cleon Throckmorton, the company's first permanent technical director and scenic designer, was paid, because his assistant, George Greenberg, received a salary.[4]

Despite the Players' intention to provide opportunities for both "scenic and costume designers," they seemed to consider costume design less important, since individual costume designers are less frequently credited than scenic designers for Provincetown productions, the term "designer" is rarely used in connection with costumes, and the Players never formed a costume committee. Apparently, actors, especially women, assumed much of the responsibility for their own costumes; however, for most of the company's history, someone, usually a woman, supervised the effort.[5] No records of costume budgets exist apart from the general comment that production costs increased after 1920, possibly because the company rarely contributed anything to costuming, especially in the first few years. There is no evidence that any costume designer was paid.

Despite limited budgets and consistently inadequate spaces, the scenic experiments at Provincetown proved fruitful. According to William Vilhauer, "[The Players] staged some of the most exciting and ingenious productions on view during this period of American theatre history. Furthermore, the Provincetown Players must be credited with several innovations in the area of technical production—the plaster dome cyclorama, frontal beam lighting in the auditorium, new experiments in the use of masks, and advances in the use of simplified Expressionistic and realistic settings."[6] Their successful designs were recognized by contemporary observer Constance D'Arcy Mackay as well: "In the matter of scenery the Provincetown Players are far more assured than in their acting. Considering the size of their stage they have given some amazing effects, notably in the one-act play, *Fog.* . . . There have also been excellent examples of scenery without perspective, and some delightfully decorative effects by the Zorachs."[7]

Although the company's contributions to theatrical design have been noted, very little is known about individual designers. Perhaps because Provincetown's scenic designers include two celebrated names (Robert Edmond Jones and Cleon Throckmorton), the others, including the six women designers, have been neglected. Costume designers, nearly all women, have received even less attention. Yet women designers for

Provincetown were also pioneers in the practice, and they deserve recognition for their share in the company's achievements in design.

Because Provincetown's women designers worked during a particularly important era in theatrical design in America, a brief review of that context provides a greater appreciation of their achievements. The year the Provincetown Players began producing plays—1915—marked a pivotal moment in American theatre design. In that year, Robert Edmond Jones's scenic design for *The Man Who Married a Dumb Wife* introduced to America both the "new stagecraft," inspired by the theories of Adolph Appia and Gordon Craig, and a new kind of theatre specialist. Both modern scenic design (i.e., design that offered individualized and suggestive settings that contributed to a play's meaning) and the profession of scenic designer (i.e., an interpretive artist responsible for conception and execution of setting) began here.[8] Also in 1915, America's first important woman designer, Aline Bernstein, began her career as a costume designer at the Neighborhood Playhouse.[9] A few years later, the profession of costume designer was boosted by the Actors' Strike of 1919. The strike's settlement required producers to supply costumes, wigs, shoes, and stockings for all women in principal roles and in the chorus, thus creating a need for a costume specialist to design, build, or acquire all costumes.[10] During the remaining years of Provincetown's operation, scenic and costume designers were increasingly recognized as specially trained professionals. In the early 1920s, scenic designers formed United Scenic Artists. In 1924, Bernstein began a long and distinguished career as a scenic designer, becoming, in 1926, the first woman to join the union. Not until 1936, however, did the union include a special section for costume designers.[11] Specialization in lighting design was somewhat slower to develop; lighting was generally handled by scenic designers or electricians.[12] Neither the commercial theatre nor the Provincetown Players credited lighting designers during these years.

Women designers of both sets and costumes enjoyed much higher rates of participation at Provincetown than did their counterparts in the commercial theatre. Of Broadway productions that credited scenic designers, only 6 percent were women. Of Provincetown productions that credited scenic designers, 15 percent were women. Forty-two percent of Broadway's credited costume designers were women, while 86 percent of Provincetown's credited costume designers were women (see graphs 3 and 4).[13]

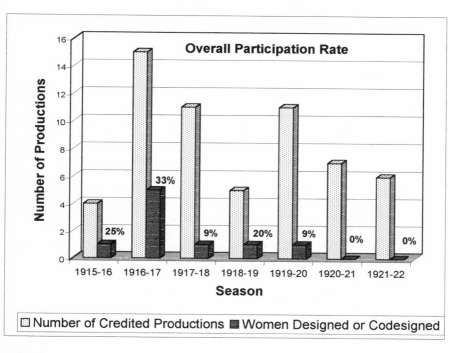

Graph 3. Number of Credited Productions Scene Designed or Codesigned by Women

The six women who designed scenery for the Provincetown Players did so between 1916 and 1919. They are Marguerite Zorach, Margaret Swain, Edith Haynes Thompson, Louise Hellstrom, Flossette Florence Heaton, and a "Miss Whittredge." Although there is no visual or verbal evidence of designs by Whittredge or Thompson, they most likely employed realistic domestic interiors. The play Whittredge designed, Saxe Commins's *The Obituary,* produced in December 1916, is lost, but the general description provided by the program (a "dramatic incident" involving a widow, her son, and an attorney) suggests a realistic interior setting. Neith Boyce's *Winter's Night,* designed by Edith Haynes Thompson in January 1917, is a three-character melodrama set in the interior of a New England farmhouse. Thompson, who owned a shop on Washington Square South that featured "many quaint and beautiful things,"[14] also provided furnishings for the first New York production of *Suppressed Desires,* set in a Village apartment.[15] Three plays designed by women employed rather challenging exterior settings. F. B. Kugelman's

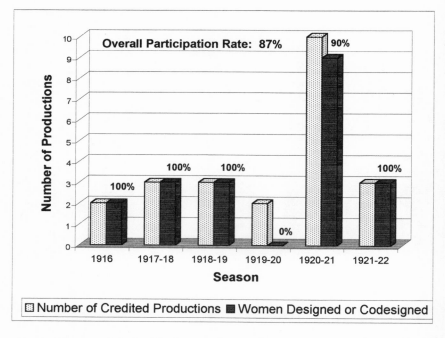

Graph 4. Number of Credited Productions Costume Designed or Codesigned by Women

*The Hermit and His Messiah,* designed by Flossette Florence Heaton in April 1918, was set in a cave in the Carpathian Mountains.[16] Louise Hellstrom's design for *Tickless Time,* a domestic comedy by Glaspell and Cook, produced in December 1918, exemplified the scenic challenges attempted by the company "in the way of country estates and other spacious effects."[17] The stage directions indicate the challenge:

> A garden in Provincetown. On the spectators' right a two-story house runs back from the proscenium—a door towards the front, a second-story window towards the back. Across the back runs a thick-set row of sunflowers nearly concealing a fence or wall. Back of this are trees and sky. There is a gate at the left rear corner of the garden. . . . A fence with sunflowers like that at the back closes off the left wing of the stage—a tree behind this left fence. The sun-dial stands on a broad step or pedestal which partly masks the digging which takes

place behind it. The position of the sun-dial is to the left of the center of the stage midway between front and back.[18]

Four of the nine scenic designs by women were collaborations with men, a circumstance which may imply that the Players were more open to women designing sets in partnership with men than independently or that women did not want the responsibility of designing independently. In January 1917, Margaret Swain codesigned Eugene O'Neill's *Fog* with Brör Nordfeldt. In O'Neill's melodrama, four passengers are adrift in a lifeboat off the banks of Newfoundland. The stage directions call for a dense fog on a still sea. The scenic design elicited Mackay's commendation: "Considering the size of their stage they have given some amazing effects, notably in the one-act play, *Fog*, with its sense of distance, of broad expanse of sea now partly revealed, now hidden by drifting mists. The scene was the work of B. J. O. [Brör] Nordfeldt."[19] Noticeably missing from this account is any mention of Swain, although she is equally credited with Nordfeldt in the program. No evidence suggests that the collaboration was anything other than an equal partnership. The program notes simply "set designed by Margaret Swain and B. J. O. Nordfeldt." But the only published contemporary review, a highly favorable one, completely erased Swain's contribution. Although we may reasonably assume that Swain did half the work, Nordfeldt got all the credit.

Provincetown's most prolific female scenic designer was Marguerite Zorach, who designed three plays in collaboration with her husband, William Zorach, and one independently. In 1915 the Zorachs joined the summer art colony at Provincetown, and the following summer they became actively involved with the Provincetown Players: "It was [the Provincetown playwrights'] first experience with the theatre and ours too, but we had no hesitations. We were full of ideas and eager to use them. . . . We were as determined to do things our way as the playwrights were to do them theirs."[20] Louise Bryant gave the Zorachs complete freedom to stage and design her *The Game*, and their "colorful mounting" contributed significantly to the play's success.[21] The backdrop, an abstract pattern of the sea, trees, the moon, and the moon's path in the water painted by Marguerite, was the set's dominant visual image.[22] Marguerite then created a linoleum cut, "Provincetown Play-

*Left to right:* John Reed, William Zorach, Martha Ryther-Fuller, and Kathleen Cannell in Louise Bryant's *The Game,* directed and designed by Marguerite and William Zorach, backdrop painted by Marguerite Zorach. 139 Macdougal Street. Courtesy Harvard Theatre Collection.

ers," inspired by her painting.[23] A reproduction of this cut appeared on Provincetown playbills for the next six years. Extant photographs and verbal descriptions of *The Game* suggest the "decorative" tendency in new stagecraft as defined by Mary Fanton Roberts: "brilliantly rich and exotic colors; unconcerned with contradictory three-dimensional actor on two-dimensional painted scenery. Not realistic."[24]

Alfred Kreymborg provided the next project suitable to the Zorachs' taste and talents, *Lima Beans,* a "fantastic treatment of commonplace themes set to a stylized rhythm."[25] Kreymborg was thrilled with their abstract and "charming" set, which featured black and white screens and brightly colored properties. The setting for *Lima Beans* apparently impressed others as well. Actress Mina Loy held back her first line "to give the set time to take effect—it was greeted with applause."[26] "*Lima Beans* was fine," reported Nani Bailey to John Reed, "wish you could have seen the Zorachs' set."[27] Kenton considered it one of the most beautiful and most effective in the company's history: "Here was a clear case of what fine synthesis an experimental stage could give when a poet wrote, when

Program cover design from "The Provincetown Players," courtesy Museum of the City of New York; linoleum cut by Marguerite Zorach, original block at National Museum of American Art, Washington, D.C.

poets spoke and when a poet-painter spoke and painted."[28] In referring to a single "poet-painter," Kenton is erasing the contribution of one of the Zorachs (both published poetry in the village's little magazines). The Zorachs next designed a forest scene for *Pan*, a two-character fantasy by Kenneth MacNichol. Years later, Nina Moise could not recall the play, now lost, but she did remember the Zorachs' design as "good."[29] The Zorachs designed and painted a backdrop of formalized waves for O'Neill's *Thirst*, but O'Neill rejected it in favor of more illusionistic crumpled canvas water.[30] The Players' preference for realistic works led the Zorachs to design costumes and sets for the Other Players bill of poetic fantasies in March 1918. Apparently, the visual elements

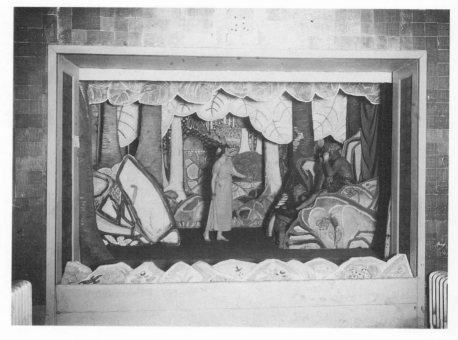

Edna James and Jig Cook in *Pan* by Kenneth MacNichol, directed by Nina Moise and designed by Marguerite and William Zorach. 139 Macdougal Street. Courtesy Brown Brothers, Sterling, Pennsylvania.

were notable; the scenes and sets were reproduced in color in several newspapers.[31]

In November 1919, Marguerite Zorach received her only independent credit for design, with William Zorach credited for "execution" of the scenery.[32] The play was Winthrop Parkhurst's domestic satire, *Getting Unmarried.* Although the text is realistic, apparently Marguerite devised another abstract visualization, described by one critic as "futurist."[33] The set provoked a somewhat left-handed compliment from Kenneth Macgowan:

> Two sets are striking. One by James Light and the other by Marguerite Zorach. The Zorach set is so striking it ought to ruin the play by drawing all the attention from its actors. The preachers for armed neutrality for scenic backgrounds have got their arguments wrong. In

spite of a play that gives the actors almost no assistance, the eternal vitality of a human being on a lighted stage platform dominates, as it always has dominated and always must. That is the eternal secret of the thing we call the stage. All honor to the Zorachs for reasserting it.[34]

This review is noteworthy as the only Provincetown review that actually named a woman scenic designer.[35]

*Getting Unmarried* marked the end of Marguerite Zorach's active association with the Provincetown Players. How and why the association ended is not clear, although William Zorach has suggested that the company's preference for realism discouraged both him and Marguerite from greater participation.[36] William also maintained that Marguerite was "frustrated" by her multiple responsibilities as artist, wife, and mother. At about this time she embarked on a new and lucrative career —designing and embroidering tapestries: "Marguerite's embroidered tapestries were our main source of income for many years and brought us unexpected security and gave us money to carry on our painting and sculpture."[37] Because these tapestries were considered a "woman's medium," they were not accorded the same respect as her oils.[38] After 1945, Marguerite returned to painting and exhibited regularly until her death in 1968.

Marguerite Zorach may also have been frustrated with a collaboration in which individual contributions were not distinguished. In these collaborations, Marguerite was first submerged and then erased by historians who assumed that her husband was the dominant partner. When Kenton referred to a single "poet-painter" responsible for *Lima Beans's* scenic design, we cannot be sure which partner she is slighting. When another historian, writing several decades later, reported that "Robert Edmond Jones and William Zorach experimented endlessly to find new methods of scenic expression," with no mention of Marguerite Zorach, we can be sure.[39] Yet the evidence suggests that Marguerite, rather than William, may have dominated the partnership. According to Alfred Kreymborg, Marguerite "surpassed" her husband in her dedication to fantasy.[40] By William's own account, it was Marguerite who designed and painted the backdrop for *The Game,* and as extant photographs show, the backdrop *is* the setting.[41] Marguerite's independent design for *Getting Unmarried* elicited, by Provincetown standards in those days, considerable comment, while William's only independent design, for *Suppressed Desires,* elicited none.

Marguerite's *Getting Unmarried,* in 1919, was the last set design by a woman at Provincetown. The lack of recognition accorded women like Zorach and Swain may have discouraged participation, but the appointment of Cleon Throckmorton as a paid designer/technical director also decreased opportunities for anyone else. Only three designers other than Throckmorton designed for Provincetown during his tenure (1920–22). They were all men.

Program records affirm that women dominated costuming at Provincetown. Official records, however, do not fully account for women's contributions in this area. Whether originally conceived and constructed, bought, or borrowed, costumes were generally acquired by the women in the company: "The costumes are not only designed by themselves," reported Constance Mackay, "but literally created by their own workmanship. They are dyed, cut, and sewn by the feminine members of the staff."[42] Like the scenic designers, Provincetown's women costume designers met extraordinary challenges; with almost nothing but imagination and energy, they outfitted Greek gods, fairy princesses, prostitutes, debutantes, gangsters, Native Americans, fifty-first-century robots, nineteenth-century spinsters, an emperor, and an ape. A full accounting of women costume designers at Provincetown must consider not only the seven women who received program credit but also those who worked without official recognition.

Although her name never appeared on any program, Kenton recognized Ellen Cook, mother of Jig ("we never called her anything but Ma-Mie"),[43] as the company's unofficial costume supervisor during the first two New York seasons: "If Jig's remarkable mother had not come from Iowa just then on a visit, I do not know how the plays would have been costumed. But she came, she looked on for a day or two, and then she appeared with a full seamstress's outfit and went to work. She sewed all through the season, made everything from a Pan's costume to a Roman crown."[44] Ellen Cook was unpaid as well as uncredited, a fact that Kenton, for one, seemed to find incongruous. In her history, Kenton named the company's four salaried officers at the beginning of the second New York season, adding, "Ellen Cook remained unsalaried head of the wardrobe and costume department."[45]

Provincetown actresses proved remarkably proficient at meeting the sometimes exotic costuming demands of the plays. Louise Bryant, who had designed little theatre sets in Oregon and was noted for "flashy dressing,"[46] contrived her own costume for the role of The Dancer in *Thirst,* a bangled outfit inspired by the local Portuguese.[47] Ida Rauh found a costume in a thrift shop for her role as a prostitute in O'Neill's *The Long Voyage Home:*

> We wanted to make her look as bad and as unattractive as possible. Well, I put on a blonde wig—such a wig as you have never seen—and I got a costume for the role at a second-hand store. It was not a cos- tumer or whatever you call them in the theatre; it was simply a second-hand clothing store around the corner on Sixth Avenue. We went there very often for our things, so I went there to find a costume for *The Long Voyage Home.* The costume I picked was a red satin full- length evening gown, décolleté, without sleeves, and covered with grease spots. It was just terrible. And I wore with it white cotton stockings and white satin shoes with high heels. You never saw such a spectacle.[48]

Mina Loy, who designed her own futurist fashions (lampshades for hats, small appliances for earrings) and had come to New York expressly to publish her couture in *Vogue* and other magazines, made a vivid im- pression with her costume for *Lima Beans.* Although Kreymborg noted that Loy's "décolleté creation" was "not in keeping with Mrs. Lima," he seemed pleased that it "served to fascinate the beholders."[49] Poet Marianne Moore has left a more detailed report: "[Loy] was very beau- tiful in the play. . . . She enunciated beautifully, wore gold slippers, a green taffeta dress, a black Florentine mosaic brooch, long gold ear- rings, and some beautiful English rings."[50] The Millay sisters and their mother, Cora, sewed their own costumes. Edna Millay, who collected and made kimonos ("I really made them right, too, studying the Japa- nese ones very carefully"),[51] almost certainly provided her costume for *The String of the Samisen* in January 1919; she was probably wearing it, too, when she won first prize in a Village costume ball "as a petite Japa- nese" that month.[52] Although the Zorachs designed costumes for *The Game,* actress Kathleen Cannell, who later became a fashion editor for the *New Yorker* in Paris, recalled constructing hers: "I had an Egyptian costume and a marvelous wig of black knotted fringe which I made myself."[53] Among these unrecognized costume designers for the Players, three were apparently sufficiently skilled to work in the commercial theatre. Mina Loy, Kathleen Millay, and Kirah Markham each costumed at least one Broadway play. In 1918, Loy designed Fania Marinoff's dress and hat for the Broadway play *Karen*. Kathleen Millay supervised costumes for *Hawk Island* in 1929. Kirah Markham designed *Fashion* (with Robert Edmond Jones) for the Experimental Theatre in 1924 and *Foolscap* on Broadway in 1933.[54]

In addition to the many women who sewed, supervised, and possibly designed without recognition, seven women received individual costuming credit for Provincetown plays. Costumes for *The Game* were based on the visual concept of Marguerite and William Zorach. Although William apparently collaborated on the concept, execution was probably primarily Marguerite's responsibility: "Needlework comes handy to her, so when I saw the great facility she had in doing those things, I quit."[55] Becky Edelson supplied Louise Bryant's costume, a gown and hat suitable for the wife of a wealthy industrialist, in John Reed's comic satire *The Eternal Quadrangle*.[56]

In the fall of 1917 the Players met Edith Unger (known professionally as "Avril") a "dandy girl who will costume plays for us."[57] Unger, a sculptress, owned one of the Village's most popular tea shops, The Mad Hatter, at 150 W. Fourth, downstairs ("eloh tibbar eht nwod," as the sign read) from Nani Bailey's famous Samovar restaurant.[58] Unfortunately, no visual or verbal records exist of the presumably fanciful costumes Unger devised for *Knotholes* by William Saphier and Maxwell Bodenheim and *The Gentle Furniture Shop* by Bodenheim. Both plays were poetic fantasies: one was set in a graveyard, the other in a "queer furniture shop."[59] In December 1918, Unger provided the gown worn by Ida Rauh in Rita C. Smith's melodrama, *The Rescue*. Despite lack of visual evidence, Unger's competence may be inferred from her employment by two other companies at about the same time as her association with the Provincetown Players. In 1917 and 1918 she designed costumes for four Washington Square Players' productions,[60] and in 1919 she designed costumes for Greenwich Village Theatre's *Hobohemia*.[61]

Helen Zagat undertook one of the company's most ambitious costuming projects, designing period costumes for the more than thirty characters in Cook's *The Athenian Women*, set in the fifth century

B.C.E.[62] Again, lacking any other evidence, the extant photographs indicate Zagat's success in acquiring costumes suitable to the style and period of the play. Another costuming challenge was met by Mabel Reber. Perhaps recruited by her sister Edna Kenton, Reber, a former society reporter for the *Chicago Tribune,* and her husband, Neil, joined the Players during their third New York season. According to Kenton, Mabel Reber was responsible for the whimsical costumes worn for Robert Allerton Parker's *5050,* set in a subterranean city of the future. Using pasteboard boxes of various shapes and sizes, Reber fashioned geometric costumes shaped like squares or pyramids "with shooting decorative angles."[63] Actress Norma Millay recalled that her costume was "a lot of fun," especially a halo/hat on the end of a wire.[64] Lucy L'Engle, a Provincetown artist and close friend to Marguerite Zorach and Susan Glaspell, costumed Cook's *The Spring* in 1921.[65] This experimental drama spanned a century between acts and required both Native American and nineteenth-century costumes. Photographs of the production suggest that L'Engle successfully met the play's requirements. Reviews of *The Spring* consistently praised its "handsome mounting" but ignored costumes as part of the stage picture. Writers mentioned only Cleon Throckmorton's setting, never L'Engle's costumes, as part of the production's visual elements.[66]

Probably the individual most responsible for costuming for the Players was Blanche Hays, who was also one of the company's most popular actresses. Married to attorney Arthur Garfield Hays, cofounder of the American Civil Liberties Union, Hays was part of the Greenwich Village radical set and frequently hosted parties at her large duplex on West Twelfth Street.[67] She received credit as costume "designer" for only one play, Edna Millay's *The Princess Marries the Page.* Her costumes for this romantic fantasy elicited rare praise: "Visually *The Princess Marries the Page* is the finest thing on the bill—C. M. Sax [has provided] a gorgeous setting—Blanche Hays contributed beautiful costumes."[68] The scarcity of critical commentary on costuming makes this tribute to Hays's costumes impressive indeed.

No other record exists of Hays as a costume designer from the production of Millay's play in November 1918 until 1920, when her name began to appear regularly on the list of staff members as the company's costume "supervisor" or "director." The nature of this position is vague: there is no record of how she was appointed, whether she was paid, or

Jig Cook's *The Athenian Women,* costumes designed by Helen Zagat. 139 Macdougal
Street. Courtesy Billy Rose Theatre Collection, New York Public Library for the
Performing Arts, Astor, Lenox and Tilden Foundations.

what her responsibilities were. Most likely Hays's responsibilities included original creation and construction as well as the coordination
and execution of the ideas of others.[69] Plays produced during her tenure
include a wide variety of genres and styles, including poetic fantasies,
contemporary satires, period melodramas, and experiments in expressionism. The company's most celebrated works (O'Neill's *The Emperor
Jones, Diff'rent,* and *The Hairy Ape* and Glaspell's *Trifles* [revival], *Inheritors,* and *The Verge*) were produced during these seasons. Reviews
and records concerning several of these productions provide some information concerning Hays's work.

In costuming *The Verge* (scenic design by Cleon Throckmorton) and
*The Hairy Ape* (scenic design by Throckmorton and Robert Edmond
Jones), Hays achieved symbolic expression in costuming that comple-
mented expressionist scenic designs.[70] Stark Young's negative reaction

*The Spring* by Jig Cook, costumes designed by Lucy L'Engle. Jeanne Powers (*standing*), Jeannie Begg (*kneeling*). 133 Macdougal Street. Courtesy Billy Rose Theatre Collection, New York Public Library for the Performing Arts, Astor, Lenox and Tilden Foundations.

to the scenic elements and Margaret Wycherly's performance in *The Verge* was rare, but perhaps enlightening: although the production failed for him, his description suggests a unified attempt from set and costume designers and performer at symbolic expression: "The production works overtime. The clouds in the sky overwork . . . the actors do too much . . . [Margaret Wycherly's] neurotic gestures were unfortunately heightened by the gleaming mass of sequins or beads or whatever it was that spread over her gown at the knees and extravagantly echoed the body and elbows."[71] Hays experimented with symbolic expression again in her costumes for *The Hairy Ape*, dressing the icy debutante Mildred

*Diff'rent* by Eugene O'Neill, costumes by Blanche Hays. *Left to right:* Elizabeth Brown, Charles Ellis, Mary Blair. 133 Macdougal Street. Courtesy Billy Rose Theatre Collection, New York Public Library for the Performing Arts, Astor, Lenox and Tilden Foundations.

Douglas in a snowy white crepe de chine gown, white cloak, and white hat with flowing veil, a stark visual contrast to the coal-blackened stokers surrounding her.[72] For the ape, Hays and her assistants (including James Light and Susan Jenkins) constructed a suit from dyed goatskins and the ape's head from papier-mâché, copied by Hays from a gorilla in the Museum of Natural History. Perhaps Hays's most clearly expressionist costuming involved the use of masks in this play. For the Fifth Avenue scene, O'Neill wanted all the aristocratic characters dressed alike—"a procession of gaudy marionettes yet with something of a relentless horror of Frankensteins in their detached, mechanical awareness."[73] "The costume part was simple," Hays recalled, "but the faces stumped me. I suggested using masks, and Gene was delighted." The masks consisted of two layers of fine cheesecloth laid over a plaster cast of a face and painted with several coats of collodion, a liquid that hardens into a skinlike substance; this process produced a featherlight mask on which the required features were painted. According to Arthur and Barbara Gelb, Hays's successful results inspired O'Neill's later experiments with masks in plays like *The Great God Brown*.[74] Despite Hays's important contribution to the overall design, reviewer Robert Gilbert Welsh failed to acknowledge her achievement, apparently assuming that Robert Edmond Jones, the scenic designer, was responsible: "The stage pictures are remarkable. . . . Robert Edmond Jones has been happier in using suggestive scenery in these sets than he was with the *Macbeth* settings of a former season. The masks of the hypocritical churchgoers have a distinct meaning."[75] Although Hays appeared on the program as "costume supervisor," her name was not mentioned in the review. Alexander Woollcott also cited the Fifth Avenue scene of "wooden-faced churchgoers" as particularly effective, but he, too, failed to credit Hays.[76]

Edna Kenton's postproduction record of *Chains of Dew* provides considerable information about costuming at Provincetown as well as the most complete description of costumes for any Provincetown production. Hays was initially cast in an acting role, but apparently director Ralph Stewart "didn't like her." Hays voluntarily and graciously left the cast, "offering to do her usual stunt with the play in costumes . . . She was altogether nice about it." Apparently, the "usual stunt" involved considerable collaboration with actors. Although some actors supplied their own costumes ("We yearned for a crisp black taffeta for Mother but compromised on a gown Miss McCarthy had of thin black silk stuff"), Hays obviously coordinated and controlled the effort: "Mrs. McIntyre had quite a vaudeville concept of her costume, but Blanche toned that down—she's in black, and Edith has an orangy gown and soft red hat—very smart." The company apparently supplied some items, notably American Beauty silk stockings (Hays "nearly fainted" at the price of $3.75). The final result was evidently impressive. Kenton especially admired one character's "pale grey office dress, flapperish but chaste" and applauded another's wig as "real and jaunty."[77] Kenton expressed her personal gratitude to Hays several weeks after the production closed: "Never, Blanche, shall I forget your good and gracious help on *Chains*. A thousand thanks to you for all you did."[78] Kenton's letters imply that Hays was probably not paid: "offering to do her usual stunt with the costumes" does not suggest a regularly paid position, and Kenton's letter of gratitude is effusive enough to be in lieu of other compensation.

In 1922, Hays moved to Paris with Elsa Schiaparelli. The two women, who had met at Woodstock in 1921, shared unhappy marriages and daughters about the same age. They also shared an interest in fashion and design. According to Schiaparelli's biographer, the two made a coat together. For Elsa, that was the beginning of a famed career in haute couture.[79] The relationship may have been personally intimate: Schiaparelli's biographer refers to Hays as "a confidante and refuge" for Schiaparelli.[80] According to Schiaparelli, Hays "took a hand in my destiny. In her usual calm and common-sense way she said: 'why don't you come to Paris with me as my guest, and there we will see what can be done?'"[81] Hays reported to Kenton that "Elsa and I are getting along famously and it threatens to last."[82] It did not last, apparently, and Hays returned to New York in 1924. Before leaving France, however, she divorced her husband, scouted plays for the Theatre Guild, tried to interest Lugné-Poe in Glaspell's *The Verge,* and received word from Kenton of the demise of the Provincetown Players: "I wept over the decease of the Provincetown Players," she wrote Kenton. "I felt those last months not as a member of a cooperating organization but as if I were in the employ of somebody but I wasn't sure who the somebody was—maybe Harry Weinberger. . . . I did my best for the little theatre that I loved with a patient mother's love, and I shall miss it, troublesome as it sometimes was. You were the one warm bright spot there last winter."[83] In 1925 Hays returned to the Provincetown Playhouse—then home to the Experimental Theatre—to design costumes for *Adam Solitaire.* Hays eventually remarried, and in 1981 she appeared as a witness in Warren Beatty's film *Reds.*[84]

Design at Provincetown reflected conventional gender expectations, which in turn reflected attitudes in the commercial theatre. The most significant difference between Provincetown and the commercial theatre regarding theatre design is that *initially* Provincetown welcomed women scenic designers, allowing women opportunities unavailable anywhere else. Provincetown's audiences and reviewers, however, seemed unable to accept women in this role. As scenic designers, women at Provincetown were ahead of their time; the woman generally accepted as America's first important scenic designer, Aline Bernstein, did not begin that career until 1924 and did not join a professional union until

1926, four years after the Provincetown Players ended production. The erasure of women scenic designers in partnership with men reveals how difficult it was for anyone to accept women in this role. Even when program credit was clear, people assumed that men were designing sets; in partnerships, it was assumed that men were doing all the work.

Scenic design at Provincetown, as we have seen, became increasingly important, specialized, and remunerated at Provincetown after the construction of the *Kuppelhorizont* in 1920. The complete absence of women scenic designers after 1920, along with diminished participation of women writers and directors, supports the well-known feminist slogan "the more money, the fewer women." If scenic design at Provincetown reflected conventional gender expectations, costuming was even more sexually segregated. Apparently, more women learned to handle paintbrushes and hammers than men needles and thread. To oversee costuming, the company found two women who manifested conventionally female attributes: Ellen Cook ("we never called her anything but Ma-Mie") and Blanche Hays (who loved the theatre "with a patient mother's love").

Provincetown accorded costuming less importance than scenic design. Perhaps *because* women dominated costuming, everyone disregarded it. We know that Ellen Cook was unpaid and uncredited. Probably Hays was not paid for her work as company costume designer. While budgets for sets escalated, especially after 1920, budgets for costumes remained minimal. Lack of precise financial records makes comparisons between set and costume budgets hazardous, but even such trifles as we have can be meaningful. It is worth noting that Blanche Hays "nearly fainted" at spending $3.75 for hosiery in 1921, yet clearly by this time in the group's history, sets were constructed for each play, and at least one cost $1,500.00. Neither paying costume designers nor providing adequate budgets for costumes seems in keeping with the company's general failure to recognize costuming as important.

Despite lack of contemporary recognition, these women designers of sets and costumes contributed prominently to the visual innovations for which Provincetown is celebrated. In her costumes for *The Verge* and *The Hairy Ape,* Hays experimented with the use of masks and expressionism. In decorative backdrops for *The Game, Lima Beans,* and *Getting Unmarried,* Zorach explored a major trend in new stagecraft. What verbal and pictorial evidence we have of women's designs at Provincetown demonstrates a considerable degree of ability. That none of Provincetown's women scenic designers ventured into the commercial theatre may indicate that their interest in scenic design was limited to their interest in the Provincetown Players. It may also indicate that their experiences at Provincetown were not sufficiently encouraging to persuade them to confront an even less hospitable environment. That a number of Provincetown's costume designers, credited and uncredited, did work in the commercial theatre indicates an interest in a commercial career but also suggests that women costume designers found the commercial theatre more welcoming than did women scenic designers.

Personal testimony exists from only one of these women. Blanche Hays's recollection that "she wept over the decease of the Provincetown Players" and that she would "miss it, troublesome as it sometimes was" echoes that of so many of this company's prominent women, who found their experiences at Provincetown, though fraught with difficulty, uniquely fulfilling.

# 7

# *Backlash and Aftermath*

To imagine [women] passing from this just perceptible dawn into another darkness does not seem to me fantastic.

—Evelyn Scott

The introduction to this study asserted an impressive overall participation rate in all areas of operation by women at Provincetown, and our examination of individual practices has demonstrated that. What has also been revealed is a recurring chronological pattern of decreasing participation within the most nontraditional roles: writing, directing, and scenic design. Despite demonstrated success, women's participation in these areas diminished significantly in the last few seasons, a shift that seems directly related to the organizational changes discussed at some length in chapters 2 and 3. But the changes within this company reflect, and may be partially explained by, changes in society at large.

Colleagues and critics saw Glaspell's *Inheritors*, which opened in March 1921, as political propaganda, a protest against conservative, antidemocratic attitudes that Kenneth Macgowan labeled "reaction." Indeed, the social climate in America had changed significantly since the summer of 1916. When America entered World War I in the spring of 1917, its military objective mandated unity at home, and dissension was harshly suppressed. *The Masses,* which had opposed American intervention since 1914, was one casualty. The magazine was forced to stop publication after December 1917, and seven members, including Eastman, Dell, and Reed, were indicted under the Espionage Act.[1] The war in Europe and the Russian Revolution of 1917 took journalists Reed, Bryant, and Vorse overseas. Vorse became a propagandist for peace and Reed and Bryant for Communism. Village restaurateur and occasional Provincetown actress Nani Bailey volunteered as a nurse and died in France.[2] Emma Goldman served twenty months in prison for "con-

spiracy to induce persons not to register" for the draft, and Stella Ballantine took over management of *Mother Earth* during her incarcera-
tion.[3] Eleanor Fitzgerald, Ida Rauh, and Susan Jenkins joined Ballantine to raise funds for the Political Prisoners Amnesty League.

In 1919 Congress established the Overman subcommittee to investigate "Bolshevism and all other forms of anti-American radicalism in
the United States." Louise Bryant, who had recently published a respected and sympathetic account of the Russian Revolution, *Six Months
in Red Russia,* was one of the first "Reds" to testify. When Senator
Overman assured her that she was going to be treated "like a lady," she
retorted that she would prefer to be treated like a human being.[4] Those
deemed too far to the Left—Emma Goldman and Alexander Berkman,
for example—were deported. In an odd historical coincidence, the day
after *The Emperor Jones* opened on Macdougal Street, 2 November 1920,
Warren G. Harding was elected president of the United States. Harding's new Republican administration promised to return America to
"normalcy," by which he meant a return to prewar economic and social
conditions, a retrogressive process that was already under way. In the
next few years, the "Red Scare," record numbers of lynchings in southern states, the Volstead Act (Prohibition), and the Anti-Immigration
Act stilled the prewar political and ideological ferment.

Suffrage for women, finally won in 1920, did not usher in a feminist
utopia, but heightened tensions between different groups of women.
African-American women were not protected from Jim Crow dis-
enfranchisement in southern states, and conflict erupted between mod-
erate reformers, who thought the battle was over, and the more radical,
like Edna Kenton, who pushed immediately for an equal rights amend-
ment, introduced in 1923 but never passed. Women's Trade Union
League leader Ethel Smith protested that feminist expectations beyond
suffrage aroused hostility: "Even to use the word feminist is to invite
from the extremists a challenge to our authenticity."[5] Just six years after
the first feminist mass meetings of 1914, one writer warned that feminist
extremism would render women unattractive to men, thereby leading to
the extinction of the human race: "The feminist camp, further and further commandeering the intelligent and self-reliant, the worthy and
purposeful of the sex, while more and more discarding the charms and
the softness thereof, will be further and further deserted by men."[6]
Susan Glaspell responds directly to this line of thinking in her descrip-

tion of her feminist protagonist of *Chains of Dew:* "Nora has short hair. This does not mean she's eccentric—it is not that kind of short hair. It curls and is young and vital and charming short hair. Nora also is young and vital and charming—devotion to a cause really doesn't hurt her looks in the least."[7] Throughout the 1920s, membership in feminist organizations plummeted, the number of women in professions declined, and (as a diversionary tactic?) the nation instituted the Miss America Beauty Pageant.[8] In the late 1920s and 1930s, a number of states, including New York and Massachusetts, enacted legislation that compelled women to take their husbands' surnames as their only legal name, making compulsory what had previously been social custom.[9] The backlash continued into the 1930s: "All about us," wrote suffragist Doris Stevens, "we see attempts being made, buttressed by governmental authority, to throw women back into the morass of unlovely dependence from which they were just beginning to emerge."[10]

Feminist historians have recently challenged the view that feminism "failed" in the 1910s and remained moribund until it was miraculously revived in the mid-1960s. These writers have pointed to important continuities in women's progressive activism, especially in social welfare legislation relating to women and children.[11] The most radical and existential strain in feminist thinking, however, that which epitomized Greenwich Village feminism, did seem seriously threatened. Having finally bestowed upon women the right to exercise their responsibilities as citizens, the country was by no means ready to grant women the more personal, and radical, options of sexual autonomy and sexual self-identification, or the equally radical self-identification as artist or genius. As America grew increasingly "normal," many of the group's most radical aesthetic and sexual adventurers left the Village for the new bohemian Mecca, Paris. Edna Millay, Djuna Barnes, Berenice Abbott, Kathleen Cannell, Louise Bryant, Mina Loy, Blanche Hays, and Evelyn Scott all spent part of the 1920s or 1930s in Paris. Barnes reported that it was "awfully hard to work in Paris, but Edna Millay is doing more than the rest of us."[12] The former "high priestess of the ultra-modernists," Marguerite Zorach, remained in America, "returning, after 1923, to a conservative, 'academic' style far removed from her avant-garde tendencies displayed in the 1910s. The scenes she chose to depict revolved around family life . . . [and were] fairly autobiographical in nature."[13]

The Zorachs' marriage endured, but many Provincetown marriages collapsed. Alice Woods Ullman and Helen Westley divorced in the 1910s, Mary Blair divorced her first husband, Charles Meredith, in 1920, and her second, editor and critic Edmund Wilson, in 1929. Rauh divorced Eastman in 1921. Margaret Wycherly and her husband (playwright Bayard Veiller) divorced in 1922, the same year Susan Jenkins divorced James Light. Blanche Hays and Kathleen Cannell obtained divorces in Paris in the 1920s. Bosworth Crocker separated from Ludwig Lewisohn in 1924, divorced him in 1938, and later sued him for libel and back alimony. Margaret and Brör Nordfeldt separated in 1938 and divorced in 1944. Jenkins and Hays eventually remarried. Those who never married include Edna Kenton, Eleanor Fitzgerald, Nina Moise, Evelyn Scott, and Mary Carolyn Davies.

The difficulties experienced by Provincetown women in restructuring personal relationships may be at least partially explained by strong opposition from the men in their lives. Glaspell's *Chains of Dew* had vividly dramatized what was being so strongly manifested among her intimate friends: the shallowness of men's commitment to real change in sexual relations. As early as 1913, Kenton had recognized that men were lagging far behind in self-transformation along feminist lines: "What a reworking of men there has to be! And when I pause to reflect that they've got to remake themselves before things are better, I see clearly that things are to be much worse."[14] Men and women had worked together in feminist causes—Dell, Reed, Hapgood, and Eastman championed pacifism, suffrage, and birth control in *The Masses* and other publications. Playwright and poet James Oppenheim's *Bread and Roses* became an anthem for working-class women. Founder Robert Rogers reported to John Reed in 1916 that he was "controlling births to beat hell."[15]

Despite their public activism, however, men proved alarmingly resistant to radical change in private relationships. For the "revolutionary" male poets, painters, and playwrights of Greenwich Village, free love sounded like a fine idea. All too soon, and all too often, however, men wanted their modern, liberated women to transform magically into traditional wives and mothers. Thus Dell, who initially embraced the new woman as a "glorious playfellow,"[16] found Edna Millay's "ideal of feminine freedom too rash."[17] By 1919 he declared: "I wanted to be married to a girl who would not put her career before children—or even before me, hideously reactionary as the thought would have seemed a few years ago."[18] What he really wanted (and eventually found, but not with Millay) was a woman who would put him first: "She must not have any fanatical ambition to be a writer, a painter, an actress, or musician."[19]

This pattern of public feminist/private sexist reappeared frequently. Eastman, publicly espousing the ideals of feminism, privately desired selfless adoration from a woman. After witnessing the slavish devotion of Madame Maxim Gorky to her husband, Eastman frankly recorded his envy: "I sensed the adoration in her tone, and my heart whispered to me: 'That is what a writer needs!'"[20] Theodore Dreiser's fictional heroines defied convention, but his personal ideal was a woman "who would forever be younger, prettier, richer, more loving, more brilliant, more sacrificing than the woman he was with."[21] Revolutionary John Reed betrayed his conservative views of gender while poetry editor of *American* magazine: "I have wreaked my fiendish worst on 'lady' bards, too—a breed which I despise, especially when they attempt to write like Kipling."[22]

Other Provincetown men, not openly engaged in feminist action, were less hypocritical but no less sexist. William Carlos Williams asked Evelyn Scott: "Can no one understand that I am a king? That I am a baby who is always right?"[23] Playwright and actor Harry Kemp, married to Mary Pyne, waxed poetical on the subject:

men differ with the titles that they wear.
a woman's just a woman everywhere . . .
give her a necklace, sweetmeat, poem, flower,
a kiss, yourself!—but never give her power![24]

Eugene O'Neill was so physically abusive that one contemporary wondered if he were trying "to beat his way out of his marriage."[25] Agnes Boulton reported one instance of O'Neill's slapping her during a cast party. According to Boulton, only Stella Ballantine came to her rescue, telling O'Neill off in her acquired British accent. Everyone else took it as a "Dionysian gesture . . . one of [the men], with an admiring look at Gene, produced another bottle." Outside, Ballantine comforted Boulton with the assurance that "it means nothing, my dear, nothing! I've had the same thing happen to me—although Teddy has so far never tried it! Genius is like that, my dear!"[26]

Both male and female Provincetowners attributed increasing antago-

nism between the sexes to feminist consciousness. Edna Kenton acknowledged feminism's militant aspect: "Feminism is sex-war; who
doubts it . . . for women are thinking at last not on man's terms, but on
their own, and thought in a slave class is always dynamic."[27] Mina Loy
concurred: "Men and women are enemies, with the enmity of the exploited for the parasite, the parasite for the exploited."[28] On behalf of
men, Hapgood protested the feminist "lie" that men had willingly op-
pressed women: "The feminist movement is lying in order to get freedom for women, which is a part of the socialist labor movement, they
have to transmit the supposition that—man—is either a devilish thing,
or somehow or other [men] conspire against women, against the social
spirit." In this speech, Hapgood warned of the "danger" in the "social
development" of formerly individualistic sex antagonism.[29] That is, a
little sexual animosity between individuals was inevitable, but general-
ized and organized anti-male bias among women as a social class was
alarming.

Eventually the women themselves began to be affected by the changing cultural climate. In "The Ballad of a Bad Girl," a poem sent to
writer Carl Van Vechten, Greenwich Village's most noted salon hostess
and member of Heterodoxy, Mabel Dodge, now Mabel Dodge Luhan,
recanted her former feminist convictions:

> Something made me sorry for what had taken place
> I took my father's silver cane and put it in the hall
> Then I lay down in the pansy bed & whispered:
> Mother! Mother me,
> And teach me how to mother and that's all, all.

As Luhan explained to Van Vechten:

> It is an indictment against all Feminism and an earnest appeal to
> women to leave off trying to steal the world away from men—and
> to return to their original function—motherhood . . . if men want
> mothers they should have them. There's enough power in that for any
> woman. Let them leave off stealing the masculine secrets of the will
> to power, magic & all the other occult-wills. They have reached to the
> godhead in their rummaging around in the man's region—trying to
> emulate his ultimate divinity. Well there destruction awaits them. Let

them turn & climb down in time—lest they be kicked down like the Bad Girl—for of course, not many women can endure her fall & survive it. Only the geniuses can Come Back—& woman genius is scarce.

Van Vechten sent a copy of the poem and Mabel's explanation to Gertrude Stein with a sardonic comment: "Aren't you happy to see Mabel functioning so nobly?"[30] Van Vechten's disdain aside, it must have been hard to hold on to feminist attitudes in an increasingly antagonistic environment, and Luhan was not alone in her feelings of regret and self-doubt. Throughout the female Provincetown community, women began to seek more traditional relationships with men and children.

In 1923, three years after John Reed's death in Russia, Louise Bryant married Ambassador William Bullitt "because I needed someone to mother."[31] In addition to mothering Bullitt, Bryant had a daughter in 1924, and also became a mentor and patron to poet Claude McKay, who dedicated "Home to Harlem" to her in 1928. According to Kitty Cannell, however, Bryant remained a feminist and had a hard time being "tactful" in her dealings with Bullitt.[32] Bryant's marriage ended in 1930 in a lurid divorce in which Bullitt named Gwen LeGallienne as corespondent and Bryant lost custody of her daughter.[33] At about the same time, Bryant began work on a biography of John Reed. Eventually, however, she handed over her materials to Granville Hicks, who became Reed's first biographer. Despite the ravaging effects of disease, alcoholism, and poverty, Bryant remained adventurous of spirit, learning to fly just before her death in 1936.[34]

In 1921, Mary Heaton Vorse married radical artist Robert Minor in the Soviet Union, a marriage not recognized in the United States. A year later she became pregnant, at the age of forty-seven, and suffered a miscarriage. As she recuperated, Minor informed her that he was leaving her for another woman who was younger, more beautiful, and more politically educable.[35] According to her biographer, Vorse suffered massive guilt in the 1920s for what she perceived as her earlier neglect of her children; her relationship with her oldest daughter, Ellen, was especially troubled. Because she had lost Minor to a younger, more traditional woman, Vorse began to doubt her former feminist convictions. In an article published in 1924, "Why I Have Failed as a Mother," Vorse repeated her friend Norman Matson's assertion that she had failed both as a writer and as a mother because she allowed her children to interrupt her work: "Do you suppose there's a man who would stand for that? You're blind if you can't see they hate your work."[36] Vorse spent the next seven years repairing relations with her children. She eventually returned to radical journalism and political activism, joining protests against the Vietnam War when she was ninety-one years old.

Evelyn Scott was less fortunate in resolving troubled domestic relationships. In an unpublished memoir, her son Creighton Scott accused his mother of both neglect and cruelty, leaving a "lurid, condemnatory child's eye view of bohemian life."[37] As Scott's biographer observed, "No witness remains to give evidence whether she was a cruel mother or simply a highly strung woman faced with two troublesome seven-year-olds."[38] Creighton Scott's resentment of his mother's liberated sexuality is most obvious in his ugly characterization of free love: "In circles where free love prevails, women are far less than chattels in my experience—they are more nearly a sort of public convenience, like the subway or the Men's Room."[39]

Like Vorse and Scott, Neith Boyce had also dealt with the struggle to reconcile a productive writing career with raising children. In Vorse's eyes, Boyce had chosen to devote herself to her family,[40] but Boyce also experienced guilt for inadequate mothering, especially relating to her oldest son's death. In 1923 Boyce published her last book, a memorial to her son, *Harry*.[41] Despite the difficulties, the Boyce/Hapgood marriage endured for forty-six years; at its best, according to Hapgood, it was like a comedy by Schnitzler.[42]

In the same year that Vorse married Robert Minor, Ida Rauh left New York with her son Daniel Eastman to live with Andrew Dasburg in Santa Fe. Rauh called herself "Mrs. Dasburg," and their closest friends thought they were married.[43] This relationship ended, abruptly and acrimoniously, in 1928, and Dasburg married another woman almost immediately. Rauh then began a relationship of ambiguous intimacy with playwright Lynn Riggs, who was more than twenty years her junior and primarily homosexual. The relationship lasted until Riggs's death in 1954.[44] Rauh died in New York in 1970.

In Paris, Millay renewed her sexual interest in women, including sculptor Thelma Wood, who later became more seriously attached to Djuna Barnes. In 1923 she rather unexpectedly married coffee importer

Eugen Boissevain, who had previously been married to suffragist leader Inez Milholland and had been psychoanalyzed to free him of any feelings of "male superiority."[45] According to Millay biographer Anne Cheney, despite Boissevain's apparently progressive attitudes, he became a "father figure" who micromanaged her professional and personal life, negotiated her contracts, read her mail, and fended off admirers and intruders, even her sister Norma. If, as Cheney has implied, Boissevain nurtured Millay to death, she at least died characteristically, with a glass of wine in one hand and a sheet of poetry in the other.[46]

In December 1919, Eleanor Fitzgerald asked to share Berkman's exile as his common-law wife. Failing that, Fitzgerald remained a faithful correspondent, visiting Berkman in exile whenever possible. She also began an intimate relationship with Berkman's attorney, Harry Weinberger, a relationship Emma Goldman pronounced disastrous: "He held onto Fitzie like one possessed and when he saw that she did not feel quite the same for him as he did for her, he became cruel, unreasonable, positively brutal, as most men do when they see the woman slip away. He tore Fitzie to pieces, waylaid her, threatened to shoot himself, made public scenes."[47]

In her biography of Jig Cook, published in 1927 and dedicated to his two children, Susan Glaspell confided her disappointment at not being able to have children of her own and her pleasure at having her stepchildren, Harl and Nilla, with them "almost every summer."[48] Tensions evidently erupted, however, between Glaspell and her precocious stepdaughter, Nilla, who later recalled, with irony, her "radical" stepmother's dating restrictions.[49] While in Greece, Glaspell apparently seriously considered leaving Jig, confessing to Boyce and Hapgood that "the difficulties of her life with Jig . . . had grown too great" and identifying Nilla's presence as a "complicating" factor.[50] In *Road to the Temple* and other aubiographical pieces, Glaspell gives the impression that she would never have written a play if Cook had not "forced" her: "I didn't want my marriage to break up, so I wrote *Trifles*."[51] She seems a passive observer, with little ambition of her own, an image distinctly at odds with her actual involvement as a writer, actor, and executive director of the company. Although the work is intended to be a biography of Cook, not an autobiography of Glaspell, her treatment of the Provincetown years manifests a tendency among women autobiographers, noted by Thomas Postlewait, to reconcile unwomanly achievement with femi-

Eleanor Fitzgerald and Alexander Berkman. Courtesy Papers of Djuna Barnes, Special Collections, University of Maryland Libraries.

nine reticence: "As they report matters, their own ambitions and contributions are seldom acknowledged. If we are to believe Marie Wilton, for example, it never once occurred to her to become a theatre manager until her brother-in-law suggested the idea.... In similar manner, Ethel Barrymore ... depended upon the intervention of Henry Irving."[52]

As Postlewait argues, "A version of sexual and social subordination gets expressed, in the voice of gratitude, as a story of need, rescue, and feminine respect for authority."[53] While Glaspell was expiating the sins of unwomanly achievement, however, she fell in love with Norman Matson, a playwright fifteen years her junior. Glaspell called herself "Mrs. Matson" during this relationship, and many thought they were legally married. Like Cook, Matson was less successful than Glaspell, and apparently even less able than Cook to tolerate that circumstance: "I loved you, God knows, and love you now. But it was strange: you

Susan Glaspell, Nilla Cook, and Jig Cook in Greece. Courtesy Beinecke Rare Book and Manuscript Library, Yale University.

supported me; you were successful and I wasn't; and then there was the age difference and no children."[54] Matson left Glaspell in 1932 to marry the nineteen-year-old daughter of one of Glaspell's closest friends.

The antagonism that Hutchins Hapgood had observed within the Provincetown Players was part of the growing backlash against feminism within the culture at large, and Kenton had been correct in predicting that things would get worse before they got better. The mood in 1922 seems considerably altered from that of 1915; we have moved from restless optimism to frustration, doubt, and guilt. In her plays in the early 1920s, Glaspell defends feminism against what seems an onslaught of reactionary thought; by the late 1920s she has, perhaps tactically, retreated. Both strategies suggest the degree of resistance these women faced in meeting their personal, professional, and political goals. The Provincetown women were at least partially aware of the forces that stalled their progress. By 1932, Evelyn Scott, describing herself as "one of the few [feminists] still in captivity," submitted an article to

*Spectator* magazine on the decline of feminism. Scott linked feminism with women's artistic self-expression and blamed the Church and Republican governments for the decline of both. Her conclusion seemed pessimistic, but it may have been intended as a challenge for a new generation to carry on the struggle: "To imagine [women] passing from this just perceptible dawn into another darkness does not seem to me fantastic."[55]

Recent feminist biographers have found enlightenment and inspiration in these women's "eerily familiar" struggles to reconcile personal and professional needs and to find fulfillment in each sphere.[56] It was a struggle fraught with disappointment, but not entirely futile. For the most part, these women enjoyed considerable professional success and at least a measure of personal happiness. For many, the years just preceding World War I, including the first few seasons of the Provincetown theatre, probably represented the nearest culmination of that feminist ideal. The struggle does not seem to be one they ever completely abandoned, however. They retreated. They compromised. They divorced, moved on, and changed careers, loves, and lives in their ongoing process of personal re-creation and fulfillment. To characterize their struggles in terms of success or failure, however, betrays the spirit of experimentation in which they lived.

# 8

## *Valedictory*

To have seen this spirit, to have lived with it, has been worth all the difficulty, all the obvious sadness at closing the book and writing "finis."

        —Eleanor Fitzgerald, "Valedictory of an Art Theatre"

Creating the Provincetown Players was part of a larger revolutionary impulse to create a new social order. Sexual equality was not the only goal of the new order, but for the members of this particular community —who were, for the most part, of a race and class already privileged—it was the most personally urgent. Male and female Provincetowners, in this mostly heterosexual group, were obsessed with relations between men and women, and feminism was embraced, at first, by both men and women as a method for perfecting those relationships.

At the outset, women were present in sufficient numbers to provide a welcoming climate for other women. Moreover, feminists were present in sufficient numbers, not only to welcome women, but to seek equity for women in all aspects of operation. Among the company's female leadership, feminists were so numerous that it is almost permissible to use the terms "women" and "feminists" interchangeably. These women composed not merely a group but an overlapping, interlinking, intimately woven network of mutual support. Their close social, professional, and personal relationships, many predating the theatre, fed the network: Westley and Wycherly were Heterodites who staged or performed in the plays of other Heterodites; Rauh recruited her political comrade Fitzgerald and her housemate Jenkins, who in turn brought in her college chum, Mary Blair; and Margaret Swain recruited her friend Nina Moise. At least three groups of sisters and several interlocking couples worked at Provincetown. There is almost no limit to the varieties of shared experience among Provincetown's women. They went to college together, traveled and lived together, sent their children to the same school, slept with many of the same men, and, occasionally, with one another. They shared political goals, social backgrounds, and personal space. The women's/feminist network helped establish Provincetown as a microcosm of the new egalitarian society Provincetown's women wished to create along feminist ideals.

The network produced singularly felicitous collaborations among women. New plays by women offered strong acting roles to women; plays by and about women attracted female directors, female critics, and female audiences. The potential political impact of a feminist play by Susan Glaspell, for example, is significantly enhanced when we consider that the leading protagonist was usually portrayed by feminist actresses like Ida Rauh or Margaret Wycherly and that feminist critics like Ruth Hale and Maida Castellun interpreted the performances. Such a network, unsurprisingly, survived the demise of the company: when Blanche Hays tried to market *The Verge* in Paris; when Nina Moise brought Edna James to Santa Barbara; when Rauh and Nordfeldt worked together in Santa Fe; when Norma Millay appeared in Barnes's *The Dove* in 1926; when Barnes became Loy's agent in New York; when six Provincetown women offered Kenton financial aid in 1933; and when Glaspell tried to bring Rauh into the Federal Theatre Project in 1937.

Provincetown gave women a place to practice public as well as private goals. Because theatre was a sphere that had historically excluded women, except as actresses, merely to seek a place in theatre as anything else had feminist implications. Provincetown provided its women a space from which to challenge sexually segregated theatrical practice by becoming directors, designers, playwrights, and managers. To the degree that they succeeded, they could claim with evidence that, in theatre, "women's place was everywhere." In addition to providing opportunities to challenge sexual segregation, a platform for feminist issues, and a laboratory in which sexual conflicts could be symbolically represented, examined, and resolved, Provincetown provided a liberating arena for aesthetic experimentation. For women in particular, aesthetic experimentation was closely related to personal goals of fulfillment, empowerment, and enrichment, but it also helped them make important artistic contributions. Women helped set the Players' artistic goals and operating procedures, and they led the move from business by consensus to business through hierarchy. Women exercised powerful control over playreading and play selection and improved standards of both staging and performance. Women controlled costuming throughout the group's history. Women wrote more than one-third of the plays produced and directed nearly one-half the plays produced. Women, always influential, dominated theatre management at Provincetown by 1918. Women playwrights contributed some of the company's most inventive and socially relevant works, works that were typically revolutionary in both form and content, introducing or promoting stylistic innovations for which there was not yet a suitable critical vocabulary and exploring ideas that many found disturbing. The combined contributions of Provincetown's women playwrights helped establish the Provincetown Players as the birthplace of modern American drama and perhaps the most important platform for feminist drama in America before the 1960s. Provincetown's actresses' commitment to naturalism and individual creation helped speed the shift in acting style then under way in American theatre. Provincetown's women directors and designers pioneered specialism in those fields. Blanche Hays, in her early experiments with expressionism and masks, and Marguerite Zorach, in her work with abstract modernism and new stagecraft, helped launch the visual innovations for which Provincetown is celebrated. In rejecting blackface casting in *The Dreamy Kid,* a decision perhaps motivated as much by a desire for realism in the theatre as for racial equality in society, Ida Rauh made an important individual contribution with aesthetic and ideological implications.

Provincetown gave women a space in which to rehearse power as well as plays. The differing ways in which women achieved influence and exercised authority at Provincetown reflected a major transition in the ways by which women were seeking power and influence in the culture at large. Women like Moise, Fitzgerald, and Hays exhibited more traditionally feminine characteristics: patience, tact, and sympathetic nurturance. Others, like Kenton, Rauh, Bryant, and Glaspell, challenged gender expectations: they relished power, unapologetically exercised authority, and resented losing it. The two types embodied a split within the larger culture, a transition from the nineteenth century's "woman movement," with its emphasis on "nurturant service" (what feminist historians now call "maternalism"), to the twentieth century's "feminist movement," with its focus on women's rights. Both strategies were, to some degree, effective in that all of these women achieved considerable influence within the company. Practitioners of the first type, however, encountered less opposition from men in the company. Men like James Light and Eugene O'Neill had little problem accepting Moise's maternal authority, but they were likely to call women like Kenton, Bryant, and Rauh unflattering names.

By Provincetown's last two seasons, women remained strong only in those areas traditionally open to them: acting and costuming. In all others, their influence declined or disappeared (see graph 5). Feminism and gender ideology are intimately implicated in both these circumstances: the unusual participation by women in all areas early on and the sharp decline in women's participation in directing, writing, and scenic design during the last two seasons. That men supported feminism, at least for a while, probably helped women attain an unprecedented degree of equality. For a few years at least, Provincetown was a promising model for a more egalitarian society. That Provincetown's men supported feminism more in theory than in practice underscores the different effects of living feminism and the sharp discrepancy between men's and women's understanding of and commitment to radical change in gender roles. Men wanted feminism to provide more interesting and sexually liberated companions. Women wanted more satisfying personal and sexual lives, too, but they also wanted to participate equally in all human endeavors. Provincetown's women understood gender politics far better than did their male partners, and they needed feminism in a way men did not. As Kenton predicted, things would get worse before they could get better, and Evelyn Scott accurately described the feminist efforts of her generation as "a just perceptible dawn."

For the women of Provincetown, feminism, although certainly concerned with specific political or legal reforms (suffrage, economic equity, reproductive rights, etc.), was more than a political affiliation; it was a secular religion. Feminism, as extolled and practiced by Edna Kenton and her colleagues, was a new way to think, to live, and to relate to other human beings. Religious metaphors and allusions have frequently been employed to describe Provincetown's passionate excesses in work and play. Robert K. Sarlós has depicted Jig Cook as a Dionysian figure, an image perhaps originating with Glaspell's attempt to immortalize Cook in her suggestively titled *Road to the Temple*.[1] Similarly, Glaspell characterized the men who eventually formed the Experimental Theatre as "alien gods."[2] Greenwich Village feminism provides a possible source of

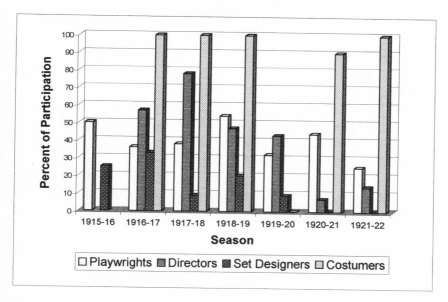

Graph 5. Overall Percentage of Participation by Women

Provincetown's religious fervor (hence Elsie Dufour's description of a Heterodoxy meeting in which she was almost "excommunicated" for criticizing *The Verge,* which the Heterodites were clearly celebrating as a feminist hymn). Alexander Woollcott also employed a religious metaphor for Provincetown's audience ("the faithful") when *The Verge* was onstage.[3] There were goddesses (perhaps "Furies" or "Danaïds") as well as gods at Provincetown. The use of religious metaphors by Provincetowners to describe both their theatre and feminism manifests their perception of the significant spiritual aspect of both. These feminists were the first generation of women to begin to understand gender as socially constructed—"Man" and "Woman" as "capitalized impersonalities." Those old ideas, those patterns of behavior, could not be legislated away. The new social order must be effected by personal transformation —men and women and all human relationships had to be transformed through a process that was intellectual, psychological, and spiritual. They used the theatre to help effect this transformation.

Women easily weathered the shift from working by consensus to working by hierarchy, for the early hierarchies included men and women in roughly equal numbers. It was not the change from consensus to hierarchy that displaced women; it was the shift from a hierarchy that included women in positions of power to one that excluded such women that spelled their doom within the organization. An undeniable factor in women's displacement was O'Neill's eventual preeminence. Always an important member, O'Neill assumed an unassailable position after the success of *The Emperor Jones*. His commercial aspirations and personal attitudes toward women helped foster an inhospitable environment for women's significant presence. The men he surrounded himself with were similarly uninterested in political or personal transformation; they were interested in professional success. As O'Neill and his group replaced the founding group, Provincetown women declined in both number and influence, but the displacement of women almost certainly did not include an overt conspiracy on the part of these men. Although O'Neill, Light, Macgowan, and others did want to get rid of particular women, no evidence suggests that they ever consciously set out to exclude women artists in general. Nor is there evidence that they ever sat down and said, "Look, we'll let the girls act and sew, but no women playwrights, directors, or designers." The sad fact is they did not have to. It takes little effort to enforce gender ideology that has been firmly in place for centuries. What requires conscious effort is challenging those assumptions. As conscious effort to challenge traditional sexual segregation in theatre practice decreased at Provincetown, the sexual division of labor came to resemble that in the mainstream commercial theatre.

Although individual career goals rarely seemed paramount among Provincetown's leading women, by 1922 a number of prominent Provincetown women had ventured into the commercial theatre. Women who made the most successful transitions from Provincetown to Broadway, however, made them in the most traditionally female fields: acting and costuming. Those who did not enter the commercial theatre at all were in the least traditionally female field: scenic design. As we have seen, this pattern is the very one observed in the last two seasons at Provincetown, when women's participation overall diminished and the participants noticeably arranged themselves around familiar, sexually approved areas of work—women in acting and costuming, men in playwriting, directing, and scenic design. The conclusion would seem to be that in the absence of active, conscious efforts to welcome women throughout the field of theatre, women will drift into—or be forced into—traditionally female fields within theatre, with men assuming the theatrical positions usually associated with control and money. What is true for the theatre may be applied to society at large. Social relations between men and women are not likely to change without conscious and active effort to investigate and challenge conventional gender ideology—without, in short, feminist consciousness and feminist activism. The decrease in conscious effort to challenge traditional gender roles at Provincetown paralleled even more overt efforts in society at large to reinforce that ideology.

Theatre always reflects society, and rarely has that relationship been more direct, immediate, and personal than in the creation and development of the Provincetown Players. This study strongly confirms the relationship between feminism and the Provincetown Players suggested by social historians and allows us to view the Provincetown Players as an important part of feminist theatre history. Just as the creation of Provincetown may be seen as one manifestation of the surge of feminist activism of the 1910s, the structural changes at Provincetown, the gradual disappearance of women, and the hushing of women's voices may also be seen as a manifestation of larger social changes, specifically, the conservative backlash of the 1920s. The watershed year in the disintegration of the Provincetown Players is 1920, a year that also marks the beginning of the decline of first-wave feminism.[4] The timing is right if, as Susan Faludi has argued, antifeminist backlash is not initiated by women's achievement of full equality but by the increased likelihood that they may win it: "It is a preemptive strike that stops women long before they reach the finish line."[5] The year 1920, when women won universal suffrage in America, was precisely such a historic moment. Threatened with disruption, the culture at large closed ranks against feminists and feminist impulses. Likewise, Provincetown men recanted their former feminist ideals. Eventually even the women began to lose faith; they felt guilty for neglecting their families. In the 1920s and 1930s, the formerly radical feminists of Provincetown wrote homages to children and husbands and looked for men to mother. The changing attitudes of women, stimulated by widespread cultural backlash to all radical political movements, is another crucial factor in their displacement.

Writing in 1926, Floyd Dell attempted to explain the feminist efforts of his generation: "We were content with what was happening to women because what we wanted was something for ourselves—a glorious playfellow . . . but they wanted something different—something for themselves. They wanted happiness—the happiness that comes from being a freely expressive and largely active personality." Dell did not believe they found it: "Not at college, nor in the professions, nor on the stage."[6] The findings of this study support Dell's perception of the differences in men's and women's desires, but not his pessimistic conclusion. Despite the seemingly disappointing results of Provincetown's feminist experiments, despite their limited impact on mainstream American theatre, and despite their inability to convert personal transformation into immediate social change, the women of Provincetown did get "something for themselves" from their experiences at Provincetown. Although the scope of this study did not call for a thorough examination of the women's individual lives, the evidence examined suggests that these women grew as individuals and as artists during these years. They lost innocence and acquired a deeper understanding of the world they had set out so blithely to remake in 1915. Their experiences at Provincetown were surely an important part of their growing enlightenment, and some of the plays are eloquent testimony to that effect: from *Trifles* to *The Verge* is a journey from an awakening to a fully aroused feminist consciousness. Personal testimonies of the company's female leadership have confirmed that their years with the organization were deeply, personally fulfilling. They used the theatre primarily for re-creation, in the profoundest sense of that word, and their theatrical achievements gave their lives meaning, excitement, joy.

Despite the fact that few of Provincetown's leading women made the transition into sustained Broadway careers, their artistic and social legacy is not inconsequential. Many of their plays enjoyed productions in noncommercial theatres around the country and in this way probably spread elements of a new drama and changed attitudes toward women, as well as art, for decades. Glaspell and Fitzgerald doubtless spread the "Provincetown ideas" in the Federal Theatre, and women working in regions of America other than New York, like Moise and Rauh, are the cultural antecedents of the women who pioneered the regional theatre movement in the 1940s and 1950s. It is possible, too, that the extent of the legacy cannot yet be assessed, for many of these women's plays, although ignored for a time, began to be rediscovered, reanalyzed, retaught, and re-produced with the advent of second-wave feminism in the 1970s. If not direct influences, Provincetown's women were harbingers of aesthetic and political changes to come. Not until the 1960s did a similarly radical counterculture emerge in America, and once again America's revolutionaries began a crusade against war and for economic, racial, and sexual equality. Theatre collectives like the Living Theatre, the Performance Group, and the Open Theatre allied themselves with the political Left and sought personal and social transformation through artistic experimentation. Self-identified feminist theatres sprang into existence across the country, a grassroots phenomenon not witnessed since the little theatre movement fifty years earlier. In one of the earliest published surveys of this feminist theatre movement, Patti Gillespie described motives and political backgrounds remarkably similar to those of Provincetown's female membership. Like the women of Provincetown, women in the 1960s and 1970s turned to the theatre for personal fulfillment, artistic experimentation, and a political platform. Also like Provincetown's women, many of them had been active in leftist political organizations that had used paratheatrical performances to promote their causes.[7] By the 1980s, these second-wave feminists were relaunching battles against the same antifeminist attitudes that Provincetown's women had faced in the 1920s, and by the end of the 1980s, few self-identified feminist theatre groups remained. In her recent retrospective analysis of second-wave feminist theatres, based largely on interviews with its practitioners, Charlotte Canning has argued that the absence of self-identified feminist theatre groups does not indicate the end of the intersection of feminism and theatre, but change in how that intersection may be manifested.[8] Her interviewees' perceptions of their experiences in feminist theatre also strongly echo that of Provincetown's female leadership: "All of them felt they had participated in something of immense importance and value."[9] In this study, Canning challenged scholars to confront contradiction and complexity in recovering women's history, reminding us that "a history, no matter how contradictory or problematic, is a crucial component of power, accomplishment, and change."[10]

Provincetown women's failure to make a mark on commercial theatre points to a continuing controversy within American theatre—and the scholars who chart it. As Helen Krich Chinoy has noted, theatre historians of the twentieth century focused primarily on mainstream,

154 ⌒ Chapter Eight

commercial theatre, thereby ignoring the achievements of most women, whose primary contributions have not been in the commercial theatre, especially not on Broadway, but in the art, little, community, educational, and children's theatres. Chinoy's argument that women who have made major contributions to American theatre have typically identified with "an idea of theatre larger than that of Broadway" is strongly reinforced by the achievements of Provincetown's women.[11] Scholars in the twenty-first century must continue to challenge the traditional measures of success or significance in theatre history, because until that happens, much will remain unrecorded and uncelebrated. We should certainly celebrate the brief but vital presence of these extraordinarily gifted women whose significant contributions in the fields of journalism, literature, drama, poetry, and painting have been widely recognized (and include three Pulitzer Prizes). That they could not, or chose not to, make the theatre their primary career is surely theatre's loss, but the combined richness of all these divergent talents produced a very fertile moment in its history.

# Appendix 1
## The Women of Provincetown

This listing represents an attempt at a comprehensive record of women's participation in every capacity at Provincetown. Sources include Deutsch and Hanau's appendix B, playbills, minutes, and published or nonpublished plays.

Abbott, Berenice—actress
Allen, Ruth Collins—actress
Anderson, Ruth—actress
Bailey, Margaret ("Nani")—actress, restaurateur
Baker, Marjory Lacey—actress, director
Ballantine, Stella—actress
Barber, Mary F.—playwright
Barleon, Amelie—actress
Barnes, Djuna—playwright
Becket, Helen—actress
Begg, Jeannie—actress
Beland, Millie—actress
Berry, Marion—actress
Blair, Mary—actress
Booth, Marie Rosalie—actress
Boris, Magda—actress
Boyce, Neith—playwright, actress, director
Bronlee, Lark—actress
Brown, Elizabeth—actress
Bryant, Louise—actress, playwright, executive committee member
Burnmore, Florence—actress
Burr, Jane—actress
Cannell, Kathleen—actress

Carr, Myra—founder
Cary, Augusta—actress
Chapin, Elsie—director
Chauvenet, Virginia—actress
Colbron, Grace Isabel—translator
Colvert, Leathe—actress
Cook, Ellen ("Ma-mie")—costume designer
Cook, Nilla—actress
Crocker, Bosworth—playwright
Davies, Mary Carolyn—playwright
Doubleday, Angelica—actress
Edelson, Becky—costume designer
Ell, Christine—actress
Enright, Florence—director
Erle, Luie [Lucy?]—actress
Ferber, Edna—playwright
Fishman, Sarah—actress
Fitzgerald, M. Eleanor—business manager
Frank, Florence Kiper—playwright
Freeman, Helen—actress
Fuller, Martha Ryther—actress
Glaspell, Susan—playwright, actress, director, executive committee member

Grant, Lillian Ward—actress
Hall, Alice—actress, director
Hall, Francis—actress
Hall, Julia—actress
Hall, Rosalys—actress
Hapgood, Beatrix—actress
Hapgood, Miriam—actress
Harding, Ann—actress
Harding, Ravida—actress
Harrison, Elsie—actress
Hays, Blanche—actress, costume designer
Heaton, Florence Flossette—scene designer
Heinemann, Eda—actress
Hellstrom, Louise—scene designer
Hoving, Greta—actress
Huffaker, Lucy—actress
Hutchenson, Josephine—actress
Hutchison, Eleanor—actress
James, Edna—actress
Javne, Leah—actress
Jenkins, Susan (Light Brown)—administrative assistant
Kent, Bertha—actress
Kenton, Edna—executive committee member
Kiper, Miriam—actress
Kittredge, Helen G.—actress
L'Engle, Lucy—costume designer
L'Engle, Tracy—actress
Lewis, Judith—actress
Loughran, Beatrix—actress
Loy, Mina (aka Imna Oly)—actress
MacDougal, Alice—actress
March, Jane—actress
Markham, Kirah (Elaine Hyman)—actress
McCarthy, Agnes—actress
Millay, Cora—actress
Millay, Edna—playwright, actress, executive committee member
Millay, Kathleen—actress
Millay, Norma—actress
Miller, Dorothy—actress
Moise, Nina—company director, actress
Moore, Dorothy—actress

Moreland, Mara—actress
Nodell, Bella—actress
Nordfeldt, Margaret—secretary-treasurer, executive committee member, actress
Pinch, Esther—actress
Potter, Grace—playwright
Powers, Jeanne—actress
Pyne, Mary—actress
Quidington, Augusta—actress
Rauh, Ida—actress, director, executive committee member
Reber, Mabel—costume designer
Rhodes, Margaret—actress
Rice, Kate—actress
Robb, Jean—actress
Rostetter, Alice—playwright, actress
Rubinstein, Dosha—actress
Rudell, Billie—actress
Savage, Clara—actress
Sawyer, Dorothy—actress
Schoonmaker, Nancy M.—actress
Scott, Evelyn—playwright
Shreve, Lucy—actress
Smith, Edna—actress
Smith, Jessica—actress
Smith, Rita Creighton—playwright
Steele, Margaret—actress
Stevens, Mary—actress
Stockton, Esther—actress
Swain, Margaret—scene designer, actress
Taft, Emily—actress
Thompson, Edith Haynes—scene designer
Tobey, Virginia—actress
Treadwell, Louise—actress
Treadwell, Sophie—director, member of producing committee
Turkel, Pauline—administrative assistant
Turner, Betty—actress
Unger, Edith (Avril)—costume designer, actress
Upjohn, Dorothy—actress
Vincent, Nell—actress
Vorse, Ellen—actress
Vorse, Mary Heaton—actress
Wehn, Josephine—actress

Wellman, Rita—actress, playwright, director
Wenclaw (Wenclawska), Ruza—actress
Westley, Helen—director
Whittredge, Miss—scene designer
Wilds, Sophie—actress

Wold, Petra—administrative secretary
Woods, Alice (Ullman)—playwright
Wycherly, Margaret—director, actress
Zagat, Helen—costume designer, actress
Zorach, Marguerite—scenic and costume designer, director

## *Appendix 2*
## Charter Members of the Provincetown Players, September 1916[1]


Edward J. Ballantine
Stella Ballantine
Neith Boyce
Louise Bryant
Frederic Burt
David Carb
Myra Musselman Carr
George Cram Cook
Floyd Dell
Charles Demuth
Max Eastman
Susan Glaspell
Alice Hall
Dr. Henry M. Hall
Hutchins Hapgood
Lucy Huffaker
Brör Nordfeldt
Margaret Nordfeldt
Eugene O'Neill
Ida Rauh
John Reed
Robert Rogers
Edwin D. Schoonmaker
Nancy Schoonmaker
Margaret Steele
Wilbur Daniel Steele
Mary Heaton Vorse
Marguerite Zorach
William Zorach

# *Appendix 3*
## Executive Committee Membership[1]

| | |
|---|---|
| 5 September 1916 | George Cram Cook, Margaret Nordfeldt, Floyd Dell, Louise Bryant, John Reed |
| 7 October 1916 | Cook, Nordfeldt, Bryant, Reed, Lucian Cary |
| 21 February 1917 | Cook, Nordfeldt, Cary, Edna Kenton, Ida Rauh |
| 21 March 1917 | Cook, Cary, Kenton, Rauh, David Carb |
| 21 April 1918 | Cook, Kenton, Rauh, Carb, Otto Liveright |
| 1918–19 | Cook, Kenton, Rauh, Liveright, Eleanor Fitzgerald |
| 1919–20 | Cook, Kenton, Rauh, Fitzgerald, Edna Millay |
| 1920–21 (first bill) | Cook, Kenton, Rauh, Fitzgerald, Millay, James Light, Charles Ellis |
| (Added, second bill) | E. J. Ballantine, Susan Glaspell, Eugene O'Neill |
| (Added, third bill) | Jasper Deeter and Cleon Throckmorton |
| 1921–22 | Cook, Kenton, Fitzgerald, Glaspell, O'Neill |

# Appendix 4
## Productions of Plays Written or Cowritten by Women

### Summer 1915 (Provincetown)

*Constancy,* Neith Boyce
*Suppressed Desires,* George Cram Cook and Susan Glaspell

### Spring 1916 (New York)

*Suppressed Desires*
*Suppressed Desires*

### Summer 1916 (Provincetown)

*Winter's Night,* Neith Boyce
*Suppressed Desires*
*The Game,* Louise Bryant
*Constancy*
*Trifles,* Susan Glaspell
*Enemies,* Neith Boyce and Hutchins Hapgood
*The Game*
*Suppressed Desires*

### 1916–1917 (New York)

*The Game*
*Enemies*
*Suppressed Desires*
*The Two Sons,* Neith Boyce
*Winter's Night*
*Barbarians,* Rita Wellman
*The People,* Susan Glaspell
*Barbarians*
*The People*
*Suppressed Desires*

### 1917–1918

*Close the Book,* Susan Glaspell
*Funiculi-Funicula,* Rita Wellman
*The Outside,* Susan Glaspell
*The Slave with Two Faces,* Mary Carolyn Davies
*About Six,* Grace Potter
*The Devil's Glow,* Alice Woods Ullman
*The Rib-Person,* Rita Wellman
*Woman's Honor,* Susan Glaspell

### 1918–1919

*The Princess Marries the Page,* Edna Millay
*Gee-Rusalem,* Florence Kiper Frank
*The Rescue,* Rita Creighton Smith
*Tickless Time,* Susan Glaspell and George Cram Cook
*The Widow's Veil,* Alice Rostetter
*The String of the Samisen,* Rita Wellman
*The Baby Carriage,* Bosworth Crocker
*The Squealer,* Mary Foster Barber
*Bernice,* Susan Glaspell
*The Widow's Veil*
*Woman's Honor*
*The Widow's Veil*
*Tickless Time*
*Tickless Time*

### 1919–1920

*Three from the Earth,* Djuna Barnes
*Aria da Capo,* Edna Millay
*The Eldest,* Edna Ferber
*An Irish Triangle,* Djuna Barnes
*Kurzy of the Sea,* Djuna Barnes
*Aria da Capo*

### 1920–1921

*Tickless Time* (curtain-raiser to *The Emperor Jones*)
*Love,* Evelyn Scott
*Inheritors,* Susan Glaspell
*Trifles*
*Suppressed Desires* (curtain-raiser to *The Emperor Jones*)
*Inheritors*
*The Widow's Veil*
*Aria da Capo*

### 1921–1922
*The Verge,* Susan Glaspell
*Chains of Dew,* Susan Glaspell

### 1915–1922
Total number of productions of plays: 145
Total number of productions of plays written by women: 60
Overall percentage of productions of plays written by women: 42 percent

# *Appendix 5*
## Provincetown Productions for Which Directing
## Credit Can Be Reasonably Established

*Credited in playbill or published in Deutsch and Hanau appendix
**Credited in first published version of play
***Credit established by letter, interview, newspaper article, or memoir

### 1916–1917

*The Game* by Louise Bryant—Marguerite Zorach and William Zorach*
*Bound East for Cardiff* by Eugene O'Neill—E. J. Ballantine***
*Trifles* by Susan Glaspell—E. J. Ballantine***
*Mother Carey's Chickens* by Henry Hall—Henry Hall and Alice Hall***
*King Arthur's Socks* by Floyd Dell—E. J. Ballantine*
*Freedom* by John Reed—Arthur Hohl*
*Enemies* by Neith Boyce and Hutchins Hapgood—Neith Boyce and Hutchins Hapgood*
*Before Breakfast* by Eugene O'Neill—Eugene O'Neill***
*Lima Beans* by Alfred Kreymborg—Alfred Kreymborg***
*Sauce for the Emperor* by John Mosher—Sophie Treadwell***
*The Obituary* by Saxe Commins—Saxe Commins*
*A Long Time Ago* by Floyd Dell—Duncan Macdougal*
*Pan* by Kenneth MacNichol—Nina Moise***
*Winter's Night* by Neith Boyce—Nina Moise***
*A Dollar* by David Pinski—Nina Moise*
*Barbarians* by Rita Wellman—Nina Moise*
*The Sniper* by Eugene O'Neill—Nina Moise*
*The People* by Susan Glaspell—Nina Moise*
*The Prodigal Son* by Harry Kemp—Frederic Burt*
*Cocaine* by Pendleton King—Margaret Wycherly*
*Suppressed Desires* by George Cram Cook and Susan Glaspell (revival)—Nina
    Moise***

Total number of productions credited: 21
Number directed or codirected by women: 12
Percentage of plays directed or codirected by women: 57 percent

## 1917–1918

*The Long Voyage Home* by Eugene O'Neill—Nina Moise*
*Close the Book* by Susan Glaspell—Nina Moise*
*Night* by James Oppenheim—Rollo Peters*
*'Ile* by Eugene O'Neill—Nina Moise*
*Funiculi-Funicula* by Rita Wellman—Nina Moise**
*The Angel Intrudes* by Floyd Dell—Nina Moise and Floyd Dell*
*The Outside* by Susan Glaspell—Nina Moise***
*Down the Airshaft* by Mike Gold—David Carb*
*The Slave with Two Faces* by Mary Carolyn Davies—Nina Moise*
*About Six* by Grace Potter—Nina Moise and Grace Potter*
*Sweet and Twenty* by Floyd Dell—Nina Moise*
*The Athenian Women* by George Cram Cook—Nina Moise*
*The Devil's Glow* by Alice Woods—Harold Parsons*
*The Rib-Person* by Rita Wellman—Rita Wellman*
*Contemporaries* by Wilbur Steele—George Cram Cook*
*The Rope* by Eugene O'Neill—Nina Moise*
*Woman's Honor* by Susan Glaspell—Nina Moise and Susan Glaspell*
*The Gentle Furniture Shop* by Maxwell Bodenheim—Nina Moise***[1]

Total number of productions credited: 18
Number directed or codirected by women: 14
Percentage of plays directed or codirected by women: 78 percent

## 1918–1919

*The Princess Marries the Page* by Edna Millay—Edna Millay*
*Where the Cross Is Made* by Eugene O'Neill—Ida Rauh*
*Gee-Rusalem* by Florence Frank—Florence Enright*
*The Moon of the Caribbees* by Eugene O'Neill—Thomas Mitchell*
*The Rescue* by Rita Smith—Ida Rauh*
*Tickless Time* by Susan Glaspell and George Cram Cook—Susan Glaspell and
    George Cram Cook*
*From Portland to Dover* by O. K. Liveright—O. K. Liveright*
*5050* by Robert A. Parker—Robert A. Parker*
*The Widow's Veil* by Alice Rostetter—George Cram Cook*
*The String of the Samisen* by Rita Wellman—Michio Itow*
*The Baby Carriage* by Bosworth Crocker—Ida Rauh***
*The Squealer* by Mary Barber—E. J. Ballantine*
*Bernice* by Susan Glaspell—E. J. Ballantine*
*Woman's Honor* by Susan Glaspell (revival)—Marjory Lacey Baker*
*Bound East for Cardiff* by Eugene O'Neill (revival)—George Cram Cook*

Total number of credited productions: 15
Number directed or codirected by women: 7
Percentage of plays directed or codirected by women: 47 percent

## 1919–1920

*The Dreamy Kid* by Eugene O'Neill—Ida Rauh*
*The Philosopher of Butterbiggins* by Harold Chapin—Elsie Chapin*
*Getting Unmarried* by Winthrop Parkhurst—Ida Rauh*
*Brothers* by Lewis Beach—James Light*
*Aria da Capo* by Edna Millay—Edna Millay*
*The Eldest* by Edna Ferber—James Light*
*An Irish Triangle* by Djuna Barnes—Helen Westley*
*Money* by Mike Gold—James Light*
*Vote the New Moon* by Alfred Kreymborg—James Light*
*Three Travellers Watch a Sunrise* by Wallace Stevens—Charles Ellis*
*Pie* by Lawrence Langner—Lawrence Langner*
*Last Masks* by Arthur Schnitzler—E. J. Ballantine*
*Kurzy of the Sea* by Djuna Barnes—Helen Westley*
*Exorcism* by Eugene O'Neill—Edward Goodman*

Total number of credited productions: 14
Number directed or codirected by women: 6
Percentage of plays directed or codirected by women: 43 percent

## 1920–1921

*Matinata* by Lawrence Langner—Lawrence Langner*
*The Emperor Jones* by Eugene O'Neill—George Cram Cook*2
*What D'You Want* by Lawrence Vail—Florence Enright*
*Diff'rent* by Eugene O'Neill—Charles O'Brien Kennedy*
*The Spring* by George Cram Cook—George Cram Cook and Jasper Deeter*
*Love* by Evelyn Scott—Rollo Lloyd*
*Inheritors* by Susan Glaspell—Jasper Deeter*
*Trifles* by Susan Glaspell (revival)—Ralph Stewart*
*Grotesques* by Cloyd Head—James Light*
*The Moon of the Caribbees* by Eugene O'Neill (revival)—Charles O'Brien Kennedy*
*Autumn Fires* by Gustav Wied—Jasper Deeter*
*Aria da Capo* by Edna Millay (spring season)—Jasper Deeter*
*The Widow's Veil* by Alice Rostetter (spring season)—Jasper Deeter*
*Suppressed Desires* by George Cram Cook and Susan Glaspell (Broadway)—George Cram Cook*

Total number of credited productions: 14
Number directed or codirected by women: 1
Percentage of plays directed or codirected by women: 7 percent

## 1921–1922

*The Verge* by Susan Glaspell—George Cram Cook*
*The Hand of the Potter* by Theodore Dreiser—Charles O'Brien Kennedy*
*A Little Act of Justice* by Norman C. Lindau—Margaret Wycherly*
*Footsteps* by Don Corley—George Cram Cook and Don Corley*

*The Stick-up* by Pierre Loving—George Cram Cook*
*The Hairy Ape* by Eugene O'Neill—James Light and Arthur Hopkins***
*Chains of Dew* by Susan Glaspell—Ralph Stewart*

Total number of credited productions: 7
Number directed or codirected by women: 1
Percentage of plays directed or codirected by women: 14 percent

### Summary for 1915–1922
Total number of credited productions: 89
Number directed or codirected by women: 41
Overall percentage of women directors: 46 percent

# Appendix 6

## Provincetown Productions for Which Scenic Design Credit Can Be Reasonably Established[1]

### 1915–1916

*Constancy* by Neith Boyce—Robert Edmond Jones*
*Suppressed Desires* by George Cram Cook and Susan Glaspell—Robert Edmond Jones*
*The Game* by Louise Bryant—Marguerite Zorach and William Zorach
*The Eternal Quadrangle* by John Reed—E. J. Ballantine*

Total number of productions credited: 4
Number designed or codesigned by women: 1
Percentage designed or codesigned by women: 25 percent

### 1916–1917

*Freedom* by John Reed—Brör Nordfeldt[2]
*Enemies* by Neith Boyce and Hutchins Hapgood—Brör Nordfeldt
*Lima Beans* by Alfred Kreymborg—Marguerite Zorach and William Zorach
*The Obituary* by Saxe Commins—Miss Whittredge
*Bored* by John Mosher—Don Corley
*Fog* by Eugene O'Neill—Brör Nordfeldt and Margaret Swain
*Pan* by Kenneth Macnichol—Marguerite Zorach and William Zorach
*Winter's Night* by Neith Boyce—Edith Haynes Thompson
*A Dollar* by David Pinski—Brör Nordfeldt
*Ivan's Homecoming* by Irwin Granich (Mike Gold)—Don Corley
*Barbarians* by Rita Wellman—Don Corley
*The Sniper* by Eugene O'Neill—Don Corley
*Cocaine* by Pendleton King—Ira Remsen and Carroll Berry
*The Prodigal Son* by Harry Kemp—George Cram Cook
*Suppressed Desires* by George Cram Cook and Susan Glaspell (revival)—William Zorach[3]

Total number of productions credited: 15
Number designed or codesigned by women: 5
Percentage designed or codesigned by women: 33 percent

## 1917–1918

*The Long Voyage Home* by Eugene O'Neill—Ira Remsen
*Night* by James Oppenheim—Rollo Peters
*'Ile* by Eugene O'Neill—Louis B. Ell
*The Angel Intrudes* by Floyd Dell—Floyd Dell and Neil Reber
*The Outside* by Susan Glaspell—Ira Remsen
*Down the Airshaft* by Irwin Granich—Louis B. Ell
*The Slave with Two Faces* by Mary Carolyn Davies—Norman Jacobsen
*About Six* by Grace Potter—Louis B. Ell
*Sweet and Twenty* by Floyd Dell—Floyd Dell
*The Athenian Women* by George Cram Cook—Ira Remsen
*The Hermit and His Messiah* by F. B. Kugelman—Flossette Florence Heaton

Total number of productions credited: 11
Number designed or codesigned by women: 1
Percentage designed or codesigned by women: 9 percent

## 1918–1919

*The Princess Marries the Page* by Edna Millay—C. M. Sax
*Gee-Rusalem* by Florence Kiper Frank—Glen Coleman
*Tickless Time* by Susan Glaspell and George Cram Cook—Louise Hellstrom
*The String of the Samisen* by Rita Wellman—Lloyd Wright
*Not Smart* by Wilbur Daniel Steele—W. G. Reinecke

Total number of productions credited: 5
Number designed or codesigned by women: 1
Percentage designed or codesigned by women: 20 percent

## 1919–1920

*The Dreamy Kid* by Eugene O'Neill—Glen Coleman
*The Philosopher of Butterbiggins* by Harold Chapin—James Light
*Three from the Earth* by Djuna Barnes—James Light
*Getting Unmarried* by Winthrop Parkhurst—Marguerite Zorach
*Brothers* by Lewis Beach—George Theodore Hartmann
*Aria da Capo* by Edna Millay—Charles Ellis
*The Eldest* by Edna Ferber—James Light
*An Irish Triangle* by Djuna Barnes—James Light
*Money* by Irwin Granich—James Light
*Vote the New Moon* by Alfred Kreymborg—Jean Paul Slusser
*Three Travellers Watch a Sunrise* by Wallace Stevens—Charles Ellis

Total number of productions credited: 11
Number designed or codesigned by women: 1
Percentage designed or codesigned by women: 9 percent

### 1920–1921
*The Emperor Jones* by Eugene O'Neill—Cleon Throckmorton
*What D'You Want* by Lawrence Vail—Cleon Throckmorton
*Diff'rent* by Eugene O'Neill—Cleon Throckmorton
*The Spring* by George Cram Cook—Cleon Throckmorton
*Love* by Evelyn Scott—Don Corley
*Grotesques* by Cloyd Head—Harry Gottlieb
*The Moon of the Caribbees* by Eugene O'Neill (revival)—Harry Gottlieb

Total number of productions credited: 7
Number designed or codesigned by women: 0
Percentage designed or codesigned by women: 0 percent

### 1921–1922
*The Verge* by Susan Glaspell—Cleon Throckmorton
*The Hand of the Potter* by Theodore Dreiser—Cleon Throckmorton
*A Little Act of Justice* by Norman C. Lindau—Cleon Throckmorton
*Footsteps* by Don Corley—Cleon Throckmorton
*The Hairy Ape* by Eugene O'Neill—Robert Edmond Jones and Cleon Throckmorton
*Chains of Dew* by Susan Glaspell—Cleon Throckmorton

Total number of productions credited: 6
Number designed or codesigned by women: 0
Percentage designed or codesigned by women: 0 percent

## Summary for 1915–1922
Total number of productions credited: 59
Number designed or codesigned by women: 9
Overall percentage of women scenic designers: 15 percent

# *Appendix 7*

## Provincetown Productions for Which Costume Design Credit Can Be Reasonably Established[1]

### 1916

*The Game* by Louise Bryant—Marguerite Zorach and William Zorach*[2]
*The Eternal Quadrangle* by John Reed—Becky Edelson* (Miss Bryant's costume and hat)

Total number of productions credited: 2
Number designed or codesigned by women: 2
Percentage designed or codesigned by women: 100 percent

### 1917–1918

*Knotholes* by Maxwell Bodenheim and William Saphier—Edith Unger (Avril)
*The Gentle Furniture Shop* by Maxwell Bodenheim—Edith Unger (Avril)
*The Athenian Women* by George Cram Cook—Helen Zagat

Total number of productions credited: 3
Number designed or codesigned by women: 3
Percentage designed or codesigned by women: 100 percent

### 1918–1919

*The Princess Marries the Page* by Edna Millay—Blanche Hays
*The Rescue* by Rita C. Smith—Edith Unger (Avril) (Miss Rauh's gown)
*5050* by Robert Allerton Parker—Mabel Reber*

Total number of productions credited: 3
Number designed or codesigned by women: 3
Percentage designed or codesigned by women: 100 percent

### 1919–1920

*Vote the New Moon* by Alfred Kreymborg—James Light and Charles Ellis
*Pie* by Lawrence Langner—Willoughby Ions (Miss Heinemann's gown)

Total number of productions credited: 2
Number designed or codesigned by women: 0
Percentage designed or codesigned by women: 0 percent

### 1920–1921

*Matinata* by Lawrence Langner—Blanche Hays[3]
*The Emperor Jones* by Eugene O'Neill—Blanche Hays
*What D'You Want* by Lawrence Vail—Blanche Hays
*Diff'rent* by Eugene O'Neill—Blanche Hays
*Trifles* by Susan Glaspell (revival)—Blanche Hays
*Inheritors* by Susan Glaspell—Blanche Hays
*Love* by Evelyn Scott—Blanche Hays
*The Spring* by George Cram Cook—Lucy L'Engle
*Grotesques* by Cloyd Head—Harry Gottlieb

Total number of productions credited: 9
Number designed or codesigned by women: 8
Percentage designed or codesigned by women: 89 percent

### 1921–1922

*The Verge* by Susan Glaspell—Blanche Hays
*The Hairy Ape* by Eugene O'Neill—Blanche Hays
*Chains of Dew* by Susan Glaspell—Blanche Hays

Total number of productions credited: 3
Number designed or codesigned by women: 3
Percentage designed or codesigned by women: 100 percent

### Summary for 1915–1922

Total number of productions credited: 22
Number designed or codesigned by women: 19
Overall percentage of women as costume designers: 86 percent

# Notes

## Introduction

1. This phrase was part of the group's articulated artistic vision. See Susan Glaspell, *The Road to the Temple* (New York: Frederick A. Stokes, 1927), 252–53.

2. Hutchins Hapgood, *A Victorian in the Modern World* (New York: Harcourt, Brace, 1939), 393. Mabel Dodge hosted one of the era's most notable salons for the discussion of new ideas at her Fifth Avenue home.

3. At a suggestion from Eugene O'Neill, the Provincetown Players added "The Playwright's Theatre" to their official title. See Edna Kenton, "The Provincetown Players: The Playwright's Theatre," ed. Travis Bogard and Jackson Bryer, *Eugene O'Neill Review* 21, nos. 1–2 (Spring–Fall 1997): 31. A slightly different version of Kenton's history exists in manuscript in the Provincetown Players Archive, Special Collections, Fales Library, New York University; whenever possible I have cited from the published version (cited below as Kenton, "Provincetown Players," *Eugene O'Neill Review*), but I have also used the unpublished version (cited below as Kenton, "Provincetown Players," Fales Library).

4. For calendar of productions, see Robert K. Sarlós, *Jig Cook and the Provincetown Players: Theatre in Ferment* (Amherst: University of Massachusetts Press, 1982), appendix A, 169–80.

5. See ibid., 153–68, and William W. Vilhauer, "A History and Evaluation of the Provincetown Players" (Ph.D. diss., University of Iowa, 1965), 765–69.

6. Sarlós, *Jig Cook,* 160.

7. These women's names are listed in appendix 1.

8. By "leading" I mean most productive.

9. See Helen Deutsch and Stella Hanau, *The Provincetown: A Story of the Theatre* (New York: Farrar, 1931); Leona Rust Egan, *Provincetown as a Stage: Provincetown, the Provincetown Players, and the Discovery of Eugene O'Neill* (Orleans, Mass.: Parnassus Imprints, 1994); Sarlós, *Jig Cook;* and Vilhauer, "History and Evaluation." Sarlós's is the most comprehensive published account of the group's activities from

1915 to 1922 and the first to make the clear distinction between the Provincetown Players and the Experimental Theatre. His appendixes include the most accurate calendar of productions (plays only), detailed descriptions of the physical theaters, and brief biographical entries of more than one hundred "founders, participants, and friends of the Provincetown Players," including thirty women.

10. See, for example, Gerhard Bach, "Susan Glaspell: A Bibliography of Dramatic Criticism," *Great Lakes Review* 3 (1977): 1–34; Gerhard Bach, "Susan Glaspell: Provincetown Playwright," *Great Lakes Review* 4 (1978): 31–43; Linda Ben-Zvi, ed., *Susan Glaspell: Essays on Her Theater and Fiction* (Ann Arbor: University of Michigan Press, 1995); Linda Ben-Zvi and J. Ellen Gainor, eds., *The Complete Plays of Susan Glaspell* (Ann Arbor: University of Michigan Press, forthcoming); C. W. E. Bigsby, ed., *Susan Glaspell: Plays* (Cambridge: Cambridge University Press, 1987); Veronica Makowsky, *Susan Glaspell's Century of American Women* (New York: Oxford University Press, 1993); Marcia Noe, *Susan Glaspell: Voice from the Heartland* (Macomb: Western Illinois University Press, 1983); Barbara Ozieblo, "Rebellion and Rejection: The Plays of Susan Glaspell," in *Modern American Drama: The Female Canon,* ed. June Schlueter (Rutherford, N.J.: Fairleigh Dickinson University Press, 1990), 66–75; and Barbara Ozieblo, *Susan Glaspell: A Critical Biography* (Chapel Hill: University of North Carolina Press, 2000); J. Ellen Gainor, *Susan Glaspell in Context: American Theater, Culture, and Politics, 1915–48* (Ann Arbor: University of Michigan Press, 2001).

11. See Robert K. Sarlós, "Nina Moise Directs Eugene O'Neill's *The Rope,*" *Eugene O'Neill Newsletter* 6, no. 3 (Winter 1982): 9–12, and Robert K. Sarlós, "Susan Glaspell and Jig Cook: Rule Makers and Rule Breakers," in *1915: The Cultural Moment,* ed. Adele Heller and Lois Rudnick (New Brunswick, N.J.: Rutgers University Press, 1991), 250–60. See also Cheryl Black, "Ida Rauh: Power Player at Provincetown," *Journal of American Drama and Theatre* 6, nos. 2–3 (Spring–Fall 1994): 63–80; Cheryl Black, "Interpretation and Tact: Nina Moise Directs the Provincetown Players," *Theatre Survey* 36, no. 1 (May 1995): 55–64; Cheryl Black, "Pioneering Theatre Managers: Edna Kenton and Eleanor Fitzgerald of the Provincetown Players," *Journal of American Drama and Theatre* 9, no. 3 (Fall 1997): 40–58. Material from the last three articles is incorporated in this study and reprinted with the kind permission of the journal editors.

12. Judith Barlow, "Susan's Sisters: The 'Other' Women Writers of the Provincetown Players," in Ben-Zvi, *Susan Glaspell,* 259–60.

13. Rosamond Gilder, *Enter the Actress: The First Women in the Theatre* (Freeport, N.Y.: Books for Libraries Press, 1931); Helen Krich Chinoy and Linda Walsh Jenkins, eds., *Women in American Theatre* (New York: Crown Publishers, 1981; rev. and expanded ed., New York: Theatre Communications Group, 1987); Albert Auster, *Actresses and Suffragists: Women in the American Theater, 1890–1920* (New York: Praeger, 1984); Tracy C. Davis, *Actresses as Working Women: Their Social Identity in Victorian Culture* (London and New York: Routledge, 1991); Charlotte Canning, *Feminist Theaters in the U.S.A.: Staging Women's Experience* (London and New York:

Routledge, 1996); Catherine Schuler, *Women in Russian Theatre: The Actress in the Silver Age* (New York and London: Routledge, 1997).

14. See Deutsch and Hanau, *The Provincetown;* Egan, *Provincetown as a Stage;* Sarlós, *Jig Cook;* Vilhauer, "History and Evaluation."

15. See Heller and Rudnick, *1915;* June Sochen, *The New Woman: Feminism in Greenwich Village, 1910–1920* (New York: Quadrangle Books, 1972).

16. See Suzanne Beal, "Mama, Teach Me That French: Mothers and Daughters in Twentieth-Century Plays by American Women Playwrights" (Ph.D. diss., University of Maryland at College Park, 1993); Barlow, "Susan's Sisters"; Kathleen L. Carroll, "Centering Women Onstage: Susan Glaspell's Dialogic Strategy of Resistance" (Ph.D. diss., University of Maryland at College Park, 1990); Anne Corey, "Susan Glaspell: Playwright of Social Consciousness" (Ph.D. diss., New York University, 1990); Ann Larabee, "First-Wave Feminist Theatre, 1890–1930" (Ph.D. diss., Graduate School of New York at Binghamton, 1988); Makowsky, *Susan Glaspell's Century;* Noe, *Susan Glaspell;* Ozieblo, "Rebellion and Rejection"; and Ellen Kay Trimberger, "The New Woman and the New Sexuality: Conflict and Contradiction in the Writings and Lives of Mabel Dodge and Neith Boyce," in Heller and Rudnick, *1915,* 98–116.

17. See Deutsch and Hanau, *The Provincetown;* Kenton, "Provincetown Players," *Eugene O'Neill Review* and Fales Library; Constance D'Arcy Mackay, *The Little Theatre in the United States* (New York: Holt, 1917); Thomas H. Dickinson, *The Insurgent Theatre* (New York: B. W. Huebsch, 1917); Kenneth Macgowan, *Footlights across America* (New York: Harcourt, Brace, 1929).

18. See Auster, *Actresses and Suffragists;* Karen Blair, *The Clubwoman as Feminist: True Womanhood Redefined, 1860–1914* (New York: Holmes and Meier, 1980); Karen Blair, *The Torchbearers: Women and Their Amateur Arts Associations in America, 1890–1930* (Bloomington: Indiana University Press, 1994).

19. Blair, *Torchbearers,* 11. See also George Kelly, *The Torch-Bearers* (New York: Samuel French, 1924).

20. Blair, *Torchbearers,* 143.

21. I use "first-wave feminism" to mean the new phase in women's emancipation beginning around 1910, roughly synonymous with Greenwich Village feminism. See Sochen, *New Woman;* and Nancy F. Cott, *The Grounding of Modern Feminism* (New Haven: Yale University Press, 1987).

## Chapter 1. Creating Women

1. Sources for anecdotes, in order: Sochen, *New Woman,* 65–66; Dee Garrison, *Mary Heaton Vorse: The Life of an American Insurgent* (Philadelphia: Temple University Press), 55–61; Mary V. Dearborn, *Queen of Bohemia: The Life of Louise Bryant* (Boston: Houghton Mifflin, 1996), 121–23; William Zorach, *Art Is My Life* (Cleveland: World, 1967), 35.

2. The charter members of the Provincetown Players are listed in appendix 2.

3. Oscar Handlin, *The Americans* (Boston: Little, Brown, 1963), 278.

4. Ibid., 341.

5. Floyd Dell, *Homecoming* (New York: Farrar and Rinehart, 1933), 251.

6. Hapgood, *Victorian*, 153.

7. Cott, *Grounding of Modern Feminism*, 37.

8. Ibid., 13–14. According to Cott, the term entered popular usage around 1913.

9. Heywood Broun, clipping from *New York Herald Tribune*, 19 February 1919, n.p., Provincetown Players Scrapbook, Harvard Theatre Collection, Houghton Library, Harvard University.

10. Steve Watson, *Strange Bedfellows: The First American Avant-Garde* (New York: Abbeville Press, 1991), 143.

11. Cott, *Grounding of Modern Feminism*, 38. The club was founded by Marie Jenney Howe and included in its membership Charlotte Perkins Gilman and Crystal Eastman. See Judith Schwarz, *Radical Feminists of Heterodoxy* (Lebanon, N.H.: New Victoria Publishers, 1982), and list of Heterodoxy founders in Edna Kenton Papers, Butler Rare Book and Manuscript Library, Columbia University.

12. See Charlotte Perkins Gilman, *Women and Economics* (New York: Small, Maynard, 1898; reprint, New York: Harper and Row, 1966); Blanche Wiesen Cook, ed., *Toward the Great Change: Crystal and Max Eastman on Feminism, Antimilitarism, and Revolution* (New York: Garland Publishing, 1976).

13. See Edward Carpenter, "Woman in Freedom," in *The Woman Question*, ed. T. R. Smith (New York: Modern Library, 1918), 137–48; see also Alice Wexler, *Emma Goldman: An Intimate Life* (New York: Pantheon Books, 1984); and Cott, *Grounding of Modern Feminism*, 35, 61.

14. See Havelock Ellis, *Psychology of Sex: A Handbook for Students* (New York: Emerson Books, 1954); "New Erotic Ethics," *Nation*, 14 March 1912, 260–62; Ellen Key, "The Right of Motherhood," in T. R. Smith, *The Woman Question*, 116–36.

15. Allen Churchill, *The Improper Bohemians* (New York: Dutton, 1959), 23–25.

16. Garrison, *Insurgent*, 45.

17. Ibid., 4.

18. Ibid., 36.

19. Ibid., 74, 87.

20. Ibid., 75.

21. Ibid., 189–91. For Vorse's life and work, see also Dee Garrison, ed., *Rebel Pen: The Writings of Mary Heaton Vorse* (New York: Monthly Review Press, 1985).

22. Max Eastman, *Enjoyment of Living* (New York: Harper and Brothers, 1948), 342.

23. Lawrence Langner, *The Magic Curtain* (New York: Dutton, 1951), 92; for Rauh's (and Eastman's) languorous movement, see Churchill, *Improper Bohemians*, 29.

24. Hapgood, *Victorian*, 313.

25. Eastman, *Enjoyment of Living*, 391.

26. Ibid., 485–90, 570–73. Although Rauh and Eastman did not divorce until 1922, their separation in 1916 was final.

27. In her entry in *Woman's Who's Who of America*, Glaspell identified herself as a Socialist who was in favor of woman suffrage. Other Provincetowners included in the volume—Alice Woods Ullman, Neith Boyce, and Edna Kenton—did not comment on the suffrage referendum. See *Woman's Who's Who of America, 1914–1915* (reprint, Detroit: Gale Research, 1976), 25, 329, 361, 453, 830.

28. Hapgood, *Victorian*, 375.

29. Kirah Markham to Louis Sheaffer, 23 July, 6 September 1962, Sheaffer-O'Neill Collection, Special Collections, Charles E. Shain Library, Connecticut College.

30. Kirah Markham to Louis Sheaffer, 6, 22 September 1962, ibid. (Glaspell might, in turn, have questioned Markham's attachment to either Theodore Dreiser or Floyd Dell). According to Marcia Noe, Jig had "amorous adventures" with Eunice Tietjens, Marjorie Jones, Rauh, and Edna Millay. See Noe, *Susan Glaspell*, 36. See also Floyd Dell regarding Rauh's relationship to Cook in "Not Roses, Roses All the Way," unpublished memoir, 2, Floyd Dell Papers, Special Collections, Newberry Library, Chicago; see also notes from Louis Sheaffer interview with William Zorach, 29 June [1960], Sheaffer-O'Neill Collection; notes from Robert K. Sarlós interviews with Norma Millay and Charles Ellis, 10 July 1963, Robert K. Sarlós Papers, Special Collections, Shields Library, University of California, Davis; Jig Cook to Ida Rauh, n.d. [1922–23], George Cram Cook Papers, Berg Collection, New York Public Library.

31. Dell, *Homecoming*, 152. This characterization of Cook is echoed in Hapgood, *Victorian*, 375.

32. Cook to Glaspell, 7 February 1923, Cook Papers.

33. Notes from George Voellmer's interview with Nina Moise for Louis Sheaffer, 20 July 1957, Sheaffer-O'Neill Collection.

34. Quoted in Ellen Kay Trimberger, ed., *Intimate Warriors: Portraits of a Modern Marriage, 1899–1944* (New York: Feminist Press, 1991), 7.

35. Hapgood, *Victorian*, 149.

36. Boyce to Hapgood, 1907, quoted in Trimberger, *Intimate Warriors*, 20.

37. Lois Rudnick, introduction to Miriam Hapgood DeWitt, *Taos: A Memory* (Albuquerque: University of New Mexico Press, 1992), xiv.

38. *Marguerite Zorach: The Early Years, 1908–1920* (Washington, D.C.: Smithsonian Institution Press, National Collection of Fine Arts, 1973), 29.

39. Zorach, *Art Is My Life*, 23.

40. Marilyn Friedman Hoffman, *Marguerite and William Zorach: The Cubist Years, 1915–1918* (Manchester, N.H.: Currier Gallery of Art, 1987), 11.

41. Zorach, *Art Is My Life*, 37; *Marguerite Zorach*, 38.

42. Zorach, *Art Is My Life*, 189–90.

43. Ibid., 61, 183.

44. Wexler, *Emma Goldman*, 105. Alternate spelling of Stella's last name, cited by Wexler, include "Cominsky" and "Commins."

45. The list includes Rauh, Florence Enright, Agnes McCarthy, Lucy Huf-

faker, Edith Haynes Thompson, Helen Westley, Dorothy Upjohn, Jean Robb, Miriam Kiper, Blanche Hays, and John Reed, whose play *Moondown* was produced by the Washington Square Players in their first season.

46. Agnes Boulton, *Part of a Long Story* (New York: Garden City, 1958), 320. Boulton, who was pregnant at the time, recorded Ballantine's "look of consternation" at Ian's eviction. Ian Ballantine, it should be noted, turned out well; he co-founded Ballantine Books.

47. Reed to Sally Robinson, 18 December 1915, in Robert A. Rosenstone, *Romantic Revolutionary: A Biography of John Reed* (New York: Knopf, 1975), 241; see also Dearborn, *Queen of Bohemia,* 40.

48. Bryant to Sara Bard Field, 12 June 1916, Sara Bard Field Correspondence, C. E. S. Wood Collection, Huntington Library, San Marino, California.

49. Max Eastman, "Poetry to Reed," in *Heroes I Have Known* (New York: Simon and Schuster, 1942), 213.

50. Hapgood, *Victorian,* 373.

51. Edna Kenton, "The Militant Women—and Women," *Century,* November 1913, 13.

52. Edna Kenton, "Feminism Will Give—Men More Fun, Women Greater Scope, Children Better Parents, Life More Charm," *Delineator,* July 1914, 17.

53. I refer to *Sister Carrie* (1900) and *Jennie* (1911). The Provincetown Players later produced Dreiser's play *The Hand of the Potter,* also condemned as morally repulsive. See Richard Lingeman, *Theodore Dreiser: An American Journey, 1908–1945* (New York: Putnam, 1986), 42, 124, 132–33.

54. Frank to Kenton, n.d., Kenton Papers.

55. Dreiser to Kenton, 11 November 1911, ibid. See also Kenton's correspondence with Cook, Dell, Dreiser, Frank, Van Vechten, and others: Kenton Papers; Carl Van Vechten Papers, Yale Collection of American Literature, Beinecke Rare Book and Manuscript Library, Yale University; and Dell Papers.

56. Handbill reprinted in Cott, *Grounding of Modern Feminism,* 12. For Kenton's role in organizing these meetings, see George Middleton, *These Things Are Mine: The Autobiography of a Journeyman Playwright* (New York: Macmillan, 1947), 130.

57. Regarding Sheffield, see Kenton to Boyce, 21, 24, 26, 28 January 1943, Hapgood Family Papers, Yale Collection of American Literature, Beinecke Rare Book and Manuscript Library, Yale University. The "beautiful and bookish" quote is from Churchill, *Improper Bohemians,* 63.

58. Cook to Kenton, n.d., Kenton Papers.

59. Cook to Kenton, n.d., ibid.; the letter indicates that Cook was living in Chicago and that Kenton's *What Manner of Man* had been recently published (1903).

60. Mina Loy, "Feminist Manifesto," in *The Last Lunar Baedeker,* ed. Roger L. Conover (Highlands, N.C.: Jargon Society, 1982), 269–71. Emphasis in original.

61. Conover, *Last Lunar Baedeker,* lxxiv.

62. "Pig Cupid," reprinted in Carolyn Burke, *Becoming Modern: The Life of Mina Loy* (New York: Farrar, Straus and Giroux, 1996), 6.

63. William Carlos Williams, *Autobiography* (New York: Random House, 1948), 138.

64. Barnes to James Scott, 15 April 1971, quoted in Philip Herring, *Djuna: The Life and Work of Djuna Barnes* (New York: Viking, 1995), 25.

65. "Corpse B" in Djuna Barnes, *Book of Repulsive Women* (Los Angeles: Sun and Moon Press, 1994), 36.

66. See "How It Feels to Be Forcibly Fed," *New York World Magazine*, 6 September 1914, in Djuna Barnes Papers, Special Collections, University of Maryland at College Park Libraries. Ann Larabee listed Barnes as a Heterodite, but Judith Schwarz (*Radical Feminists*) did not include her, and Barnes is not included in Kenton's list or the album at Radcliffe. See Ann Larabee, "Death in Delphi: Susan Glaspell and the Companionate Marriage," *Mid-American Review* 2 (1987): 93.

67. Barnes to Emily Coleman, 27 October 1935, quoted in Herring, *Djuna*, xix.

68. James Light was an actor and director for the Provincetown Players, married to Susan Jenkins; Lawrence Vail was a playwright and painter who later married Peggy Guggenheim; Charles Ellis was an actor and designer who married Norma Millay. Biographical details come from Herring, *Djuna*, and interviews and correspondence with Susan Jenkins and Kirah Markham, Sheaffer-O'Neill Collection. For Barnes's relationship with Pyne, see also Markham to Agnes Boulton O'Neill, 17 April 1959, Eugene O'Neill Papers, Yale Collection of American Literature, Beinecke Rare Book and Manuscript Library, Yale University.

69. Published in Anne Cheney, *Millay in Greenwich Village* (Tuscaloosa: University of Alabama Press, 1975), 9.

70. Edna Millay to family, 9 May 1913, Millay Family Papers, Berg Collection, New York Public Library.

71. Millay's brief engagement to Dell is revealed in Norma Millay to Kathleen Millay, "Monday," January 1918, ibid.

72. See Dell, "Not Roses"; notes from Robert K. Sarlós interview with Floyd Dell, 18 July 1963, Sarlós Papers.

73. For Scott's biography I have relied principally upon D. A. Callard, *Pretty Good for a Woman: The Enigmas of Evelyn Scott* (London: Jonathan Cape, 1985).

74. See Emma Goldman, *Living My Life*, vol. 2 (New York: Knopf, 1931), 518–20, 532. See also notes from Sheaffer interview with Pauline Turkel, n.d. [1957–62], Sheaffer-O'Neill Collection.

75. See Lingeman, *Theodore Dreiser*, 77–83; Markham correspondence with Louis Sheaffer, Sheaffer-O'Neill Collection; Markham file, Billy Rose Theatre Collection, New York Public Library for the Performing Arts, Astor, Lenox and Tilden Foundations. Lloyd Wright was a landscape gardener and the son of architect Frank Lloyd Wright. See Robert K. Sarlós to Nilla Cram Cook, 27 November 1976, Sarlós Papers.

76. Florence Kiper, "Some American Plays from the Feminist Viewpoint," *Fo-*

*rum* 51, no. 6 (June 1914): 931. Kiper married Jerome Frank in 1914 and thereafter used "Kiper Frank" as a surname. Actress Miriam Kiper was her sister.

77. We may possibly add to this list Djuna Barnes (see note 66). Louise Bryant occasionally attended meetings as a guest of suffragist Sara Bard Field. See Dearborn, *Queen of Bohemia*, 44; see also Bryant/Field correspondence in the Bard Field Correspondence.

78. Louis Sheaffer, *O'Neill: Son and Playwright* (Boston: Little, Brown, 1968), 326.

## Chapter 2. Managing Women

1. This phrase occurs throughout Jig Cook's writings; see Glaspell, *Road to the Temple*, 252. See also Sarlós, *Jig Cook*, 9.

2. Nilla Cram Cook to Robert K. Sarlós, 5 February 1975, 2, Sarlós Papers.

3. Mary Heaton Vorse, *Time and the Town* (New York: Dial, 1942), 124.

4. Glaspell, *Road to the Temple*, 248. According to Rauh's husband, Max Eastman, Rauh had long "envisioned a subscription theatre which could ignore box office and adhere to pure standards of art." In 1914, Rauh had sought that goal by creating, along with Lawrence Langner and Albert Boni, the Washington Square Players; artistic disagreements with her cofounders, however, led Rauh to resign within a year. See Eastman, *Enjoyment of Living*, 521.

5. Boyce to her father-in-law, July 1915, Hapgood Family Papers, quoted in Egan, *Provincetown as a Stage*, 129.

6. Glaspell, *Road to the Temple*, 252–53.

7. See Constitution and Resolutions of the Provincetown Players, 5 September 1916, *Minutes of the Provincetown Players*, Billy Rose Theatre Collection, New York Public Library for the Performing Arts, Astor, Lenox and Tilden Foundations. See also Minutes, 4 September 1916. Although the group chose four members to draft a constitution (Reed, Cook, Freddie Burt, and Max Eastman), the work was primarily that of Reed. See Eastman, *Enjoyment of Living*, 564.

8. Kenton, "Provincetown Players," Fales Library, 16–17, 23, 27.

9. Rauh made the suggestion in October. In December the Players elected a producing committee that included Rauh. See Minutes, 22 October, 11 December 1916.

10. Kenton, "Provincetown Players," *Eugene O'Neill Review*, 28.

11. See Minutes, 22 October, 22 November, 6, 11 December 1916.

12. Vilhauer, "History and Evaluation," 212.

13. Executive committee members and their tenures are listed in appendix 3. According to the Players' constitution, executive committee members were to be elected annually and were subject to recall by a majority vote of active members; because records of general membership meetings end after the spring of 1918, there is no way to know how long this policy was observed.

14. Van Deren Coke, *Nordfeldt the Painter* (Albuquerque: University of New Mexico Press, 1972), 52.

15. Kenton, "Provincetown Players," Fales Library, 61.

16. The contrasting attributes ascribed to Cook and Nordfeldt are from ibid., 32. See also Margaret Nordfeldt to Robert K. Sarlós, 8 December 1963, Sarlós Papers.

17. Minutes, 21 March 1917. David Carb was elected to replace Nordfeldt as secretary-treasurer.

18. Kenton to Margaret Nordfeldt, 1 January 1929, Provincetown Players Archive, Special Collections, Fales Library, New York University.

19. Moise to Kenton, 16 October 1933, ibid.

20. The roles Bryant performed were Estelle in *The Eternal Quadrangle* and The Dancer in *Thirst.*

21. Biddle quoted in Dearborn, *Queen of Bohemia,* 308. La Passionaria (Dolores Ibarruri) was a leader of the Spanish Communist Party during the Spanish Civil War noted for fiery eloquence; her "No pasaran!" ("They shall not pass!") became the party's battle cry. I am grateful to Robert K. Sarlós for this identification.

22. Louise Bryant, "Christmas in Petrograd, 1917," 8, Granville Hicks Papers, Special Collections, Syracuse University Library. I believe Bryant used the term "director" to mean "leader," not stage director. Bryant was not a stage director or a salaried officer. As a member of the executive committee, however, she was probably justified in considering herself one of the leading members of the group at that time.

23. Bryant/Reed correspondence, fall 1916, John Reed Collection, Houghton Library, Harvard University.

24. Bryant to Reed, "Tuesday," fall 1916, and Alfred Kreymborg to Louise Bryant, n.d., ibid.

25. Bryant to Reed, "Wednesday Night," fall 1916, ibid.

26. Bryant to Reed, Thanksgiving Day (1916), ibid.

27. Bryant to Reed, 12 June 1916, ibid.

28. Bryant to Reed, "Tuesday," November 1916, ibid.

29. According to E. J. Ballantine, Stella complained to Vorse that "just because she's sleeping with Jack Reed is no reason to do her play." See notes from Sheaffer interview with E. J. Ballantine, Sheaffer-O'Neill Collection.

30. See notes from Sheaffer interview with Robert Parker, 23 January 1964, Sheaffer-O'Neill Collection. See also Robert K. Sarlós to Nilla Cram Cook, 29 June 1975, Sarlós Papers.

31. Eastman, *Enjoyment of Living,* 566.

32. Mary Heaton Vorse, quoted in Dearborn, *Queen of Bohemia,* 114. Susan Jenkins Brown made similar statements; see notes from Shaeffer interview with Susan Jenkins Brown, n.d. [1960], Sheaffer-O'Neill Collection.

33. Eastman, *Enjoyment of Living,* 527.

34. Margaret Nordfeldt to Robert K. Sarlós, 8 December 1963, Sarlós Papers.

35. Notes from Voellmer interview with Moise, 20 July 1957, Sheaffer-O'Neill Collection; Margaret Nordfeldt to Robert K. Sarlós, 8 December 1963, and Susan

Jenkins Brown to Robert K. Sarlós, 17 February 1965, Sarlós Papers; Vilhauer, "History and Evaluation," 76.

36. By this time, Cook was considered the general director of the company, a position roughly analogous to what we now call "artistic director" and not to be confused with Nina Moise's position as company stage director.

37. Ida Rauh played Mabel in *Suppressed Desires*, which served as curtain-raiser to *The Emperor Jones*. Playbill in Provincetown Players Scrapbook, Billy Rose Theatre Collection, New York Public Library for the Performing Arts, Astor, Lenox and Tilden Foundations. Carl Van Vechten reported that Rauh was scheduled to travel to London with *The Emperor Jones*. See Carl Van Vechten to Fania Marinoff, 24 April 1921, in *Letters of Carl Van Vechten*, ed. Bruce Kellner (New Haven: Yale University Press, 1987), 38.

38. See Sarlós, *Jig Cook*, 131–37, 147–52.

39. Glaspell to Agnes Boulton, 21 November [1919], O'Neill Papers. *Diff'rent* opened in December 1919, *Power of Darkness* in January 1920.

40. Minutes, 10 September 1921.

41. Deeter to Kenton, n.d. [1921], Provincetown Players Manuscript Collection, Harvard Theatre Collection, Houghton Library. In the spring of 1921, Deeter had directed Gustav Wied's *Autumn Fires* on a bill that also included plays by Glaspell, Millay, and Alice Rostetter.

42. Only Cook served longer (1916–22).

43. Kenton, "Provincetown Players," Fales Library, 20, 23, 27, 37-a, 53, 65.

44. Ibid., 65.

45. Kenton, "Provincetown Players," *Eugene O'Neill Review*, 56.

46. Kenton, "Provincetown Players," Fales Library, 37-a.

47. It is unclear precisely when Kenton began to receive a salary for playreading and publicity, but Cook reported to Glaspell in August 1921 the company's decision to "keep her [Edna] on for PP [Provincetown Players] publicity. . . . the job combined with playreading." See Cook to Glaspell, 27 August 1921, Cook Papers. The Minutes of 10 September 1921 record that the executive committee voted to "engage" Kenton to "read all plays—sort out and return impossible ones and hold possible ones." A letter from Fitzgerald to Kenton mentions their salaries (not specific amounts), 6 December 1922, Provincetown Players Archive.

48. An unidentified newspaper clipping dated 27 February 1920 reported that plays were "pouring in from east, west, north, and south." In Provincetown Players Scrapbook, Harvard Theatre Collection.

49. Kenton, "Provincetown Players," *Eugene O'Neill Review*, 46.

50. Glaspell to Fitzgerald, 31 May 1924, Provincetown Players Manuscript Collection.

51. Kenton, "Provincetown Players," *Eugene O'Neill Review*, 46.

52. Deutsch and Hanau, *The Provincetown*, 130.

53. The two were Arthur Schnitzler's *Last Masks*, directed by James Light, and Wied's *Autumn Fires*, noted above.

54. Kenton, "Provincetown Players," *Eugene O'Neill Review*, 129–31, 139–41. Following *The Emperor Jones*, the Players moved *Diff'rent, The Spring*, and *The Hairy Ape* into Broadway houses.

55. Glaspell to Fitzgerald, 31 May 1924.

56. According to Kenton, the company gathered at John Reed's to draft the first circular. Some wanted to appoint a committee to draft it; others protested: "There was a tolerable amount of abstract discussion on this line before we were brought back to the appointing of a committee." Kenton, "Provincetown Players," Fales Library, 23.

57. See Minutes, 15 March 1917. Kenton probably drafted, or helped draft, a number of circulars, but there are few specific records. The Minutes of 10 September 1921 show that Kenton drafted a fall announcement to increase membership. Her correspondence with Cook and Glaspell in the spring of 1922 (Provincetown Players Manuscript Collection) indicates that Kenton was acting as a press liaison at the time, although she may have shared this responsibility with Fitzgerald and others.

58. Kenton, "Unorganized, Amateur, Purely Experimental," *Boston Evening Transcript*, 27 April 1918, sec. 2, pp. 8–9.

59. See Cook to Glaspell, 27 August 1921.

60. Kenton to Cook, 8 May 1921, Provincetown Players Archive.

61. Fitzgerald probably recruited Weinberger; he was an intimate friend and had defended Goldman, Berkman, and other political radicals.

62. Kenton to Cook and Glaspell, 19 June 1922, Provincetown Players Manuscript Collection.

63. Kenton to Cook and Glaspell, 5 May 1922, ibid.

64. Kenton, "Provincetown Players," Fales Library, 205.

65. Light's pursuit of Barnes is reported by Susan Jenkins Brown to Louis Sheaffer, 11 January 1969, Sheaffer-O'Neill Collection. See also Herring, *Djuna*, 107.

66. Kenton to Glaspell and Cook, 5 May 1922.

67. *Taboo*, set in the southern United States and Africa, included a large cast of African characters and would probably have been staged, like *The Emperor Jones*, with Charles Gilpin surrounded by Villagers in blackface.

68. Kenton to Cook and Glaspell, 5 May 1922. Kenton seems to have been right about *Taboo*, which played only four matinee performances, despite the efforts of Paul Robeson and Margaret Wycherly in leading roles. Retitled *Voodoo*, the play also failed in England (with Robeson and Mrs. Patrick Campbell). See Martin Duberman, *Paul Robeson: A Biography* (New York: The New Press, 1989), 43–46.

69. See Fitzgerald to Kenton, 23 June, 4 October, 6 December 1922, Kenton to "Miss Robbins," 7 April 1922, Kenton to "Miss Ryan," 13 April 1922, and Kenton to Adolph Klauber, 20 June 1922, Provincetown Players Archive; see also Kenton to Cook and Glaspell, 5, 7, 13 May 1922, Provincetown Players Manuscript Collection; Kenton, "Provincetown Players," Fales Library, 197–212.

70. See Minutes, Executive Committee Meeting, 23 February 1922; see also correspondence between Fitzgerald and Kenton, summer 1922, Provincetown Players Archive, and correspondence among Fitzgerald, Kenton, Cook, and Glaspell, summer 1922, Provincetown Players Manuscript Collection.

71. Kenton to Cook and Glaspell, 5 May 1922.

72. See Glaspell, *Road to the Temple*, 309–10.

73. See Arthur Gelb and Barbara Gelb, *O'Neill* (New York: Harper and Row, 1973), 513–14.

74. Kenton to Cook and Glaspell, 24 September 1923, Provincetown Players Manuscript Collection.

75. O'Neill to Kenton, 26 May 1924, ibid.

76. Kenton to Glaspell, 28 May 1924, ibid.

77. Ibid.

78. Glaspell to Fitzgerald, 31 May 1924, ibid.

79. See Kenton, "The Provincetown Players and the Playwright's Theatre," *Billboard*, 5 August 1922, 6–7, 13–15.

80. Kenton's history is finally being published in book form by McFarland, edited by Jackson R. Bryer (forthcoming).

81. Kenton to Stella Hanau, 5 August 1931, Provincetown Players Archive.

82. See Inez Haynes Irwin to Carl Van Vechten, 13 December 1933, Van Vechten Papers.

83. Fitzgerald's nickname is also frequently spelled "Fitzi." I have chosen "Fitzie" as that is how I decipher her handwritten signature.

84. See M. Eleanor Fitzgerald, "Valedictory of an Art Theatre," *New York Times*, 22 December 1929, sec. 8, p. 1. Fitzgerald may have met other members through her association with Goldman.

85. Deutsch and Hanau, *The Provincetown*, 81.

86. Fitzgerald to Erwin Piscator, 1 January 1950, reprinted in "In Memory of Fitzie," booklet compiled by Pauline Turkel, in Margaret Wycherly clippings file, Billy Rose Theatre Collection, New York Public Library for the Performing Arts, Astor, Lenox and Tilden Foundations.

87. Goldman to Alexander Berkman, 4 September 1925, in *Nowhere at Home: Letters from Exile of Emma Goldman and Alexander Berkman*, ed. Anna Maria Drinnon and Richard Drinnon (New York: Schocken Books, 1975), 132.

88. Ibid., 81.

89. See notes from Shaeffer interview with Pauline Turkel, n.d. [1957–63], and Susan Jenkins Brown to Louis Sheaffer, 9 February 1970; Susan Jenkins Brown, then married to company member James Light, recalled that Rauh, "being a Lucy Stoner, put me down in the program as 'Susan Jenkins.'" Sheaffer-O'Neill Collection. Turkel joined the Provincetown staff sometime after 10 September 1921. See Minutes, Executive Committee Meeting, 10 September 1921.

90. e. e. cummings, in "In Memory of Fitzie."

91. Notes from Shaeffer interview with James Light, 21 May 1960, Sheaffer-O'Neill Collection.

92. In the fall of 1918, the Players moved from 139 Macdougal to a slightly larger space at 133 Macdougal, which eventually became known as the "Provincetown Playhouse."

93. Notes from Sheaffer interview with Jasper Deeter, Sheaffer-O'Neill Collection.

94. See Cook to Glaspell, 27 August 1921; Kenton, "Provincetown Players," *Eugene O'Neill Review*, 144.

95. Nilla Cram Cook to Robert K. Sarlós, 5 February 1975, Sarlós Papers.

96. Deutsch and Hanau, *The Provincetown*, 81.

97. Djuna Barnes, "Days of Jig Cook: Recollections of Ancient Theatre History but Ten Years Old," *Theatre Guild Magazine* 6 (January 1929): 32.

98. Sheaffer interview with Light, 21 May 1960, Sheaffer-O'Neill Collection.

99. Ibid.

100. Cook to Kenton, 23 July 1922, Susan Glaspell Collection, Special Collections, Clifton Waller Barrett Library, University of Virginia.

101. Kenton to Cook, 5 August 1921, Provincetown Players Manuscript Collection.

102. Kenton to Cook and Glaspell, 3 May 1922, ibid.

103. Fitzgerald to Kenton, 24 October 1922, Provincetown Players Archive.

104. Cook to Fitzgerald, from Greece, n.d. [1922–24], Cook Papers.

105. Notes from Sheaffer interviews with Pauline Turkel and Susan Jenkins, Sheaffer-O'Neill Collection. Those who earned Fitzgerald's disdain were not named.

106. Fitzgerald to Glaspell, 1 May 1929, Provincetown Players Archive.

107. Goldman to Berkman, 4 September 1925, in Drinnon and Drinnon, *Letters from Exile*, 132.

108. The "triumvirate" (O'Neill, Macgowan, and Robert Edmond Jones) disbanded in 1925 when those three moved operations to the Greenwich Village Theatre. The Experimental Theatre continued at 133 Macdougal under the leadership of Light, Cleon Throckmorton, Harold McGee, Henry Alsberg, and Fitzgerald. In 1929 Light and Fitzgerald moved uptown to the Garrick Theatre under the official and (as Glaspell commented) "architecturally clumsy" heading "The Provincetown Playhouse in the Garrick Theatre"). This venture lasted only one season.

109. Fitzgerald, "Valedictory," 4.

110. See Fitzgerald to Glaspell, 6 April, and Glaspell to Kenton, 30 April 1929, Provincetown Players Archive.

111. Fitzgerald, "Valedictory," 1, 4.

112. Fitzgerald to James Light, 18 October 1931, Sheaffer-O'Neill Collection.

113. Fitzgerald to Deutsch and Hanau, 16 October, 10 November 1931, ibid.

114. "Radical Men" by Verna Weskoff, as performed by the New Feminist The-

atre in 1969. See Roz Regelson, "Is Motherhood Holy? Not Anymore," *New York Times*, 18 May 1969, 3. See also Marlene Nade, "Radical Women," *Village Voice*, 15 May 1969, 1.

### Chapter 3. Writing Women

1. Most of the plays produced by the Players were one-acts. For a complete listing of Provincetown's repertory, see Sarlós, *Jig Cook*, 169–80. Excluding the Other Players plays and the guest appearance by the Ellen Van Volkenburg–Maurice Brown Repertory Company, the Provincetown plays number ninety-six. Plays by women are listed in appendix 4.

2. Women wrote or cowrote 36 percent of Provincetown's plays. The percentage for the 1915–16 season is tabulated from Burns Mantle and Garrison P. Sherwood, eds., *The Best Plays of 1909–1919* (New York: Dodd, Mead, 1943). Tabulating from Mantle's *Best Plays* series, the average percentage of plays by women on Broadway for 1915–22 was 15.57 percent.

3. Dickinson, *Insurgent Theatre*, 227–43.

4. This figure includes only plays produced from 1912 to 1917 and excludes dance dramas or music festivals. See Alice Lewisohn Crowley, *The Neighborhood Playhouse* (New York: Theatre Arts Books, 1959), 252–60.

5. See Barlow, "Susan's Sisters."

6. Frequently produced European writers included Maeterlinck, Shaw, Synge, Ibsen, Galsworthy, Strindberg, Lord Dunsany, and Lady Augusta Gregory. See Dickinson, *Insurgent Theatre*, and Mackay, *Little Theatre*.

7. For Washington Square's rejection of *Suppressed Desires* (cowritten by Glaspell and Cook), see Glaspell, *Road to the Temple*, 250–51. Boyce reported her efforts to find a producer for *Constancy* in several letters to Hutchins Hapgood, Hapgood Family Papers.

8. See Barlow, "Susan's Sisters," 262. The following overview is drawn from Barlow's essay and my own research. Brief descriptions of all available plays are also included in the general histories of Sarlós and Vilhauer. Three Provincetown plays written or cowritten by women are lost: *About Six* by Grace Potter, *The Devil's Glow* by Alice Woods Ullman, and *Barbarians* by Rita Wellman. Barlow's essay does not treat *Love* by Evelyn Scott (available in Sarlós Papers) or *Barbarians*, which is discussed in some detail in Kenton's history and in interviews with company members conducted by Vilhauer, Sarlós, and Louis Sheaffer.

9. Barlow, "Susan's Sisters," 262.

10. Callard, *Pretty Good for a Woman*, 57.

11. Both Robert K. Sarlós and Barlow have noted similar parallels between Boyce's *Winter's Night* and *Beyond the Horizon*. See Sarlós, *Jig Cook*, 21, and Barlow, "Susan's Sisters," 264.

12. See Boyce's *Winter's Night*, Glaspell's *Trifles* and *The Verge*, and Scott's *Love*. In *Trifles* the man is dead at opening.

13. Larabee, "First-Wave Feminist Theatre," 165.

14. I do not mean to imply that Provincetown's women playwrights were the only stylistic innovators. A number of Provincetown's male playwrights also employed nontraditional structures and abstract styles.

15. Barlow, "Susan's Sisters," 264–65.

16. Ludwig Lewisohn, *Nation*, 14 December 1921, 708.

17. Clipping in Ida Rauh clippings file, n.d., n.p., Billy Rose Theatre Collection, New York Public Library for the Performing Arts, Astor, Lenox and Tilden Foundations.

18. Kenton described in some detail audience participation in selecting a "review bill" for the first season; it is not clear, however, whether this was the manner of selection for every season. See Kenton, "Provincetown Players," Fales Library, 57–58. A sample audience voting ballot (undated) can be found in the Provincetown Players Scrapbook, Harvard Theatre Collection.

19. The twelve plays written or cowritten by women revived at least once were Boyce's *Constancy, Winter's Night,* and *Enemies;* Bryant's *The Game;* Glaspell's *Trifles, Suppressed Desires, Tickless Time, The People,* and *Woman's Honor;* Wellman's *Barbarians;* Millay's *Aria da Capo;* and Rostetter's *The Widow's Veil.* Those produced three or more times were *The Widow's Veil, Aria da Capo, Tickless Time, Suppressed Desires,* and *The Game.* See appendix 4.

20. The season selected by Deeter included Glaspell's *Inheritors,* Rostetter's *The Widow's Veil,* Millay's *Aria da Capo,* and the second (and last) European play, *Autumn Fires* by Gustav Wied.

21. The plays by women were Kiper Frank's *Gee-Rusalem,* Millay's *The Princess Marries the Page,* Rostetter's *The Widow's Veil,* and Glaspell's *Woman's Honor* and *Bernice.* Gorham Munson, "The Theatre," *The Modernist,* November 1919, 43.

22. A typical article, written in 1921, is headed "Susan Glaspell and Eugene O'Neill Are the Pillars on Which the Provincetown Players Rest"; another listed O'Neill, Glaspell, Millay, and Harold Chapin as the group's "best" playwrights. Both articles are in Provincetown Players Scrapbook, Billy Rose Theatre Collection. Kenneth Macgowan, in the *New York Globe,* declared "O'Neill and Susan Glaspell are the stars," but cited Djuna Barnes's "curiously interesting flavor." Macgowan's article is in Provincetown Players Scrapbook, Harvard Theatre Collection.

23. For response to *Aria da Capo* see Alexander Woollcott, "There Are War Plays and War Plays," *New York Times,* 14 December 1919, sec. 8, p. 2, and Deutsch and Hanau, *The Provincetown,* 54; for response to *The Widow's Veil* see Heywood Broun, *New York Tribune,* 23 January 1919, 9, *New York Dramatic Mirror,* 8 February, 1919, n.p., *New York Morning Telegraph,* 20 January, 1919, n.p., and *Brooklyn Eagle,* 18 February 1919, n.p., in Provincetown Players Scrapbook, Harvard Theatre Collection; for response to *Gee-Rusalem,* see Munson, "The Theatre," 42, and *New York Herald,* 21 December 1918, n.p., Provincetown Players Scrapbook, Harvard Theatre Collection; for response to *Suppressed Desires,* see Heywood Broun, *New York Tribune,* 30 January 1917, 9, and Louis Sherwin, "Plots, Playwrights, Actors,

and Things," *New York Globe*, n.d. [1917], n.p., in Provincetown Players Scrapbook, Billy Rose Theatre Collection; for response to *Suppressed Desires* and *Trifles*, see John Corbin, *New York Times*, 11 November 1917, sec. 8, p. 6, and Herbert Gorman, "New Vogue of the Printed Play," *New York Times Book Review*, 18 July 1920, 2; for response to *Bernice*, see John Corbin, *New York Times*, 30 March 1919, sec. 8, p. 2, Rebecca Drucker, *New York Tribune*, 20 April 1919, sec. 4, p. 2, T. H., "Little Theatres," *Nation*, 3 May 1919, 703, and Heywood Broun, "Realism Has Special Thrills of Its Own," *New York Tribune*, 30 March 1919, sec. 4, p. 1.

24. Heywood Broun, 30 January 1917, n.p., in Provincetown Players Scrapbook, Billy Rose Theatre Collection.

25. Review by Heywood Broun, *New York Tribune*, n.d., n.p., in Cook Papers.

26. Kenton, "Provincetown Players," Fales Library, 40, 53. The play's director, Nina Moise, and leading actress, Ida Rauh, recalled both the cast's excitement and their hope to be arrested for saying "goddamn" onstage. See Robert K. Sarlós, "The Provincetown Players: Experiments in Style" (Ph.D. diss., Yale University, 1965), 126. They were not arrested, presumably saved by their official status as a private club. The play's author, Rita Wellman, was the first of Provincetown's women playwrights produced on Broadway; her *The Gentile Wife* was staged by Arthur Hopkins at the Vanderbilt Theatre in 1918.

27. Nani Bailey to John Reed, December 1916, Reed Collection.

28. Barlow, "Susan's Sisters," 288–89.

29. See Sarlós, *Jig Cook*, 128–29.

30. Kenton to Glaspell and Cook, 5 May 1922, Provincetown Players Manuscript Collection.

31. Although *The Emperor Jones* is shorter than most full-length plays, it is considerably longer than the one-acts previously produced by the Players. Before *The Emperor Jones*, the Players had produced only three full-length plays (*The Athenian Women, Bernice,* and *Gee-Rusalem*).

32. Before the end of the year, O'Neill had two plays running on Broadway and a Pulitzer Prize for *Beyond the Horizon*. In 1921 he picked up another Pulitzer for *Anna Christie*.

33. Deutsch and Hanau, *The Provincetown*, 78.

34. Kenton, "Provincetown Players," *Eugene O'Neill Review*, 135.

35. Callard, *Pretty Good for a Woman*, 56–61. Drama's loss may have been literature's gain. Scott's recently reprinted *The Wave* is now considered one of the finest novels of the Civil War.

36. Act 2 stage directions, *The Verge*, in Bigsby, *Susan Glaspell: Plays*, 78. David Sievers has suggested that the expressionistic set depicted a womb. See Sievers, *Freud on Broadway* (New York: Hermitage House, 1955), 71–72.

37. Some might disagree that Robert Edmond Jones was "an outsider." He occupied a uniquely ambiguous position in Provincetown's history. Although he was clearly a central figure in the Players' first summer season (1915), his name does not appear on the list of founders in 1916 or on any other membership list. After

the summer of 1915, he was not actively involved in a production until the spring of 1922.

38. O'Neill to George Tyler, 15 December 1920, quoted in Sarlós, *Jig Cook,* 134.

39. Lingeman, *Theodore Dreiser,* 207. I have discovered no other record of the Provincetown Players paying royalties to writers. Those whose plays moved to Broadway as curtain-raisers to O'Neill's longer works received royalties from the Broadway producer, usually Hopkins.

40. Executive committee members are listed in appendix 3.

41. Kenton, "Provincetown Players," *Eugene O'Neill Review,* 152–53.

42. Both quotations are from John Corbin, "The One-Act Play," *New York Times,* 19 May 1918, sec. 4, p. 8.

43. John Corbin, "Little Theatre Plays," *New York Times,* 11 November 1917, sec. 8, p. 6.

44. M. C. D., "Drama: Women and the American Theatre," *Nation,* 1 June 1918, 665.

45. "Drama," *Greenwich Villager,* 16 November 1921, 7.

46. Kenneth Macgowan, review of *The Dreamy Kid, New York Globe,* 3 November 1919, 9.

47. Corbin, "The One-Act Play," 19 May 1918. Corbin does not credit Cook as coauthor of *Suppressed Desires.* The O'Neill play referred to is *'Ile.*

48. For Floyd Dell, it was one of two plays that justified the company's existence. Dell, *Homecoming,* 267. The other was Millay's *Aria da Capo. Inheritors* was Jasper Deeter's favorite Provincetown play; he revived it regularly at his Hedgerow Theatre. See notes from Sarlós interview with Deeter, Sarlós Papers. For favorable critical responses, see Ludwig Lewisohn, *Nation,* 6 April 1921, 515; Kenneth Macgowan, *New York Globe,* 24 March 1921, 12, Provincetown Players Archive; Stephen Rathbun, *New York Sun,* 26 March 1921, 4, in Cook Papers.

49. James Patterson, "Inheritors," *Billboard,* 2 April 1921, 19, in Provincetown Players Scrapbook, Billy Rose Theatre Collection. For a similar opinion, see Alexander Woollcott, *New York Times,* 27 March 1921, sec. 7, p. 1.

50. *Weekly Review,* 13 April 1921, in Provincetown Players Scrapbook, Billy Rose Theatre Collection.

51. Edith [Unger? Haynes Thompson?] to Agnes Boulton O'Neill, 25 March 1921, O'Neill Papers. Glaspell's *Inheritors* did not have an uptown run, but the Players did present a benefit performance of *Inheritors* for Friends of Freedom for Indian Hindu Students. Program in *Inheritors'* file, Billy Rose Theatre Collection, New York Public Library for the Performing Arts, Astor, Lenox and Tilden Foundations.

52. Maida Castellun, "Susan Glaspell's *Inheritors* Directed against Reaction," *New York Call,* 27 March 1921, 4; and Kenneth Macgowan, "Susan Glaspell Attacks Reaction in *Inheritors," New York Globe and Commercial Advertiser,* 24 March 1921, 12.

53. I refer to *The Hairy Ape* and *The Emperor Jones.* O'Neill's Provincetown

transfers were much more experimental in form than his concurrent Broadway successes that did not originate on Macdougal Street (*Beyond the Horizon* and *Anna Christie*).

54. Alexander Woollcott, *New York Times,* 11 November 1921, 23. Robert A. Parker described the audience as a "feminine majority." *New York Independent,* 17 December 1921, 296. Clipping in Provincetown Players Scrapbook, Billy Rose Theatre Collection.

55. Alexander Woollcott, *New York Times,* 15 November 1921, 23.

56. Alexander Woollcott, "Second Thoughts on First Nights," *New York Times,* 20 November 1921, sec. 6, p. 1, and unidentified clipping, 23 November 1921, n.p., in Provincetown Players Scrapbook, Billy Rose Theatre Collection.

57. Percy Hammond, *New York Herald,* 15 November 1921, 12; *Boston Evening Transcript,* 16 November 1921, sec. 1, p. 11; Weed Dickinson, *New York Evening Telegraph,* 15 November 1921, n.p.; and other, unsigned reviews in Provincetown Players Scrapbook, Billy Rose Theatre Collection.

58. Hapgood, *Victorian,* 377, 428.

59. Woollcott, *New York Times,* 15 November 1921, 23.

60. Woollcott, "Second Thoughts on First Nights," 1.

61. For reviews of *The Verge,* see Woollcott, *New York Times,* 15 November 1921; Jay Rankin Towse, *New York Evening Post,* 15 November 1921, 9; Robert A. Parker, *New York Independent,* 17 December 1921, 296, and *Brooklyn Daily Eagle,* 17 November 1921, 7; and Weed Dickinson, *New York Evening Telegraph,* 15 November 1921, n.p., all in Provincetown Players Scrapbook, Billy Rose Theatre Collection.

62. Robert A. Parker, *New York Independent,* 17 December 1921, 296. Presumably this is the same Robert A. Parker who wrote *5050,* produced by the Provincetown Players in January 1919.

63. Kenneth Macgowan, "Seen on the Stage," *Vogue,* 15 January 1922, 48–49. Macgowan's individual review had been generally favorable, naming the play a "remarkable dramatic document." See Macgowan, "The New Play," *New York Evening Globe,* 15 November 1921, n.p., in Provincetown Players Scrapbook, Billy Rose Theatre Collection.

64. Dufour quoted by Hapgood, *Victorian,* 377. In reporting the events of a Heterodoxy meeting, Dufour broke the club's rule of silence.

65. Ruth Hale, letter to the dramatic editor, *New York Times,* 20 November 1921, sec. 6, p. 1.

66. Maida Castellun, *New York Call,* 16 November 1921, 4, in Provincetown Players Scrapbook, Billy Rose Theatre Collection.

67. "Drama," *New York World,* 28 April 1922, 11, quoted in Bach, "Glaspell: A Bibliography," 24.

68. Maida Castellun, "The Plays That Pass," *New York Call,* 30 April 1922, 4, in Provincetown Players Scrapbook, Billy Rose Theatre Collection.

69. Ludwig Lewisohn, *Nation,* 24 May 1922, 627.

70. Alexander Woollcott, *New York Times,* 28 April 1922, 20.

71. This generalization is based on nine reviews—two favorable, the others negative (of play and performance). Reviews in Provincetown Players Scrapbook, Billy Rose Theatre Collection.

72. Kenton to Glaspell and Cook, 5 May 1922.

73. Ibid. Kenton had previously asked Margaret Wycherly, Mary Shaw, and Roland Young, who were all unavailable. Stewart had directed a revival of *Trifles* the previous season.

74. Ibid.

75. Ibid. Kenton's first choice, Clara Savage, who had appeared in *Close the Book* and *'Ile*, was unable to take the role because she was pregnant. The "adequate" actress cast was Agnes McCarthy from the Neighborhood Playhouse.

76. Glaspell to Kenton, 11 May 1922, and undated letter to Kenton, Glaspell Collection.

77. [*New York Herald*], 28 April 1922, "Susan Glaspell's 'Chains of Dew' Is Sharp Satire," clipping in Glaspell Collection.

78. Kenton to Glaspell, 5 May 1922.

79. Ibid. This is the ending that appears in the only version of *Chains of Dew* I am aware of, the one at the Library of Congress. Kenton's letters are the only evidence we have of the changes made by its director.

80. Kenton to Glaspell and Cook, 22 May 1922, Provincetown Players Manuscript Collection. According to this letter, Kenton mailed the "cut script" on 18 May.

81. Glaspell expressed gratitude to all in her letter to Kenton dated 29 May 1922; for reaction to script's arrival, see 26 June 1922, both letters in Glaspell Collection.

82. Cook died of glanders, apparently contracted from their puppy, which had recently died; glanders is extremely rare in humans. See Glaspell, *Road to the Temple*, 433–41.

83. *New York World Telegram*, 5 May 1931, n.p., in Cook Papers.

84. Barnes, "Days of Jig Cook," 32.

85. Published plays include Barnes's *An Irish Triangle* and *Three from the Earth;* Boyce's *The Two Sons, Enemies,* and *Winter's Night;* Bryant's *The Game;* all of Glaspell's except *Chains of Dew;* Crocker's *The Baby Carriage;* Davies's *The Slave with Two Faces;* all three of Millay's plays; Rostetter's *The Widow's Veil;* Smith's *The Rescue;* and Wellman's *Funiculi-Funicula* and *The String of the Samisen.*

86. Plays subsequently produced nationwide include *Trifles, Suppressed Desires, Aria da Capo, The Game, The Two Sons, Woman's Honor, The People, Close the Book, Inheritors, The Verge, The Slave with Two Faces, The Rescue, The Baby Carriage, The Eldest,* and *The Princess Marries the Page.* This information was obtained from individual files on plays at the Billy Rose Theatre Collection and is by no means comprehensive.

87. Emma Goldman to Alexander Berkman, in Drinnon and Drinnon, *Nowhere at Home,* 235. Goldman was also a great admirer of Evelyn Scott. In this letter,

Goldman reminded Berkman of this opinion, which he had apparently expressed to Stella Ballantine.

88. One was a revival of *Fashion* by Anna Cora Mowatt, the other *East Lynne* by Mrs. Henry Wood. See Vilhauer, "History and Evaluation," 798–800.

89. Gretchen Cryer, "Where Are the Women Playwrights?" *New York Times*, 20 May 1973, 50.

### Chapter 4. Performing Women

1. Barnes, "Days of Jig Cook," 31.

2. Cook to Glaspell, 6 October 1921, Cook Papers.

3. Markham to Louis Sheaffer, 23 July 1962, Sheaffer-O'Neill Collection. Markham played Mrs. Hale in *Trifles* and the Aunt in *Inheritors*.

4. Benjamin McArthur, *Actors and American Culture, 1880–1920* (Philadelphia: Temple University Press, 1984), 170–77. See also James McTeague, *Before Stanislavsky: American Professional Acting Schools and Acting Theory, 1875–1925* (Metuchen, N.J.: Scarecrow Press, 1993), ix–xvii.

5. McTeague, *Before Stanislavsky*, xi, 245. McTeague lists the Lyceum Theatre School (which became the American Academy of Dramatic Arts), the St. James Theatre School, and the Madison Square Theatre School as typical.

6. *Boston Transcript*, 30 August 1916, in Vilhauer, "History and Evaluation," 50–51.

7. Glaspell, *Road to the Temple*, 218.

8. Sheaffer, *Son and Playwright*, 205.

9. Those actresses were Susan Glaspell, Mary Heaton Vorse, Neith Boyce, Ida Rauh, Alice Hall, Louise Bryant, Nancy Schoonmaker, Margaret Nordfeldt, Margaret Steele, Stella Ballantine, and Lucy Huffaker. Sources for this list include all general histories of the company, original published versions of plays, and typescripts of *The Eternal Quadrangle* (Reed Collection) and *Change Your Style* (George Cram Cook Collection, Special Collections, Clifton Waller Barrett Library, University of Virginia).

10. The four were Nancy Schoonmaker, Margaret Nordfeldt, Susan Glaspell, and Ida Rauh. Mary Heaton Vorse was apparently offered a role in Saxe Commins's *The Obituary* in December 1916 but turned it down because she thought it was misogynistic. Tracy L'Engle to Louis Sheaffer, n.d. [1960], Sheaffer-O'Neill Collection. L'Engle performed the role. Saxe Commins was Stella Ballantine's brother—their name is variously spelled Comyn, Commins, Comminsky, and Comynsky.

11. Kenton reported at the beginning of the 1919–20 season that "if anything was left over after bills were paid, actors were to be paid." Kenton, "Provincetown Players," *Eugene O'Neill Review*, 106. A financial record for this season lists $1,524.90 as an expenditure for "actors' salaries." In Provincetown Players Archive. The Provincetown Players apparently never had a set policy regarding actor sala-

ries; the highest salary recorded is Charles Gilpin's at $50/week for *The Emperor Jones*. See Deutsch and Hanau, *The Provincetown*, 67.

12. Langner, *The Magic Curtain*, 111.

13. Hapgood, *Victorian*, 399.

14. Deutsch and Hanau, *The Provincetown*, 23. Pyne and Eugene O'Neill had apparently listened tactfully and then ignored O'Neill Sr.'s "old fogey" approach. See Gelb and Gelb, *O'Neill*, 322–23.

15. Bailey to Reed, December 1916, Reed Collection.

16. Langner, *The Magic Curtain*, 111.

17. Hapgood, *Victorian*, 430.

18. These roles include the maid in Saxe Commins's *The Obituary*, Sarah in Neith Boyce's *Winter's Night*, The Heroine in David Pinski's *A Dollar*, Elena in Mike Gold's *Ivan's Homecoming*, and Rachel in Harry Kemp's *The Prodigal Son*.

19. Heywood Broun, *New York Tribune*, 18 March 1917, Cook Papers.

20. Minutes, 15 March 1917.

21. Playbill in Cook Papers. The role had previously been played by Margaret Nordfeldt and Lucy Huffaker.

22. William Brevda, *Harry Kemp* (Lewisburg, Pa.: Bucknell University Press, 1986), 100.

23. This information comes from Mantle and Sherwood, *Best Plays of 1909–1919*, 619, 628.

24. Untitled clipping from *New York Dramatic Mirror*, Provincetown Players Scrapbook, Harvard Theatre Collection; Heywood Broun, *New York Tribune*, 23 January 1919, 9.

25. *Brooklyn Eagle*, 26 January 1919, n.p., in O'Neill Papers.

26. See Herring, *Djuna*, 74. For Kemp anecdote, see Maude Kivlen to Louis Sheaffer, 30 March 1958, Sheaffer-O'Neill Collection. Kivlen was a close friend of Eugene O'Neill's brother, Jim.

27. Miriam Gurko, *Restless Spirit: The Life of Edna St. Vincent Millay* (New York: Crowell, 1962), 61–64.

28. Edna Millay to Norma Millay, 20 June 1917, in *Letters of Edna St. Vincent Millay*, ed. Allan Ross Macdougall (New York: Harper and Brothers, 1952), 67.

29. Dell, *Homecoming*, 299.

30. Norma Millay to Kathleen Millay, n.d., Millay Family Papers.

31. Ibid.

32. Churchill, *Improper Bohemians*, 209.

33. Langner, *The Magic Curtain*, 69.

34. Notes from Voellmer interview with Moise, 20 July 1957, Sheaffer-O'Neill Collection.

35. Dell, *Homecoming*, 301.

36. *Brooklyn Eagle*, 26 January 1919, n.p., O'Neill Papers.

37. Dell quoted in Churchill, *Improper Bohemians*, 264.

38. Clipping in Provincetown Players Scrapbook, Harvard Theatre Collection.

39. Deutsch and Hanau, *The Provincetown,* 49.

40. Edna Millay to W. Adolphe Roberts, January 1919, in Macdougall, *Letters,* 87–88. Roberts was an author, editor, and Millay admirer.

41. *Brooklyn Eagle,* 4 November 1919, n.p., and *New York Call,* 2 November 1919, n.p., both in Provincetown Players Scrapbook, Harvard Theatre Collection; see also Kenneth Macgowan, *New York Evening Globe,* 3 November 1919, 9.

42. Clippings in Provincetown Players Scrapbook, Billy Rose Theatre Collection.

43. Edna Millay to Kathleen Millay, 23 January 1918, Millay Family Papers.

44. The Washington Square Players reorganized to become the Theatre Guild in 1919.

45. Churchill, *Improper Bohemians,* 262.

46. This includes the offstage singing for O'Neill's *The Moon of the Caribbees.*

47. "Norma Millay Remembers Provincetown's Early Days," *Village Voice,* 1 February 1977, 20, in Millay Family Papers. To avoid confusion between the two sisters, I will refer to Norma Millay by her first name.

48. Norma Millay's additional appearances include the revival of Dell's *The Angel Intrudes* (playbill in Cook Papers), Parkhurst's *Getting Unmarried,* Rita Wellman's *The Rib-Person,* Glaspell's *Woman's Honor,* Florence Kiper Frank's *Gee-Rusalem,* Glaspell and Cook's *Tickless Time,* Robert Allerton Parker's *5050,* Edna Ferber's *The Eldest,* Langner's *Matinata,* and Lawrence Vail's *What D'You Want?*

49. Kenneth Macgowan, *New York Evening Globe,* 3 November 1919, 9. See also Heywood Broun, *New York Tribune,* 25 November 1918, n.p.; Heywood Broun, *New York Tribune,* 23 December 1918, 9; *New York Call,* 2 November 1919, n.p., Provincetown Players Scrapbook, Harvard Theatre Collection. See also Heywood Broun, *New York Tribune,* 24 November 1920, Provincetown Players Scrapbook, Billy Rose Theatre Collection.

50. See notes from Sarlós interview with Norma Millay and Charles Ellis, 10 July 1963, Sarlós Papers. See also "Norma Millay Remembers . . . ," *Village Voice,* 1 February 1977, 20.

51. Ibid. See also Norma Millay file, Billy Rose Theatre Collection, New York Public Library for the Performing Arts, Astor, Lenox and Tilden Foundations; Gil Patten to Norma Millay, 2 August 1920, Millay Family Papers. In 1973 she founded the Millay Colony for the Arts in Austerlitz, New York. Barnes's play was part of the Little Theatre Tournament of 1926.

52. See Heywood Broun, *New York Tribune,* 23 February 1919, sec. 7, p. 1. See also Heywood Broun, *New York Tribune,* 17 November 1919, n.p., unsigned review from *New York Evening Sun,* 19 January 1920, n.p., and unsigned review from *SRO,* all in Provincetown Players Scrapbook, Harvard Theatre Collection. See also unsigned review from *Weekly Review,* n.d., n.p., in Provincetown Players Scrapbook, Billy Rose Theatre Collection.

53. Heywood Broun, *New York Tribune,* 15 January 1920, 11. Hays also per-

formed roles in Mary Carolyn Davies's *The Slave with Two Faces,* O. K. Liveright's *From Portland to Dover,* Robert Allerton Parker's *5050,* Rita Wellman's *String of the Samisen,* Wilbur Daniel Steele's *Not Smart,* Glaspell's *Bernice* and *The Verge,* Glaspell and Cook's *Tickless Time,* Barnes's *Kurzy of the Sea,* Lawrence Vail's *What D'You Want,* and Norman Lindau's *A Little Act of Justice.*

54. Heywood Broun, 23 January 1919, *New York Tribune,* 9. See also unsigned review from *New York Dramatic Mirror,* 8 February 1919, n.p., unsigned review from *New York Morning Telegraph,* 20 January 1919, n.p., and unsigned review from *Brooklyn Eagle,* 18 February 1919, n.p., Provincetown Players Scrapbook, Harvard Theatre Collection.

55. Playbill for revival of *Tickless Time* in Cook Papers (Rostetter replaced Jean Robb). In *Woman's Honor,* Rostetter replaced Dorothy Upjohn. Rostetter repeated her most successful role (of Mrs. Phelan in *The Widow's Veil*) in its two revivals. Playbills in Provincetown Players Scrapbook, Billy Rose Theatre Collection.

56. See Deutsch and Hanau, *The Provincetown,* 285. I have been unable to discover any further information on Rostetter's life.

57. Glaspell's roles were Henrietta in *Suppressed Desires,* Mrs. Hale in *Trifles,* the Woman from Idaho in *The People,* Mrs. Root in *Close the Book,* the Cheated One in *Woman's Honor,* Abbie in *Bernice,* and Allie Mayo in *The Outside.*

58. Moise to Kenton, 16 October 1933, Provincetown Players Archive. See also notes from Voellmer interview with Moise, 20 July 1957, Sheaffer-O'Neill Collection.

59. Notes from Sheaffer interview with William and Marguerite Zorach, 29 June [1960], Sheaffer-O'Neill Collection.

60. Zorach, *Art Is My Life,* 7.

61. Kenton, "Provincetown Players," Fales Library, 66.

62. Heywood Broun, *New York Tribune,* n.d., n.p., in Cook Papers.

63. Heywood Broun, *New York Tribune,* 30 March 1919, sec. 4, p. 1.

64. Unsigned review from *New York Daily Times,* 15 April 1919, n.p., Cook Papers.

65. Norman Paul, "Copeau Looks at the American Stage," *Educational Theatre Journal* 29 (March 1977): 67–68. Jacques Copeau (1879–1949), founder of Théâtre du Vieux Colombier, was France's premier stage director during the interwar years.

66. Ibid., 68.

67. Ibid., 69.

68. Clippings in Provincetown Players Scrapbook, Billy Rose Theatre Collection.

69. Clipping in ibid.

70. Review quoted in Deutsch and Hanau, *The Provincetown,* 72.

71. Clippings in Provincetown Players Scrapbook, Billy Rose Theatre Collection.

72. Notes from Sheaffer interview with Kenneth Macgowan, 24 October [1960], Sheaffer-O'Neill Collection.

73. Notes from Sheaffer interview with Light, 21 May 1960, ibid. The role was played by Carlotta Monterey, who became Eugene O'Neill's third and last wife.

74. See Deutsch and Hanau, *The Provincetown*, appendix B, and Mary Blair file, Billy Rose Theatre Collection, New York Public Library for the Performing Arts, Astor, Lenox and Tilden Foundations.

75. Kenton, "Provincetown Players," Fales Library, 183. See also Ann Harding clipping in Provincetown Players Scrapbook, Billy Rose Theatre Collection.

76. Ludwig Lewisohn, *Nation*, 6 April 1921, 515.

77. Deutsch and Hanau, *The Provincetown*, 79.

78. "Behind the Scenes," *New York Evening Telegram*, 31 October 1921, 6. Clipping in Provincetown Players Scrapbook, Billy Rose Theatre Collection.

79. Reviews by Maida Castellun, Kenneth Macgowan, Alexander Woollcott, Jay Ranken Towse, Stark Young, and Stephen Rathbun in Provincetown Players Scrapbook, Billy Rose Theatre Collection.

80. Maida Castellun, *New York Call*, 16 November 1921, 4, in Provincetown Players Scrapbook, Billy Rose Theatre Collection.

81. McTeague, *Before Stanislavsky*, 47, 51.

82. Hays and Norma Millay each performed thirteen roles during the same period. James Light holds the record for male performers (seventeen roles). Sources for this information include Deutsch and Hanau's *The Provincetown*, playbills, interviews conducted by Sarlós and Sheaffer, and cast lists in published versions of plays.

83. Eastman, *Enjoyment of Living*, 342.

84. Mabel Dodge Luhan, *Intimate Memories*, vol. 3 (New York: Harcourt, Brace, 1936), 199.

85. Joseph Foster, *D. H. Lawrence in Taos* (Albuquerque: University of New Mexico Press, 1972), 220.

86. Boulton, *Long Story*, 27.

87. Eastman, *Enjoyment of Living*, 342. Maude Kivlen also recalled Rauh's beautiful speaking voice. Maude Kivlen to Louis Sheaffer, 28 July 1958, Sheaffer-O'Neill Collection.

88. Floyd Dell, *Love in Greenwich Village* (New York: George H. Doran, 1926), 32.

89. "Workers Should Produce Their Own Plays," *New York Call*, 29 February 1920, in Provincetown Players Scrapbook, Harvard Theatre Collection.

90. Rauh played Myrtle Dart in Cook's *Change Your Style*, the Mother and/or the youth (Sam) in Wilbur Daniel Steele's *Contemporaries*, and Estelle in John Reed's *The Eternal Quadrangle*. See Sarlós, *Jig Cook*, 19, 209 n. 35. See also Deutsch and Hanau, *The Provincetown*, appendix B.

91. Rauh's roles include Neith Boyce's *Enemies* and *Winter's Night*, Dell's *A Long Time Ago*, Rita Wellman's *Barbarians*, O'Neill's *The Sniper*, Kemp's *The Prodigal Son*, Pendleton King's *Cocaine*, O'Neill's *The Long Voyage Home*, James Oppenheim's *Night*, Wellman's *Funiculi-Funicula* and *The Rib-Person*, Glaspell's

*Woman's Honor* and *The Outside,* Mary Carolyn Davies's *The Slave with Two Faces,* and Cook's *The Athenian Women.* Deutsch and Hanau, *The Provincetown,* appendix B.

92. Rauh to Sara Bard Field, 22 April [1918], Bard Field Correspondence. Rauh's comment that "the street is filled with flying flags—conscription is being loaded upon us" indicates that the letter was written while the United States was at war.

93. Rauh appeared in O'Neill's *Where the Cross Is Made,* Rita Creighton Smith's *The Rescue,* Mary Barber's *The Squealer,* Wilbur Daniel Steele's *Not Smart,* and Glaspell's *Bernice.*

94. Rauh appeared in the Broadway *Suppressed Desires/ The Emperor Jones* production.

95. In the 1919–20 season the Players presented nineteen plays (including a review bill); in the 1920–21 season, thirteen; in the 1921–22 season, eight.

96. Rauh directed five plays for the Players in the 1918–19 and 1919–20 seasons.

97. Kenneth Macgowan is quoted in Deutsch and Hanau, *The Provincetown,* vii; additional complimentary comments by Thomas Buchanan and Henry Kolker are quoted in circular, November 1917, Cook Papers. See also "Shockers from Provincetown," clipping in Provincetown Players Scrapbook, Harvard Theatre Collection.

98. Quoted in Deutsch and Hanau, *The Provincetown,* 51. Although the label was subsequently and frequently invoked as a tribute to Rauh, heap may not have meant it has a compliment: "[Duse] has always given me a large pain." heap, quoted in Margaret Anderson, *My Thirty Years' War* (New York: Covici, Friede, 1930), 107.

99. "How Experimental Theaters May Avoid the Pitfalls of Professionalism," *Current Opinion* 65 (July 1918): 28–29.

100. Munson, "The Theatre," 42.

101. Broun's reviews of *The Athenian Women* and *Bernice* are in Cook Papers. For review of *Where the Cross Is Made,* see *New York Tribune,* 25 November 1918, 9; for review of *The Squealer,* see *New York Tribune,* 23 February 1919, sec. 7, p. 1.

102. Review by Rebecca Drucker, *New York Tribune,* in Barnes Papers.

103. *Toledo News,* 7 November 1919, n.p., in Rauh clippings file.

104. Reviews in Cook Papers.

105. Heywood Broun, "Realism Has Special Thrills of Its Own," *New York Tribune,* 30 March 1919, sec. 4, p. 2.

106. Heywood Broun, "All-American Dozen of Our Best Actresses," *New York Tribune,* 13 April 1919, n.p., in Cook Papers.

107. "Critics Declare She's a Genius," *Cleveland Press,* 9 May 1919, in Provincetown Players Scrapbook, Harvard Theatre Collection.

108. Clipping in Provincetown Players Scrapbook, Billy Rose Theatre Collection.

109. Heywood Broun, *New York Tribune,* 23 February 1919, sec. 7, p. 1.

110. Bjorkman's review is in Provincetown Players Scrapbook, Billy Rose Theatre Collection.

111. Markham to Louis Sheaffer, 22 September 1962, Sheaffer-O'Neill Collection.

112. Carl Van Vechten to Kenton, 1924, Van Vechten Papers. See also Rauh to Sara Bard Field, "Thursday—Taos," Bard Field Correspondence.

113. The list includes Kirah Markham, Nilla Cook, Ruza Wenclawska, Marion Berry, Helen Freeman, Edna James, Ruth Chorpenning, Lucy Shreve, Jeannie Begg, Eda Heineman, Agnes McCarthy, Edna James, and possibly Pauline Turkel. See Deutsch and Hanau, *The Provincetown*, appendix B.

## Chapter 5. Staging Women

1. See Toby Cole and Helen Krich Chinoy, eds., *Directing the Play: A Sourcebook of Stagecraft* (New York: Bobbs-Merrill, 1953), 38–39. According to Chinoy and Cole, David Belasco, who began his directing career around 1900, was the "first significant directorial figure" in America. My observations on the ambiguous use of terms to identify directors and general lack of recognition for directing are based on extensive examination of newspaper and magazine articles during this era and from Burns Mantle's *Best Plays of 1909–1919*. The Provincetown Players were among those who frequently used the term "producer" to mean "stage director" and the term "director" to mean what we would now call "artistic director" or "managing director."

2. See Shirlee Hennigan, "The Woman Director in the Contemporary Professional Theatre" (Ph.D. diss., Washington State University, 1983), 12–13.

3. "Resolutions of the Provincetown Players," 5 September 1916, reprinted in Vilhauer, "History and Evaluation," 775–78.

4. The Resolutions, adopted in September 1916, authorized Cook to "cooperate with the author in producing the play under the author's direction." Casting was discussed by the active membership, with playwrights presumably having the final say. The decision to allow interested active members to attend dress rehearsals and offer suggestions was made in October 1916. See Minutes, 5 September, 14, 22 October 1916.

5. Kenton, "Provincetown Players," *Eugene O'Neill Review*, 56.

6. E. J. Ballantine, one of the few professional actors in the company, apparently helped "coach" the first productions of *Bound East for Cardiff* and *Trifles*. See "Original Director for O'Neil [*sic*] Tells of First Night," *New York Tribune*, 6 January 1929, sec. 7, p. 5; notes from Sarlós interview with Alice Hall, 27 June 1963, Sarlós Papers. Bryant's play was "officially" directed (i.e., credited) by Marguerite and William Zorach. See playbill, "The Provincetown Players Will Give Two Special Performances," September 1916, Cook Papers.

7. Kenton, "Provincetown Players," Fales Library, 53.

8. Only one month after instituting the policy requiring playwrights to direct

their own plays, the members created a producing committee to interest other producers (i.e., directors) in working with them. Minutes, 22 October 1916.

9. Minutes, 21 March 1917.

10. See Helen Housley, "The Female Director's Odyssey: The Broadway Sisterhood," unpublished paper, 1991, table 1 and appendix. I know of no comparable study of women's participation as directors in noncommercial theatres.

11. Provincetown directing credits are listed in appendix 5.

12. See Hennigan, "Woman Director," 11–35.

13. Ibid., 25–35, and Helen Housley, "To Inherit the Wind: Margo Jones as Director" (Ph.D. diss., University of Maryland, 1991), 39. Agnes Morgan (1879–1976), an alumna of G. P. Baker's 47 Workshop, began her professional career as a playwright in 1910 but joined the Neighborhood Playhouse as a director in 1912. After the Playhouse closed in 1927, Morgan worked as a director on Broadway, with the Federal Theatre Project, and with Actor-Managers, Inc., a producing organization cofounded by Morgan, her partner, Helen Arthur, and Neighborhood Playhouse designer Aline Bernstein. In 1940 Morgan became company di-rector of the Paper Mill Playhouse, a position she retained until her retirement in 1968.

14. See playbill, "The Provincetown Players Will Give Two Special Performances," September 1916, Cook Papers.

15. Playbill, November 1916, Museum of the City of New York.

16. Deutsch and Hanau, *The Provincetown,* 13.

17. Both Zorachs preferred abstraction to reality. See notes from Sheaffer interview with the Zorachs, 29 June [1960], Sheaffer-O'Neill Collection; see also Zorach, *Art Is My Life,* 40–50. The Zorachs, along with Alfred Kreymborg and Edna Millay, briefly formed a separate organization, the Other Players, to present nonrealistic works at the Playwright's Theatre in March 1918.

18. Deutsch and Hanau, *The Provincetown,* 26.

19. Besides codirecting *Mother Carey's Chickens,* Alice Hall acted in the first production of *Trifles* in the summer of 1916. For information on the rehearsal and performance of this play, see Sarlós, *Jig Cook,* 28–30, narrative compiled from correspondence with Julia Ward Stickney and Charles Hapgood, interview with Alice Hall, and a telephone conversation with Rosalys Hall, 1963, in Sarlós Papers.

20. See Louise Bryant to John Reed, "Thanksgiving Day," 1916, Reed Collection; see also Minutes, 11 December 1916. Although Bryant recorded Treadwell's first name as "Susie," "Sophie Treadwell" is listed as a member of the producing committee in 1916.

21. See Sophie Treadwell clippings file, Billy Rose Theatre Collection, New York Public Library of the Performing Arts, Astor, Lenox, and Tilden Foundations.

22. Mary Heaton Vorse to John Reed, 2 December 1916, Reed Collection.

23. Cook to Glaspell, 11 December 1916, Cook Papers.

24. Moise played small roles in *The People* and *The Athenian Women* (also di-

recting both those plays) and a leading role in Alice Woods Ullman's *The Devil's Glow*, for which no director is recorded.

25. These events are related in Moise to Kenton, 16 October 1933, Province-town Players Archive. See also notes from Voellmer interview with Moise, 20 July 1957, Sheaffer-O'Neill Collection.

26. The company voted to create this position in March 1917, but precisely when Moise assumed the responsibility is not recorded. See Minutes, 21 March 1917. She clearly held the position throughout the second season (1917–18). The other salaried positions included president (Cook), stage manager (Louis Ell), and secretary (David Carb).

27. This information comes from "History of the School of Oratory," North-western University Archives. As the Los Angeles branch was established by a student of the school's original founder, Robert McClean Cumnock, and as the Los Angeles branch kept the name, I have assumed that both schools maintained es-sentially the same standards and curricula.

28. In her letter of 16 October 1933 to Kenton, Moise mentioned a "flop" stock engagement in Massachusetts. According to Moise, the company closed, obliging her to seek work elsewhere (hence her move to New York in January 1917). Al-though Moise did not mention the name of the company, evidence suggests a pos-sible candidate. *American Theatre Companies* lists four stock companies operating in Massachusetts during that time, describing one of these, the Northampton Players, as "close to extinction" in their 1916–17 season. Northampton produced thirty-one plays (primarily one-acts) in thirty-one weeks; its repertory consisted of new come-dies, light drama, and the occasional classic. Its repertory and schedule are compa-rable to those of most stock companies operating during this era. See Weldon Dur-ham, ed., *American Theatre Companies: 1888–1930* (New York: Greenwood Press, 1987), 332–39. In 1933 the *New York Times* reported that Moise once worked with Jessie Bonstelle, who directed the Northampton Players from 1912 to 1917. See *New York Times*, 26 July 1933, n.p., Nina Moise clippings file, Billy Rose Theatre Collec-tion, New York Public Library for the Performing Arts, Astor, Lenox and Tilden Foundations.

29. At Provincetown, Moise directed plays from almost every dramatic genre: drama, melodrama, comedy, satire, farce, and poetic fantasy. For complete list, see appendix 5.

30. See Kenton, "Provincetown Players," Fales Library, 47–48.

31. Notes from Sarlós interview with Dell, 24 July 1963, Sarlós Papers.

32. Gelb and Gelb, *O'Neill*, 325.

33. Ibid.

34. Sheaffer, *Son and Playwright*, 401.

35. O'Neill to Moise, 9 April 1918, in *Selected Letters of Eugene O'Neill*, ed. Travis Bogard and Jackson R. Bryer (New Haven: Yale University Press, 1988), 80.

36. O'Neill to Moise, 14 April 1918, ibid., 82. Here, presumably, O'Neill uses "producer" to mean "director."

37. Ibid., 81–82.

38. See notes from Sarlós interview with Light, 18 July 1963, Sarlós Papers.

39. Heywood Broun, *New York Tribune*, 18 March 1917, sec. 4, p. 3.

40. *Brooklyn Globe*, 24 April 1918, n.p., Provincetown Players Scrapbook, Billy Rose Theatre Collection.

41. *New York Clipper*, 1 May 1918, 10, ibid.; Heywood Broun, "Brilliant One-Act Play Called *The Rope* Provincetown Feature," *New York Tribune*, 29 April 1918, 9.

42. Alfred Kreymborg, *Troubadour* (New York: Liveright, 1925), 305.

43. See notes from Voellmer interview with Moise, 20 July 1957, Sheaffer-O'Neill Collection.

44. Taylor Jantzen to author, 12 August 1994, Employment Verification, Paramount Pictures.

45. Moise directed in the original space at 139 Macdougal. In the fall of 1918, the Players moved into a somewhat larger facility at 133 Macdougal.

46. Kenton, "Provincetown Players," *Eugene O'Neill Review*, 54. See Voellmer interview with Moise, 20 July 1957, Sheaffer-O'Neill Collection; see also playbills in Washington Square Players Scrapbook, Billy Rose Theatre Collection, New York Public Library for the Performing Arts, Astor, Lenox and Tilden Foundations.

47. Kenton, "Provincetown Players," Fales Library, 79. The same comment appears in Kenton, "Unorganized," 8–9.

48. Heywood Broun, *New York Tribune*, 4 March 1918, 9.

49. Kenton, "Unorganized," 8. In this article Kenton refers to Moise specifically as "the producer for the Players."

50. O'Neill to Moise, 17 January 1919, O'Neill Papers. Thomas Mitchell directed the first production of *Moon of the Caribbees*.

51. Moise to Kenton, 16 October 1933. Moise was referring to her first meeting with Jig Cook at Nani Bailey's restaurant. See also Sheaffer, *Son and Playwright*, 377.

52. Boulton, *Long Story*, 32.

53. Moise to Kenton, 16 October 1933, Provincetown Players Archive.

54. See notes from Voellmer interview with Moise, 20 July 1957, Sheaffer-O'Neill Collection.

55. Kenton, "Provincetown Players," Fales Library, 50.

56. See notes from Sheaffer interview with Light, 21 May 1960, Sheaffer-O'Neill Collection.

57. See Voellmer interview with Moise, 20 July 1957, and George Voellmer to Louis Sheaffer, 27 July 1957, Sheaffer-O'Neill Collection.

58. Sheaffer, *Son and Playwright*, 395.

59. Apparently O'Neill tried to seduce Moise, at one point imploring, "Don't think it over, feel it over." Moise told Voellmer she did not think her recollections necessarily belonged in an O'Neill biography, but "would belong in a biography of Nina Moise." See Voellmer interview with Moise, 20 July 1957, Sheaffer-O'Neill Collection.

60. Newspaper clippings and programs, Santa Barbara Historical Society.

61. Notes from Sarlós interview with Nina Moise, 8 November 1963, Sarlós Papers.

62. Sheldon Cheney, *The Art Theatre* (New York: Knopf, 1925), 125–26.

63. Sharon Smith, *Women Who Make Movies* (New York: Hopkinson and Blake, 1975), 24. See also *New York Sun,* 28 August 1933, n.p., and *New York Times,* 26 July 1933, n.p., Moise clippings file.

64. Copy of Moise's FBI file (dated 24 May 1948) in author's possession. The FBI recorded that Moise associated with Communists, notably Melvyn Douglas, but she was never the subject of a serious investigation.

65. Moise to Kenton, 18 August 1933, Provincetown Players Archive. See also Kenton to Cook and Glaspell, 8 September 1922, Provincetown Players Manuscript Collection.

66. Boyce and Glaspell first acted in Provincetown's two summer seasons. Potter may have acted in the Liberal Club's "communal rituals."

67. Kreymborg, *Troubadour,* 314.

68. Churchill, *Improper Bohemians,* 263.

69. Deutsch and Hanau, *The Provincetown,* 54.

70. "Woman's Honor Acted," unsigned review of Greenwich Village Theatre production, *New York Times,* 21 May 1918, 13.

71. Heywood Broun, *New York Tribune,* 18 March 1917, sec. 4, p. 3. Favorable comments by Thomas Buchanan and Henry Kolker were quoted in announcement for third season, O'Neill Papers. *Cocaine* was included in two review bills.

72. Reviews in Provincetown Players Scrapbook, Billy Rose Theatre Collection.

73. Kenton to Glaspell and Cook, 13 May 1922, Provincetown Players Manuscript Collection.

74. Wycherly codirected and starred in *Floriani's Wife* in the 1923–24 season and directed *The Unchastened Woman* in the 1925–26 season.

75. See reviews in Provincetown Players Scrapbook, Harvard Theatre Collection.

76. Notes from Sarlós interview with Norma Millay, 10 July 1963, Sarlós Papers. Millay was probably referring to her role as a robotic character in *5050,* written and directed by Robert A. Parker. *5050* ran in January 1919, *Gee-Rusalem* in November 1918.

77. See Djuna Barnes, "The Confessions of Helen Westley," in *Interviews,* ed. Alyce Barry (Washington, D.C.: Sun and Moon Press, 1985), 249.

78. See Heywood Broun, *New York Herald Tribune,* 15 January 1920, 11. Additional reviews in Provincetown Players Scrapbook, Harvard Theatre Collection.

79. Langner, *The Magic Curtain,* 93–94.

80. Bryant to John Reed, 2 December 1916, Reed Collection.

81. Cook to Glaspell, 24 October 1918, Cook Papers.

82. Gelb and Gelb, *O'Neill,* 384.

83. Kenton, "Provincetown Players," *Eugene O'Neill Review*, 88.

84. Boulton, *Long Story*, 242.

85. Sheaffer, *Son and Playwright*, 342.

86. Doris Alexander, *The Tempering of Eugene O'Neill* (New York: Harcourt, Brace, and World, 1962), 266.

87. Heywood Broun, "Provincetown Players Give Fine Thrill in a Sea Play," *New York Tribune*, 25 November 1918, 9.

88. O'Neill to Moise, 17 January 1919, O'Neill Papers.

89. O'Neill himself portrayed the mulatto sailor in *Thirst* (1916), and white actors in blackface played the West Indian prostitutes in *Moon of the Caribbees* (1918). In *The Emperor Jones* (1920), the play frequently cited as pivotal in introducing African-American actors in serious roles, Charles Gilpin was the only African-American actor. The other "native" roles were performed by white actors in blackface.

90. Vilhauer, "History and Evaluation," 245. Vilhauer cited an interview with Rauh on 11 December 1962.

91. Rebecca Drucker, *New York Tribune*, 16 November 1919, sec. 4, p. 7. See also Burns Mantle, *New York Mail*, 3 November 1919, n.p.; Jay Kaufman, *New York Globe*, 3 November 1919, n.p., in Barnes Papers; *Boston Transcript*, 5 November 1919, n.p., in Provincetown Players Scrapbook, Billy Rose Theatre Collection; and Alexander Woollcott, *New York Times*, 9 November 1919, sec. 8, p. 2.

92. Simmelkjaer appeared in *Taboo* (along with Margaret Wycherly and Paul Robeson) in April 1922. Allen Woll, ed., *Dictionary of the Black Theatre* (Westport, Conn.: Greenwood Press, 1983), 164.

93. Notes from Sarlós interview with James Light, 18 July 1963, Sarlós Papers.

94. Clipping in Provincetown Players Scrapbook, Billy Rose Theatre Collection.

95. Vilhauer, "History and Evaluation," 261.

96. Norma Millay to Kathleen Millay, 23 October 1919, Millay Family Papers. *Getting Unmarried* opened 31 October 1919.

97. Glaspell to Hallie Flanagan, 23 August 1938, Federal Theatre Project Papers, National Archives, Washington, D.C. I am grateful to Michael O'Hara for bringing this letter to my attention. I do not know whether Rauh requested Glaspell's help in obtaining work with the Federal Theatre Project, and I have not discovered any evidence of such employment. Riggs and O'Neil were playwrights in the 1930s and 1940s. O'Neil's *American Dream*, produced by the Theatre Guild in 1933, was denounced as immoral and communistic. Riggs enjoyed considerable success, especially with *Green Grow the Lilacs* (1930), the dramatic source for Rodgers and Hammerstein's phenomenally successful musical *Oklahoma!*

98. Phyllis Cole Braunlich, *Haunted by Home: The Life and Letters of Lynn Riggs* (Norman: University of Oklahoma Press, 1988), 15–16. Before this, as a student, Riggs had written one other one-act, which had been produced at the University of Oklahoma in 1923.

99. Riggs to Rauh, 8 July 1937, Lynn Riggs Papers, Yale Collection of American Literature, Beinecke Rare Book and Manuscript Library, Yale University. See also Braunlich, *Haunted by Home,* 140. The professional and personal relationship between Rauh and Riggs lasted until his death in 1954. Ibid., xiii.

100. The producer was the American Show Shop. See Burns Mantle, *Best Plays of 1937–38* (New York: Dodd, Mead, 1938), 462–63.

101. Harold Chapin was a fairly well known playwright; Elsie Chapin was his sister. I have been unable to discover any other information about her.

102. *Brooklyn Eagle,* 4 November, 1919, n.p., and *New York Call,* 2 November, 1919, n.p., both in Provincetown Players Scrapbook, Harvard Theatre Collection; see also Kenneth Macgowan, *New York Evening Globe,* 3 November 1919, 9.

103. Broadway and off-Broadway directors are listed in Hennigan, "Woman Director," appendix C.

104. Housley, "Female Director's Odyssey," table 1. Her study spanned the years 1900–1990.

105. Gordon Craig, whose career began around the turn of the century, probably introduced the practice, and Robert Edmond Jones, whose career began in 1915, occasionally combined the two roles. The designer/director did not appear as a category in Hennigan's study.

106. Johnson is quoted in Deutsch and Hanau, *The Provincetown,* 71.

107. Housley, who recorded a peak participation rate for women directors on Broadway as 16.3 percent (in 1948), attributed this dearth to sexual stereotyping. See Housley, "Female Director's Odyssey," table 1, and "To Inherit the Wind," 45.

108. See Deutsch and Hanau, *The Provincetown,* appendix B.

109. If Wycherly had been able to direct *Chains of Dew,* the percentage of women directing in the last season would have doubled (to 28.5 percent).

110. Helen Krich Chinoy, "If Not an Actress, What . . . ?" in Chinoy and Jenkins, *Women in American Theatre,* 192.

## Chapter 6. Designing Women

1. Announcement for first New York season, 1916–17, reprinted in Vilhauer, "History and Evaluation," 93.

2. See Minutes, 22 October, 11 December 1916, 21 February 1917.

3. The financial repercussions of *The Emperor Jones*'s move to Broadway in 1920 are revealed in correspondence between Kenton, Fitzgerald, Cook, and Glaspell, 1921–22, in Provincetown Players Manuscript Collection and Provincetown Players Archive. Programs for the last two seasons reflect the considerable increase in technical staff. In her history, Kenton maintained that although royalties from plays that moved uptown (all O'Neill's) brought in additional resources, even more money went out in the attempt to upgrade production values to match Broadway's standards. See Kenton, "Provincetown Players," Fales Library, 40-a, 172–77, 181, 187; see also Sarlós, *Jig Cook,* 134–35; Vilhauer, "History and Evaluation," 170–73, 282–84.

4. Vilhauer, "History and Evaluation," 274–75. Vilhauer cited an interview

with George Greenberg, 27 November 1962, who reported that he was paid ten to fifteen dollars weekly to assist Throckmorton and to stage-manage.

5. Provincetown designers and credits are listed in appendixes 6 and 7.

6. Vilhauer, "History and Evaluation," 290.

7. Mackay, *Little Theatre*, 53.

8. See Robert Black, "Robert Edmond Jones: Poetic Artist of the New Stage-craft" (Ph.D. diss, University of Wisconsin, Madison, 1955), 2–7; see also Bobbi Owen, *Scenic Design on Broadway: Designers and Their Credits, 1915–1990* (New York: Greenwood Press, 1991), introduction. Contemporaries of Jones who also pioneered the new practice include Norman Bel Geddes, Lee Simonson, Cleon Throckmorton, and Aline Bernstein.

9. Alice M. Robinson, Vera Mowry Roberts, and Milly S. Barranger, eds., *Notable Women in the American Theatre: A Biographical Dictionary* (New York: Greenwood Press, 1989), 69.

10. Owen, *Scenic Design*, xiv.

11. Ibid., xiv–xv.

12. The union recognized lighting as a specialization in the 1960s. Ibid., xv, 156.

13. I have relied on Owen, *Scenic Design*, and Owen, *Costume Design on Broadway* (New York: Greenwood Press, 1987), to tabulate these statistics. Owen, relying primarily on program records, provides an alphabetical listing of individuals who received any sort of design credit (including collaboration) on Broadway from 1915 to 1990 for scenic designers and from 1915 to 1985 for costume designers. Provincetown design credits are presented in graph 5 and in appendixes 6 and 7.

14. Advertisement in program for the Washington Square Players, 1916–17 season, Washington Square Players Scrapbook.

15. Thompson was a committee member of the Washington Square Players in 1915, but her artistic contributions to that company are unknown. See programs for 1915–16 season, ibid.

16. Heaton's contribution is neglected in Kenton's listing for scenic designers for the 1917–18 season. Kenton listed Rollo Peters, Neil Reber, Ira Remsen, and Norman Jacobsen only, excluding also Floyd Dell and Louis Ell. Kenton, "Provincetown Players," Fales Library, 49. *The Hermit and His Messiah* is unpublished. The description of its setting comes from Sarlós, *Jig Cook*, 90.

17. Kenton, "Provincetown Players," *Eugene O'Neill Review*, 93.

18. Ibid.

19. Mackay, *Little Theatre*, 53.

20. Zorach, *Art Is My Life*, 45.

21. Deutsch and Hanau, *The Provincetown*, 13.

22. Zorach, *Art Is My Life*, 46. See also notes from Sheaffer interview with the Zorachs, 29 June [1960], Sheaffer-O'Neill Collection.

23. The block for this work is held by the National Museum of American Art, Washington, D.C.

24. Mary Fanton Roberts, "The Artist in the American Theatre," *Touchstone* 5

(April 1919): 76–79, quoted in Mike A. Barton, "Aline Bernstein: A History and Evaluation" (Ph.D. diss., Indiana University, 1971), 32. Roberts described three major trends in new stagecraft: the decorative (defined above), the plastic (reduced to essential architectural shapes and forms), and the decorative-plastic (a combination of the two).

25. Kreymborg, *Troubadour,* 242. The playbill described the piece as a "conventional scherzo."

26. Ibid., 311.

27. Bailey to Reed, n.d. [December 1916], Reed Collection,

28. Kenton, "Provincetown Players," *Eugene O'Neill Review,* 48.

29. See notes from Sarlós interview with Moise, 8 November 1963, Sarlós Papers.

30. Deutsch and Hanau, *The Provincetown,* 15. According to William Zorach, they also clashed with O'Neill concerning a painted stove for one of his sets; O'Neill went out and got a real stove. Zorach, *Art Is My Life,* 45.

31. Zorach, *Art Is My Life,* 46. Zorach does not mention specific newspapers; as far as I know, they are not available.

32. Earlier, William Zorach had produced his only independent design, for a spring 1917 revival of *Suppressed Desires.* I found no comments concerning this design by either reviewers or colleagues.

33. *Boston Evening Transcript,* 5 November 1919, n.p., in Provincetown Players Scrapbook, Billy Rose Theatre Collection.

34. Kenneth Macgowan, *New York Globe,* 3 November 1919, 9.

35. Reviewers frequently neglected to mention the names of designers or directors, even when commenting on their specific contributions. Male designers named in reviews include C. M. Sax, Brör Nordfeldt, Ira Remsen, James Light, Charles Ellis, Cleon Throckmorton, and Robert Edmond Jones.

36. Zorach, *Art Is My Life,* 45–50; notes from Sheaffer interview with the Zorachs, 29 June [1960], Sheaffer-O'Neill Collection; notes from Sarlós interview with the Zorachs, 16 March 1962, Sarlós Papers.

37. Zorach, *Art Is My Life,* 56–58.

38. Hoffman, *Marguerite and William Zorach,* 26, 32.

39. Churchill, *Improper Bohemians,* 208.

40. Kreymborg, *Troubadour,* 308.

41. Zorach, *Art Is My Life,* 46. See also notes from Sheaffer interview with the Zorachs, 29 June [1960], Sheaffer-O'Neill Collection.

42. Mackay, *Little Theatre,* 49.

43. Kenton, "Provincetown Players," *Eugene O'Neill Review,* 41.

44. Ibid., 40–41.

45. Ibid., 65. Ellen Cook died in Iowa in 1918.

46. Dearborn, *Queen of Bohemia,* 21.

47. Bryant, "Christmas in Petrograd, 1917," 8, Hicks Papers. This and the fol-

lowing anecdotes are selective, but I have not selected to exclude men. I found no such recollections of costuming by male members.

48. Vilhauer, "History and Evaluation," 286. Vilhauer cited an interview with Rauh, 11 December 1962.

49. Kreymborg, *Troubadour,* 309–10.

50. Marianne Moore to H.D., 11 January 1921, in *The Selected Letters of Marianne Moore,* ed. Bonnie Costello (New York: Knopf, 1997), 141. The play is most likely Vail's *What D'You Want.*

51. Edna Millay to Witter Bynner, 29 October 1920, in Macdougall, *Letters,* 104.

52. Unidentified newspaper clipping dated 26 January 1919, n.p., Provincetown Players Scrapbook, Harvard Theatre Collection. *The String of the Samisen* ran 17–23 January 1919.

53. Cannell to Robert K. Sarlós, [1965], Sarlós Papers. Cannell danced under the stage name Rihani.

54. Deutsch and Hanau, *The Provincetown,* appendix B, and Owen, *Costume Design,* 99, 104, 110.

55. Transcript, "The Reminiscences of William Zorach," Oral History Collection, Columbia University, 259. Zorach specifically credited Marguerite for designing and constructing costumes for the Other Players' productions in the spring of 1918 and also recorded that she made "everything we wore" and "exotic imaginative costumes for [the Village balls]." Zorach, *Art Is My Life,* 46, 53–54.

56. See *The Eternal Quadrangle,* TS, Reed Collection.

57. Cook to Glaspell, 24 September 1917, Cook Papers.

58. Churchill, *Improper Bohemians,* 163–65.

59. Edith Unger also performed three roles for the Players: "the young girl" in *The Gentle Furniture Shop;* the free-spirited Jhansi in Glaspell's *Close the Book;* and "young girl" in Rita Wellman's *Funiculi-Funicula.*

60. The plays were *Blind Alley, The Avenue, Habit* (with Rose Windsor), and *Youth.* Programs in Washington Square Players Scrapbook.

61. Owen, *Costume Design,* 159.

62. Zagat, a modern dancer, also performed in the revival of *Barbarians* in the spring of 1918 (playbill in Cook Papers). She later became a minister in the Church of Divine Unity and published several religious works. See Sarlós, *Jig Cook,* 199.

63. Kenton, "Provincetown Players," *Eugene O'Neill Review,* 96.

64. See notes from Sarlós interview with Norma Millay, 10 July 1963, Sarlós Papers.

65. L'Engle (1889–1978) became a well-known painter with numerous exhibits. She studied in Paris and New York, and lived for the most part in Provincetown and Truro (Massachusetts) with her husband, artist William L'Engle. Lucy L'Engle was given a retrospective in the fall of 1997 in Truro.

66. Heywood Broun, *New York Tribune,* n.d., n.p., Kenneth Macgowan, *New*

*York Call*, 10 February 1921, Alexander Woollcott, *New York Times*, 15 November 1921, 23, *Vogue*, 1 April 1921, 96, *Theatre Arts Magazine*, July 1921, 183, all in Provincetown Players Archive.

67. Hays separated from Arthur Hays during her Provincetown days and was romantically involved with Provincetown actor Hutch Collins until his death during the influenza epidemic of 1919.

68. Heywood Broun, *New York Tribune*, 25 November 1918, 9.

69. See notes from Sheaffer interview with Blanche Hays, n.d. [1957–63], Sheaffer-O'Neill Collection; see also Gelb and Gelb, *O'Neill*, 495–96; Kenton to Cook and Glaspell, 8 May 1922, Provincetown Players Manuscript Collection.

70. According to *Theatre Arts Magazine*, *The Hairy Ape* was "the first produced example of Expressionism" in New York. *Theatre Arts Magazine*, July 1922, 187. Arguably, this distinction belongs to *The Verge*, produced in 1921.

71. Review by Stark Young, *New Republic*, 7 December 1921, 47.

72. Gelb and Gelb, *O'Neill*, 495–96.

73. Eugene O'Neill, *The Hairy Ape* (New York: Boni and Liveright, 1922), 54.

74. This information comes primarily from Gelb and Gelb, *O'Neill*, 495–96. See also notes from Sheaffer's interview with Hays, n.d. [1957–63], Sheaffer-O'Neill Collection. According to Fuerst and Hume, masks were first used in theatre design in America in 1916 (Robert Edmond Jones, *Caliban*). See Walter R. Fuerst and Samuel J. Hume, *Twentieth-Century Stage Decoration*, vol. 1 (New York: Knopf, 1929; reprint, New York: Dover, 1967), 85.

75. Welsh quoted in Deutsch and Hanau, *The Provincetown*, 87–88.

76. Alexander Woollcott, *New York Times*, 20 March 1922, in Bernard Beckerman and Howard Siegman, eds., *On Stage: Theatre Reviews from the "New York Times"* (New York: New York Times Books, 1971), 27.

77. Kenton to Cook and Glaspell, 8 May 1922, Provincetown Players Manuscript Collection.

78. Kenton to Hays, 22 June 1922, Provincetown Players Archive.

79. Palmer White, *Elsa Schiaparelli: Empress of Fashion* (London: Aurum Press, 1986), 44–57.

80. Ibid., 44.

81. Elsa Schiaparelli, *Shocking Life* (London: J. M. Dent and Sons, 1954), 36.

82. Hays to Kenton, 25 September [1922], Provincetown Players Archive.

83. Ibid. Lugné-Poe was the director of Paris's Théâtre de l'Oeuvre.

84. I am grateful to Kenneth Cameron for alerting me to Hays's appearance in *Reds*. I have been unable to find an obituary for Blanche Hays Fagen but assume she is deceased.

## Chapter 7. Backlash and Aftermath

1. Edna Millay attended the trial with Floyd Dell but was distracted by the more dashing John Reed.

2. Bailey appeared in Wilbur Daniel Steele's *Not Smart* (summer 1916) and David Pinski's *A Dollar* (winter 1917) and owned and operated one of the Province-towners' most popular restaurants, the Samovar.

3. Wexler, *Emma Goldman,* 255.

4. Dearborn, *Queen of Bohemia,* 125. Bryant actually spent four, not six, months in Russia.

5. Smith quoted in Cott, *Grounding of Modern Feminism,* 134.

6. Arabella Kenealy, *Feminism and Sex-Extinction* (New York: Dutton, 1920), 256.

7. Glaspell, stage directions, *Chains of Dew,* Library of Congress, 1–2.

8. Susan Faludi, *Backlash: The Undeclared War against American Women* (New York: Doubleday, 1991), 46–51.

9. See Una Stannard, *Mrs. Man* (San Francisco: Germanbooks, 1977), 192, 197, 212, 218.

10. Doris Stevens, "Tribute to Alva Belmont," *Equal Rights,* 15 July 1933, 189, quoted in William L. O'Neill, *Everyone Was Brave: A History of Feminism in America* (New York: Quadrangle/New York Times Book Co., 1969), 293.

11. See Robyn Muncy, *Creating a Female Dominion in American Reform, 1890–1935* (New York: Oxford University Press, 1991), introduction.

12. Andrew Field, *Djuna: The Life and Times of Djuna Barnes* (New York: Putnam, 1983), 116.

13. Efram L. Burk, "Testament to American Modernism: The Prints of William and Marguerite Zorach" (Ph.D. diss., Pennsylvania State University, 1998), 30. The "high priestess" designation comes from the *Provincetown Advocate,* 25 August 1915, quoted in Egan, *Provincetown as a Stage,* 132.

14. Kenton to Boyce, 22 July 1913, Hapgood Family Papers.

15. Rogers to Reed, November 1916, Reed Collection. Rogers was a charter member of the Provincetown Players.

16. Floyd Dell, *Intellectual Vagabondage* (New York: George H. Doran, 1926), 165.

17. Dell, "Not Roses," 10. See also notes from Sarlós interview with Dell, 18 July 1963, Sarlós Papers.

18. Dell quoted in Garrison, *Insurgent,* 82.

19. Dell, handwritten note, Dell Papers. Dell evidently found such a paragon in B. Marie Gage, whom he married in 1919. Apparently Gage did devote herself to him and their children; they stayed married until his death.

20. Eastman, *Enjoyment of Living,* 369.

21. Lingeman, *Theodore Dreiser,* 134.

22. Reed to Edward Hunt, n.d., Reed Collection.

23. Quoted in Callard, *Pretty Good for a Woman,* 56.

24. Harry Kemp, *Don Juan's Notebook* (New York: privately printed, 1929), 5. In 1931, Kemp published a Provincetown roman à clef that wallows in unabashed mi-

sogyny. See Harry Kemp, *Love among the Cape-Enders* (New York: MacCaulay, 1931).

25. Sheaffer interview with George Frame Brown, Sheaffer-O'Neill Collection. No doubt some of these stories were exaggerated for dramatic effect as the O'Neill legend grew, but many incidents of abuse are reported by Provincetown/Greenwich Village natives. See notes from interviews with the Zorachs, Betty Collins, Madeline Boyd, Margery Boulton, and Maude Kivlen, all in Sheaffer-O'Neill Collection.

26. Boulton, *Long Story*, 226. Ballantine apparently spoke from experience: "You are again in distress about Teddy—that is the price we pay for intense love—talented men make anything but ideal husbands, but one must be strong enough to face it." Emma Goldman to Ballantine, 30 June 1925, Emma Goldman Papers, New York Public Library.

27. Kenton, "Militant Women," 15.

28. Loy, "Feminist Manifesto," 270.

29. Hutchins Hapgood, quoted in Luhan, *Intimate Memories*, 3:237. Hapgood's speech on sex antagonism occurred at one of Luhan's evenings. According to Luhan, she hired a stenographer to record the event.

30. The poem and explanation are included in Van Vechten to Stein, 13 June 1924, in Edward Burns, ed., *The Letters of Gertrude Stein and Carl Van Vechten, 1913–1946*, vol. 1 (New York: Columbia University Press, 1986), 100.

31. Bryant to Frank Walsh, 17 May 1930, in Dearborn, *Queen of Bohemia*, 204. Walsh was a radical lawyer and intimate friend to Bryant.

32. Virginia Gardner, *"Friend and Lover": The Life of Louise Bryant* (New York: Horizon Press, 1982), 310.

33. The stepdaughter of poet Richard LeGallienne, Gwen LeGallienne was legally but not biologically related to actress/director Eva LeGallienne.

34. In 1927 Bryant had been diagnosed with Durcum's Disease, an incurable, disfiguring, and debilitating illness that led to an increased dependence on alcohol to relieve physical and emotional pain involved. See Dearborn, *Queen of Bohemia*, 243–49.

35. Garrison, *Insurgent*, 181–84. Vorse had never been completely sympathetic to Minor's radical communism.

36. Ibid., 193.

37. Callard, *Pretty Good for a Woman*, 62.

38. Ibid., 74. Scott was "stepmother" to Thomas Merton for a number of years, when she lived with Owen Merton.

39. Creighton Scott, "Confessions of an American Boy," unpublished MS, quoted in Callard, *Pretty Good for a Woman*, 64. The son of Ruth Hale and Heywood Broun published a milder but also critical account of childhood in Bohemia. See Heywood Hale Broun, *Whose Little Boy Are You?* (New York: St. Martin's Press, 1983).

40. Garrison, *Insurgent,* 190.

41. His name was Boyce, but he had adopted "Harry" as a nickname.

42. DeWitt, *Taos,* 98.

43. See Kenton to Carl Van Vechten, 1928, Van Vechten Papers.

44. See Braunlich, *Haunted by Home.* See also correspondence between Riggs and Rauh, Riggs Papers.

45. A. Cheney, *Millay in Greenwich Village,* 119. See also Allan Ross Macdougal, "Husband of a Genius," *Delineator,* October 1934, 40–41.

46. A. Cheney, *Millay in Greenwich Village,* 106–9, 137, 140.

47. Emma Goldman to Alexander Berkman, 4 September 1925, in Drinnon and Drinnon, *Nowhere at Home,* 132.

48. Glaspell, *Road to the Temple,* 239.

49. Nilla Cram Cook, *My Road to India* (New York: Furman, 1939), 9. See also Noe, *Susan Glaspell,* 50.

50. Hapgood, *Victorian,* 486.

51. Glaspell, unpublished autobiographical sketch, "Here's the Piece," n.d., Cook Papers. See also Glaspell, *Road to the Temple,* 255.

52. Thomas Postlewait, "Autobiography and Theatre History," in *Interpreting the Theatrical Past,* ed. Thomas Postlewait and Bruce A. McConachie (Iowa City: University of Iowa Press, 1989), 260.

53. Ibid., 262.

54. Matson to Glaspell, October 1932, quoted in Noe, *Susan Glaspell,* 63. Anna Walling was pregnant when she and Matson married in 1932. Ibid., 62.

55. Quoted in Callard, *Pretty Good for a Woman,* 137. Although Callard described this article and quoted from it, he did not provide bibliographic information; presumably it exists in manuscript in the Scott Papers, University of Texas, Austin.

56. Trimberger uses the phrase "eerily familiar" in *Intimate Warriors,* 2. See also biographies of Bryant, Glaspell, Loy, Millay, Scott, Vorse, in bibliography.

## Chapter 8. Valedictory

1. Robert K. Sarlós, "Dionysus in 1915: A Pioneer Theatre Collective," *Theatre Research International* 3 (October 1977): 33–53.

2. Glaspell to Fitzgerald, 31 May 1924, Provincetown Players Manuscript Collection.

3. See Elsie Dufour's anecdote, quoted by Hapgood, *Victorian,* 37; Alexander Woollcott, *New York Times,* 11 November 1921, 23.

4. See W. O'Neill, *Everyone Was Brave,* 225–94.

5. Faludi, *Backlash,* xx.

6. Dell, *Intellectual Vagabondage,* 139.

7. See Patti P. Gillespie, "Feminist Theatre: A Rhetorical Phenomenon," *Quarterly Journal of Speech* 64 (1978): 286–94.

8. Canning, *Feminist Theaters,* 202.
9. Ibid., 6.
10. Ibid., 9.
11. Helen Krich Chinoy, introduction to Chinoy and Jenkins, *Women in American Theatre,* 4.

## Appendix 2
1. This list appears in the *Minutes of the Provincetown Players* and is reprinted in Vilhauer, "History and Evaluation," 771.

## Appendix 3
1. Record compiled from Minutes, Kenton's history, and program listings. Although Kenton lists Petra Wold as having replaced Margaret Nordfeldt as secretary in March 1917, the Minutes record both Nordfeldt's resignation and David Carb's election on the same day. See Kenton, "Provincetown Players," *Eugene O'Neill Review,* 65, and Minutes, 21 March 1917. Petra Wold is listed as a member in the Minutes of 8 November 1917; the Players decided in the spring of 1918 to hire a paid secretary exclusive of committee membership, to be appointed by the executive committee; Wold may have served in that capacity. When Fitzgerald joined in the fall of 1918, the two functions were apparently reintegrated. See Minutes, 8 November 1917, 21 April 1918.

## Appendix 5
1. In the Voellmer interview, Moise recalled directing one of Bodenheim's plays but did not name the title. In 1918 the Players produced one play (*The Gentle Furniture Shop*) written by Bodenheim and one play (*Knotholes*) cowritten by Bodenheim and William Saphier.
2. Although no other director is formally recorded, several other (male) company members claimed credit for directing or codirecting with Cook. See Robert K. Sarlós, "Producing Principles and Practices of the Provincetown Players," *Theatre Research/Recherches Theatrales* 10 (1969): 100. Sarlós cited interviews with over a dozen former members.

## Appendix 6
1. Credit is generally established by program credit or Deutsch and Hanau, *The Provincetown,* appendix B; other sources (memoir, interview, play MSS) are indicated by an *. In these instances there is generally no way to corroborate assertions.
2. The program credits read: "directed by Arthur Hohl, staged by Brör Nordfelt." Probably the Players used "staging" in this instance to refer to "setting the stage," that is, to designing the set.
3. As in other appendixes, I list revivals when there is a change of director or designer.

## Appendix 7

1. Credit is generally established by program credit or Deutsch and Hanau, *The Provincetown*, appendix B; other sources (memoir, interview, play MSS) are indicated by an *. In these instances there is generally no way to corroborate assertions. This listing does not include Ellen Cook, Cora Millay, or the many actresses who built or bought their own costumes because their specific contributions are impossible to tabulate. Their general contributions are examined in chapter 6.

2. Program credit for *The Game* reads "staged and decorated by William and Marguerite Zorach" without distinguishing scenic and costume design. William Zorach's memoir and interviews establish their responsibility for all visual elements.

3. Hays is credited throughout the last two seasons as "costume supervisor" or "costume director," even though four productions during those seasons include additional credit for costume designers. My assumption is that Hays alone was responsible for costumes when no other credit is given, and that she also supervised or coordinated costuming for other designers.

# Selected Bibliography

## Primary Sources

### Special Collections

Bard Field, Sara. Correspondence. C. E. S. Wood Collection, Huntington Library, San Marino, California.

Barnes, Djuna. Papers. Special Collections, University of Maryland at College Park Libraries.

Cook, George Cram. Collection. Special Collections, Clifton Waller Barrett Library, University of Virginia.

———. Papers. Berg Collection, New York Public Library.

Dasburg, Andrew. Papers. Archives of American Art, Museum of American Art, Washington, D.C.

Dell, Floyd. Papers. Special Collections, Newberry Library, Chicago.

Federal Theatre Project Papers. National Archives, Washington, D.C.

Glaspell, Susan. Collection. Special Collections, Clifton Waller Barrett Library, University of Virginia.

Goldman, Emma. Papers. Manuscript Collections, New York Public Library.

Hapgood Family Papers. Yale Collection of American Literature, Beinecke Rare Book and Manuscript Library, Yale University.

"Heterodoxy to Marie" Album. Schlesinger Library, Radcliffe College.

Hicks, Granville. Papers. Special Collections, Syracuse University Library.

Kenton, Edna. Papers. Butler Rare Book and Manuscript Library, Columbia University.

———. "The Provincetown Players: The Playwright's Theatre." Unpublished manuscript. Provincetown Players Archive, Special Collections, Fales Library, New York University.

Millay Family Papers. Berg Collection, New York Public Library.

*Minutes of the Provincetown Players.* Hardbound volume. Billy Rose Theatre Collection, New York Public Library for the Performing Arts, Astor, Lenox and Tilden Foundations.

Moise, Nina. Clippings file. Billy Rose Theatre Collection, New York Public Library for the Performing Arts, Astor, Lenox and Tilden Foundations.

O'Neill, Eugene. Papers. Yale Collection of American Literature, Beinecke Rare Book and Manuscript Library, Yale University.

Provincetown Players Archive. Special Collections, Fales Library, New York University.

Provincetown Players Manuscript Collection Bms Thr 367. Harvard Theatre Collection, Houghton Library, Harvard University.

Provincetown Players Scrapbook. Billy Rose Theatre Collection, New York Public Library for the Performing Arts, Astor, Lenox and Tilden Foundations.

Provincetown Players Scrapbook. Harvard Theatre Collection, Houghton Library, Harvard University.

Rauh, Ida. Clippings file. Billy Rose Theatre Collection, New York Public Library for the Performing Arts, Astor, Lenox and Tilden Foundations.

Reed, John. Collection. Houghton Library, Harvard University.

Riggs, Lynn. Papers. Yale Collection of American Literature, Beinecke Rare Book and Manuscript Library, Yale University.

Sarlós, Robert K. Papers. Special Collections, Shields Library, University of California, Davis.

Sheaffer-O'Neill Collection. Special Collections, Charles E. Shain Library, Connecticut College.

Van Vechten, Carl. Papers. Yale Collection of American Literature, Beinecke Rare Book and Manuscript Library, Yale University.

Vorse, Mary Heaton. "Reminiscences of Mary Heaton Vorse." Oral History Collection, Columbia University.

Washington Square Players Scrapbook. Billy Rose Theatre Collection, New York Public Library for the Performing Arts, Astor, Lenox and Tilden Foundations.

Zorach, William. Papers. Library of Congress, Washington, D.C.

——. "Reminiscences of William Zorach." Oral History Collection, Columbia University.

## PLAYS

Barber, Mary Foster. *The Squealer.* TS. Copyright office, Library of Congress.

Barnes, Djuna. *An Irish Triangle.* In *Playboy* 7 (May 1921).

——. *Kurzy of the Sea.* Unpublished MS. Papers of Djuna Barnes, Special Collections, University of Maryland at College Park Libraries, 1920.

——. *Three from the Earth.* In *A Book.* New York: Boni and Liveright, 1923.

Boyce, Neith. *Constancy.* In *The Provincetown Players: A Choice of the Shorter Works,* ed. Barbara Ozieblo. Sheffield, England: Sheffield Academic Press, 1994.

——. *The Two Sons.* In *The Provincetown Plays, Third Series,* ed. Frank Shay. New York: Frank Shay, 1916.

———. *Winter's Night.* In *Fifty More Contemporary One-Act Plays,* ed. Frank Shay. New York: Appleton, 1934.

Boyce, Neith, and Hutchins Hapgood. *Enemies.* In *The Provincetown Plays,* ed. George Cram Cook and Frank Shay. Cincinnati: Stewart Kidd, 1921.

Bryant, Louise. *The Game.* In *The Provincetown Plays, First Series,* ed. Frank Shay. New York: Frank Shay, 1916.

Chapin, Harold. *The Philosopher of Butterbiggins.* London and Glasgow: Gowans and Gray, Ltd.; Boston: Leroy Phillips, 1921.

Cook, George Cram. *The Athenian Women.* TS. Berg Collection, New York Public Library.

———. *Change Your Style.* In *1915: The Cultural Moment,* ed. Adelle Heller and Lois Rudnick. New Brunswick, N.J.: Rutgers University Press, 1991.

———. *The Spring.* New York: Frank Shay, 1921.

Cook, George Cram, and Susan Glaspell. *Suppressed Desires.* In *The Provincetown Plays,* ed. George Cram Cook and Frank Shay. Cincinnati: Stewart Kidd, 1921.

Crocker, Bosworth. *The Baby Carriage.* In *Fifty Contemporary One-Act Plays,* ed. Frank Shay. New York: Frank Shay, 1916.

Davies, Mary Carolyn. *The Slave with Two Faces.* In *Fifty Contemporary One-Act Plays,* ed. Frank Shay. New York: Frank Shay, 1916.

Dell, Floyd. *A Long Time Ago.* In *King Arthur's Socks and Other Village Plays.* New York: Knopf, 1922.

Ferber, Edna. *The Eldest.* In *The American Scene,* ed. Barrett H. Clark and Kenyon Nicholson. New York: Appleton, 1930.

Frank, Florence Kiper. *Gee-Rusalem.* TS. Copyright office, Library of Congress.

Glaspell, Susan. *Bernice, Close the Book, The Outside,* and *Woman's Honor.* In *Plays.* Boston: Small, Maynard, 1922.

———. *Chains of Dew.* TS. Copyright office, Library of Congress.

———. *Inheritors.* Boston: Small, Maynard, 1921.

———. *The Verge.* Boston: Small, Maynard, 1921.

Glaspell, Susan, and George Cram Cook. *Tickless Time.* In Glaspell, *Plays.* Boston: Small, Maynard, 1920.

Head, Cloyd. *Grotesques.* In *Poetry* 9 (October 1916): 1–32.

Kelly, George. *The Torch-Bearers.* New York: Samuel French, 1924.

Kemp, Harry. *The Prodigal Son.* In *Smart Set* 52 (July 1917): 83–93.

King, Pendleton. *Cocaine.* In *The Provincetown Plays,* ed. George Cram Cook and Frank Shay. Cincinnati: Stewart Kidd, 1921.

Kreymborg, Alfred. *Lima Beans.* In *Representative One-Act Plays by American Authors,* ed. Margaret Mayorga. Boston: Little, Brown, 1922.

———. *Vote the New Moon.* In *Plays for Merry Andrews.* New York: The Sunwise Turn, 1920.

Kugelman, F. B. *The Hermit and His Messiah.* TS. Yale University Library.

Langner, Lawrence. *Matinata, Pie.* In *Five One-Act Comedies.* Cincinnati: Stewart Kidd, 1922.

Lindau, Norman. *A Little Act of Justice*. TS. Copyright office, Library of Congress.

Loving, Pierre. *The Stick-up*. In *A Treasury of Plays for Men*, ed. Frank Shay. Boston: Little, Brown, 1928.

Millay, Edna St. Vincent. *Aria da Capo*. In *Fifteen American One-Act Plays*, ed. Paul Kozelka. New York: Simon and Schuster, 1961.

——. *The Princess Marries the Page*. New York: Harper, 1920.

——. *Two Slatterns and a King*. In *Three Plays*. New York: Harper, 1926.

Mosher, John Chapin. *Sauce for the Emperor*. In *Smart Set* 51 (1917): 199–208.

O'Neill, Eugene. *The Dreamy Kid, The Long Voyage Home, The Sniper*, and *Where the Cross Is Made*. In *Complete Plays: 1913–1920*. New York: Literary Classics, 1988.

——. *The Moon of the Caribbees and Six Other Plays of the Sea*. New York: The Modern Library, 1923.

——. *The Plays of Eugene O'Neill*. New York: Random House, 1955.

Oppenheim, James. *Night*. In *The Provincetown Plays*, ed. George Cram Cook and Frank Shay. Cincinnati: Stewart Kidd, 1921.

Parkhurst, Winthrop. *Getting Unmarried*. In *Smart Set* 54 (April 1918): 91–99.

Pinski, David. *A Dollar*. In *Contemporary One-Act Plays*, ed. Benjamin Roland Lewis. New York: Scribner, 1922.

Reed, John. *The Eternal Quadrangle*. TS. John Reed Collection, Houghton Library, Harvard University.

Rostetter, Alice. *The Widow's Veil*. In *The Provincetown Plays*, ed. George Cram Cook and Frank Shay. Cincinnati: Stewart Kidd, 1921.

Scott, Evelyn. *Love*. TS. Sarlós Papers, Special Collections, The University Library, University of California, Davis.

Smith, Rita Creighton. *The Rescue*. In *Plays of the Harvard Dramatic Club*, ed. George P. Baker. New York: Brentano's, 1918.

Steele, Wilbur. *Not Smart*. In *The Provincetown Plays*, ed. George Cram Cook and Frank Shay. Cincinnati: Stewart Kidd, 1921.

Stevens, Wallace. *Three Travelers Watch a Sunrise*. In *Fifty Contemporary One-Act Plays*, ed. Frank Shay and Pierre Loving. New York: Appleton, 1920.

Vail, Laurence. *What D'You Want?* TS. Sarlós Papers, Special Collections, The University Library, University of California, Davis.

Wellman, Rita. *Funiculi-Funicula*. In *Representative One-Act Plays by American Authors*, ed. Margaret G. Mayorga. Boston: Little, Brown, 1922.

——. *The Rib-Person*. TS. Copyright office, Library of Congress.

——. *The String of the Samisen*. In *The Provincetown Plays*, ed. George Cram Cook and Frank Shay. Cincinnati: Stewart Kidd, 1921.

### REVIEWS AND ARTICLES

Beckerman, Bernard, and Howard Siegman, eds. *On Stage: Theatre Reviews from the "New York Times."* New York: New York Times Books, 1971.

Block, Ralph. "The Provincetown Players Reopen in Macdougal Street." *New York Tribune*, 3 November 1917, 13.

Britt, George. "Montmartre in Manhattan." *New York World Telegram,* 20 May 1932, n.p. In Cook Papers, Berg Collection, New York Public Library.

*Brooklyn Daily Eagle.* Unsigned review of *Bound East for Cardiff* and *The Long Voyage Home.* 19 May 1918, sec. 3, p. 7.

Broun, Heywood. "All-American Dozen of Our Best Actresses." *New York Tribune,* 13 April 1919, n.p. In Cook Scrapbook, Berg Collection, New York Public Library.

———. "Clever Satire Comes Disguised as Farce." *New York Tribune,* 4 May 1919, sec. 4, p. 2.

———. "Interesting Bill Is Given by Provincetown Players." *New York Tribune,* 23 January 1919, 9.

———. "Looking Up, Down and Around with the Provincetown Players—Susan Glaspell and *The People*." *New York Tribune,* 18 March 1917, n.p. In Cook Scrapbook, Berg Collection, New York Public Library.

———. "Provincetown Players Give Fine Thrill in a Sea Play." *New York Tribune,* 25 November 1918, 9.

———. "Realism Has Special Thrills of Its Own." *New York Tribune,* 30 March 1919, sec. 4, p. 2.

———. Review of *Not Smart, The Squealer* and *The Baby Carriage. New York Tribune,* 23 February 1919, sec. 7, p. 1.

———. Review of *The Athenian Women. New York Tribune,* 4 March 1918, 9.

———. Review of *The Rope* and *Woman's Honor. New York Tribune,* 29 April 1918, 9.

———. "Short Plays at the Provincetown in Good Bill." *New York Tribune,* 15 January 1920, 11.

———. "Susan Glaspell and George Cook Have Bright One-Act Play." *New York Tribune,* 23 December 1918, 9.

———. "Two New Plays at Comedy." *New York Tribune,* 14 May 1918, 2.

Corbin, John. "Little Theatre Plays." *New York Times,* 11 November 1917, sec. 8, p. 6.

———. "The One-Act Play." *New York Times,* 19 May 1918, sec. 4, p. 8.

———. "Plays and Players." *New York Times,* 30 March 1919, sec. 4, p. 2.

Drucker, Rebecca. "Provincetown Players Show Their Best." *New York Tribune,* 20 April 1919, sec. 4, p. 2.

———. Review of *Three from the Earth. New York Tribune,* 16 November 1919, sec. 4, p. 7.

"Funereal Drama and Childish Skit in the Village." Unsigned review of *Bernice. New York Herald,* 24 March 1919, 9.

"How Experimental Theaters May Avoid the Pitfalls of Professionalism." *Current Opinion* 65 (July 1918): 28–29.

Kaufman, Jay. "Round the Town." *New York Globe,* 3 November 1919.

Kenton, Edna. "The Provincetown Players and the Playwright's Theatre." *Billboard,* 5 August 1922, 6–7, 13–15.

———. "Unorganized, Amateur, Purely Experimental." *Boston Evening Transcript,* 27 April 1918, sec. 2, pp. 8–9.

Lewisohn, Ludwig. Review of *Love. Nation,* 16 March 1921, n.p. In Provincetown Players Scrapbook, New York Library of the Performing Arts.

Macgowan, Kenneth. Review of *The Dreamy Kid, Getting Unmarried,* and *Three from the Earth. New York Globe,* 3 November 1919, 9.

Mantle, Burns. Review of *Three from the Earth* by Djuna Barnes and *The Dreamy Kid* by Eugene O'Neill. *New York Mail,* n.d., n.p. In Papers of Djuna Barnes, Special Collections, University of Maryland at College Park Libraries.

Munson, Gorham. "The Theatre." *The Modernist,* November 1919, 43.

*New York Daily Times.* Review of *Bernice.* 15 April 1919, n.p. In Cook Papers, Berg Collection, New York Public Library.

*New York Globe.* Unsigned review of *'Ile.* 24 April 1918, n.p. In clippings file, New York Library of the Performing Arts.

"Only the Captain's Daughter Stays Sane." Review of *Where the Cross Is Made. New York Morning Telegraph,* 23 November 1918, 12.

O'Rourke, Barry. "At the Sign of the Sock and the Buskin." *New York Morning Telegraph,* 16 February 1919, 3.

"Provincetown Pioneer Dies." Ida Rauh obituary. *New York Times,* 12 March 1970, n.p. In clippings file, New York Library of the Performing Arts.

Sayler, Lucie. "The Playwright's Theatre." *The Drama* 12 (October–November 1921): 25–27, 40.

*Theatre Magazine.* Unsigned review of *Love* by Evelyn Scott. March 1921, 340. In Provincetown Players Scrapbook, New York Library of the Performing Arts.

*Town Topics.* Unsigned review of *Love* by Evelyn Scott. 10 March 1921, n.p. In Provincetown Players Scrapbook, New York Library of the Performing Arts.

Unsigned, undated review of *The Squealer* and *Not Smart.* In clippings file, New York Library of the Performing Arts.

"Woman's Honor Acted." Unsigned review. *New York Times,* 21 May 1918, 13.

Woollcott, Alexander. "The Play." Review of *The Power of Darkness. New York Times,* 22 January 1920, 22.

——. "The Provincetown Plays." *New York Times,* 9 November 1919, sec. 8, p. 2.

——. "Second Thoughts on First Nights." *New York Times,* 4 April 1920, sec. 4, p. 6.

——. "Second Thoughts on First Nights." *New York Times,* 27 March 1921, sec. 7, p. 1.

——. "There Are War Plays and War Plays." *New York Times,* 14 December 1919, sec. 8, p. 2.

## Autobiographical and Firsthand Accounts

Anderson, Margaret. *My Thirty Years' War.* New York: Covici, Friede, 1930.

Barnes, Djuna. *The Book of Repulsive Women.* Los Angeles: Sun and Moon Press, 1994.

——. "Days of Jig Cook: Recollections of Ancient Theatre History but Ten Years Old." *Theatre Guild Magazine* 6 (January 1929): 31–32.

——. *Interviews.* Ed. Alyce Barry. Washington, D.C.: Sun and Moon Press, 1985.

———. *New York.* Ed. Alyce Barry. Los Angeles: Sun and Moon Press, 1989.

———. *Smoke and Other Early Stories.* Ed. Douglas Messerli. College Park, Md.: Sun and Moon Press, 1987.

Boulton, Agnes. *Part of a Long Story.* New York: Garden City, 1958.

Broun, Heywood Hale. *Whose Little Boy Are You?* New York: St. Martin's Press, 1983.

Bryer, Jackson R., ed. *The Theatre We Worked For: The Letters of Eugene O'Neill to Kenneth Macgowan.* New Haven: Yale University Press, 1982.

Burns, Edward, ed. *The Letters of Gertrude Stein and Carl Van Vechten: 1913–1946.* Vol. 1. New York: Columbia University Press, 1986.

Carpenter, Edward. "Woman in Freedom." In *The Woman Question,* ed. T. R. Smith, 137–48. New York: Modern Library, 1918.

Chapin, Anna Alice. *Greenwich Village.* New York: Dodd, Mead, 1917.

Cheney, Sheldon. *The Art Theater.* New York: Knopf, 1925.

Cook, George Cram. *Greek Coins.* New York: George H. Doran, 1925.

Cook, Nilla Cram. *My Road to India.* New York: Furman, 1939.

Crowley, Alice Lewisohn. *The Neighborhood Playhouse.* New York: Theatre Arts Books, 1959.

Degan, Marie Louise. *The History of the Woman's Peace Party.* New York: Burt Franklin Reprints, 1974.

Dell, Floyd. *Homecoming.* New York: Farrar and Rinehart, 1933.

———. *Intellectual Vagabondage.* New York: George H. Doran, 1926.

———. *Love in Greenwich Village.* New York: George H. Doran, 1926.

———. *Women as World Builders: Studies in Modern Feminism.* 1913. Westport, Conn.: Hyperion Press, 1976.

Deutsch, Helen, and Stella Hanau. *The Provincetown: A Story of the Theater.* New York: Farrar, 1931.

DeWitt, Miriam Hapgood. *Taos: A Memory.* Albuquerque: University of New Mexico Press, 1992.

Dickinson, Thomas H. *The Insurgent Theatre.* New York: B. W. Huebsch, 1917.

Eastman, Max. *Enjoyment of Living.* New York: Harper and Brothers, 1948.

———. *Great Companions.* New York: Farrar, Straus and Cudahy, 1942.

———. *Heroes I Have Known.* New York: Simon and Schuster, 1942.

———. *Love and Revolution.* New York: Random House, 1964.

Eastman, Yvette. *Dearest Wilding: A Memoir.* Philadelphia: University of Pennsylvania Press, 1995.

Ellis, Havelock. *Psychology of Sex: A Handbook for Students.* New York: Emerson Books, 1954.

Foner, Philip S. *The Case of Joe Hill.* New York: International Publishers, 1965.

Feuer, Lewis S., ed. *Marx and Engels: Basic Writings on Politics and Philosophy.* London: Collins, 1969.

Fuerst, Walter R., and Samuel J. Hume. *Twentieth-Century Stage Decoration.* New York: Knopf, 1929. Reprint, New York: Dover, 1967.

Gallup, Donald, ed. *The Flowers of Friendship: Letters Written to Gertrude Stein.* New York: Knopf, 1958.

Gilman, Charlotte Perkins. *Women and Economics.* New York: Small, Maynard, 1898. Reprint, New York: Harper and Row, 1966.

Glaspell, Susan. *The Road to the Temple.* New York: Frederick A. Stokes, 1927.

Goldman, Emma. *Living My Life.* Vols. 1 and 2. New York: Knopf, 1931.

Hapgood, Hutchins. *A Victorian in the Modern World.* New York: Harcourt, Brace, 1939.

Hartley, Marsden. "Farewell, Charles." In *The New Caravan.* New York: Norton, 1936.

Kemp, Harry. *Don Juan's Notebook.* New York: privately printed, 1929.

———. *Love among the Cape-Enders.* New York: MacCaulay, 1931.

———. *More Miles: An Autobiographical Novel.* New York: Boni and Liveright, 1926.

Kenton, Edna. "Feminism Will Give—Men More Fun, Women Greater Scope, Children Better Parents, Life More Charm." *Delineator,* July 1914, 17.

———. "The Militant Women—and Women." *Century,* November 1913, 13–15.

———. "The Provincetown Players: The Playwright's Theatre." Ed. Travis Bogard and Jackson R. Bryer. *Eugene O'Neill Review* 21, nos. 1–2 (Spring–Fall 1997): 15–160.

Key, Ellen. *Love and Marriage.* New York: Putnam, 1911.

———. "The Right of Motherhood." In *The Woman Question,* ed. T. R. Smith, 116–36. New York: Modern Library, 1918.

Kirchwey, Freda, ed. *Our Changing Morality: A Symposium.* New York: Albert and Charles Boni, 1930.

Kreymborg, Alfred. *Troubadour.* New York: Liveright, 1925.

Langner, Lawrence. *The Magic Curtain.* New York: Dutton, 1951.

Loy, Mina. *The Last Lunar Baedeker.* Ed. Roger L. Conover. Highlands, N.C.: Jargon Society, 1982.

Luhan, Mabel Dodge. *Intimate Memories.* Vols. 1–3. New York: Harcourt, Brace, 1936.

———. *Lorenzo in Taos.* New York: Knopf, 1969.

Macgowan, Kenneth. *Footlights across America.* New York: Harcourt, Brace, 1929.

Mackay, Constance D'Arcy. *The Little Theatre in the United States.* New York: Holt, 1917.

Mantle, Burns, and Garrison P. Sherwood, eds. *The Best Plays of 1909–1937.* New York: Dodd, Mead, 1943.

McAlmon, Robert. *Being Geniuses Together: 1920–1930.* 1968. San Francsico: North Point Press, 1984.

Middleton, George. *These Things Are Mine: The Autobiography of a Journeyman Playwright.* New York: Macmillan, 1947.

Millay, Edna St. Vincent. *Letters of Edna St. Vincent Millay.* Ed. Allan Ross Macdougall. New York: Harper and Brothers, 1952.

Moore, Marianne. *The Selected Letters of Marianne Moore.* Ed. Bonnie Costello. New York: Knopf, 1997.

"New Erotic Ethics." *Nation,* 14 March 1912, 260–62.

O'Neill, Eugene. *Selected Letters of Eugene O'Neill.* Ed. Travis Bogard and Jackson R. Bryer. New Haven: Yale University Press.

Perry, Clarence Arthur. *The Work of the Little Theatres.* New York: Russell Sage Foundation, 1933.

Powys, Llewelyn. *The Verdict of Bridlegoose.* New York: Harcourt, Brace, 1926.

Sanger, Margaret. *Margaret Sanger.* New York: Dover, 1938. Reprint, New York: Dover, 1971.

Schiaparelli, Elsa. *Shocking Life.* London: J. M. Dent and Sons, 1954.

Scott, Evelyn. *Escapade.* New York: Seltzer, 1923.

Simonson, Lee. "Scenic Design in the USA." *The Studio,* June 1944, 196.

Smith, T. R., ed. *The Woman Question.* New York: Modern Library, 1918.

Sterne, Maurice. *Shadow and Light.* New York: Harcourt, 1965.

Stevens, Doris. *Jailed for Freedom.* New York: Boni and Liveright, 1920.

Tietjens, Eunice. *The World at My Shoulder.* New York: Macmillan, 1938.

Van Vechten, Carl. *Letters of Carl Van Vechten.* Ed. Bruce Kellner. New Haven: Yale University Press, 1987.

Vorse, Mary Heaton. *A Footnote to Folly.* New York: Farrar and Rinehart, 1935.

———. *Time and the Town.* New York: Dial, 1942.

Williams, William Carlos. *Autobiography.* New York: Random House, 1948.

Wilson, Edmund. *The Twenties.* New York: Farrar, Straus and Giraux, 1975.

Young, Art. *On My Way.* New York: Liveright, 1928.

Zorach, William. *Art Is My Life.* Cleveland: World, 1967.

Zurier, Rebecca. *Art for "The Masses": A Radical Magazine and Its Graphics, 1911–1917.* Philadelphia: Temple University Press, 1988.

## Secondary Sources
### BOOKS, ARTICLES, AND DISSERTATIONS

Abrahams, Edward. *The Lyrical Left: Randolph Bourne, Alfred Stieglitz, and the Origins of Cultural Radicalism in America.* Charlottesville: University Press of Virginia, 1986.

Alexander, Doris. *The Tempering of Eugene O'Neill.* New York: Harcourt, Brace, and World, 1962.

Auster, Albert. *Actresses and Suffragists: Women in the American Theater, 1890–1920.* New York: Praeger, 1984.

Bach, Gerhard. "Susan Glaspell: A Bibliography of Dramatic Criticism." *Great Lakes Review* 3 (1977): 1–34.

———. "Susan Glaspell: Provincetown Playwright." *Great Lakes Review* 4 (1978): 31–43.

Barlow, Judith E. "Susan's Sisters: The 'Other' Women Writers of the Provincetown Players." In *Susan Glaspell: Essays on Her Theater and Fiction*, ed. Linda Ben-Zvi, 259–300. Ann Arbor: University of Michigan Press, 1995.

——, ed. *Plays by American Women: The Early Years.* New York: Avon, 1981.

——. *Plays by American Women: 1900–1930.* New York: Applause Theatre Book Publishers, 1985.

Barton, Mike A. "Aline Bernstein: A History and Evaluation." Ph.D. diss., Indiana University, 1971.

Baskin, Alex. *John Reed: The Early Years in Greenwich Village.* New York: Archives of Social History, 1990.

Beal, Suzanne. "'Mama, Teach Me That French': Mothers and Daughters in Twentieth-Century Plays by American Women Playwrights." Ph.D. diss., University of Maryland at College Park, 1993.

Benstock, Shari. *Women of the Left Bank: Paris, 1900–1940.* Austin: University of Texas Press, 1987.

Ben-Zvi, Linda. "Susan Glaspell and Eugene O'Neill." *Eugene O'Neill Newsletter* 6, no. 2 (Summer–Fall 1982): 21–29.

——. "Susan Glaspell and Eugene O'Neill: The Imagery of Gender." *Eugene O'Neill Newsletter* 10, no. 1 (Spring 1986): 22–27.

——, ed. *Susan Glaspell: Essays on Her Theater and Fiction.* Ann Arbor: University of Michigan Press, 1995.

Bigsby, C. W. E. "Introduction." In *Susan Glaspell: Plays*, ed. C. W. E. Bigsby, 1–31. Cambridge: Cambridge University Press, 1987.

——. "Provincetown: The Birth of Twentieth-Century American Drama." In *A Critical Introduction to Twentieth-Century American Drama: Vol. 1, 1900–1940*, ed. Bigsby, 1–35. Cambridge: Cambridge University Press, 1982.

Black, Cheryl. "Ida Rauh: Power Player at Provincetown." *Journal of American Drama and Theatre* 6, nos. 2–3 (Spring–Fall 1994): 63–80.

——. "Interpretation and Tact: Nina Moise Directs the Provincetown Players." *Theatre Survey* 36, no. 1 (May 1995): 55–64.

——. "Pioneering Theatre Managers: Edna Kenton and Eleanor Fitzgerald of the Provincetown Players." *Journal of American Drama and Theatre* 9, no. 3 (Fall 1997): 40–58.

——. "The Women of Provincetown: 1915–1922." Ph.D. diss., University of Maryland, 1998.

Black, Robert. "Robert Edmond Jones: Poetic Artist of the New Stagecraft." Ph.D. diss., University of Wisconsin, Madison, 1955.

Blair, Karen. *The Clubwoman as Feminist: True Womanhood Redefined, 1860–1914.* New York: Holmes and Meier, 1980.

——. *The Torchbearers: Women and Their Amateur Arts Associations in America, 1890–1930.* Bloomington: Indiana University Press, 1994.

Bogard, Travis. *Contour in Time: The Plays of Eugene O'Neill.* New York: Oxford University Press, 1972.

Braunlich, Phyllis Cole. *Haunted by Home: The Life and Letters of Lynn Riggs*. Norman: University of Oklahoma Press, 1988.

Brevda, William. *Harry Kemp*. Lewisburg, Pa.: Bucknell University Press, 1986.

Brittin, Norman. *Edna St. Vincent Millay*. New York: Twayne, 1967.

Bucco, Martin. *Wilbur Daniel Steele*. New York: Twayne, 1972.

Buhle, Mary Jo. *Women and American Socialism: 1870–1920*. Urbana: University of Illinois Press, 1981.

Burk, Efram L. "Testament to American Modernism: The Prints of William and Marguerite Zorach." Ph.D. diss., Pennsylvania State University, 1998.

Burke, Carolyn. *Becoming Modern: The Life of Mina Loy*. New York: Farrar, Straus and Giroux, 1996.

Callard, D. A. *Pretty Good for a Woman: The Enigmas of Evelyn Scott*. London: Jonathan Cape, 1985.

Campbell, Barbara Kuhn. *The "Liberated" Woman of 1914*. Detroit: UMI Research Press, 1979.

Canning, Charlotte. *Feminist Theaters in the U.S.A.: Staging Women's Experience*. London and New York: Routledge, 1996.

Carroll, Kathleen L. "Centering Women Onstage: Susan Glaspell's Dialogic Strategy of Resistance." Ph.D. diss., University of Maryland at College Park, 1990.

Ceplair, Larry. *Charlotte Perkins Gilman: A Nonfiction Reader*. New York: Columbia University Press, 1991.

Cheney, Anne. *Millay in Greenwich Village*. Tuscaloosa: University of Alabama Press, 1975.

Chinoy, Helen Krich. "The Impact of the Stage Director on American Plays, Playwrights, and Theatres: 1860–1930." Ph.D. diss., Columbia University, 1963.

Chinoy, Helen Krich, and Linda Walsh Jenkins, eds. *Women in American Theatre*. New York: Crown Publishers, 1981. Reprint, Theatre Communications Group, 1987.

Churchill, Allen. *The Improper Bohemians*. New York: Dutton, 1959.

Clayton, Douglas S. *Floyd Dell: The Life and Times of an American Rebel*. Chicago: Ivan R. Dee, 1994.

Coke, Van Deren. *Andrew Dasburg*. Albuquerque: University of New Mexico Press, 1979.

———. *Nordfeldt the Painter*. Albuquerque: University of New Mexico Press, 1972.

Cole, Toby, and Helen Krich Chinoy, eds. *Directing the Play: A Sourcebook of Stagecraft*. New York: Bobbs-Merrill, 1953.

Cook, Blanche Wiesen. "Female Support Networks and Political Activism: Lillian Wald, Crystal Eastman, Emma Goldman." *Chrysalis* 3 (1977): 43–60.

———, ed. *Toward the Great Change: Crystal and Max Eastman on Feminism, Antimilitarism, and Revolution*. New York: Garland Publishing, 1976.

Corey, Anne. "Susan Glaspell: Playwright of Social Consciousness." Ph.D. diss., New York University, 1990.

Cosgrove, Stuart, Ewan MacColl, and Raphael Samuel. *Theatres of the Left: 1880–1935*. London: Routledge and Kegan Paul, 1985.

Cott, Nancy F. *The Grounding of Modern Feminism*. New Haven: Yale University Press, 1987.

Davis, Tracy C. *Actresses as Working Women: Their Social Identity in Victorian Culture*. London and New York: Routledge, 1991.

Dearborn, Mary V. *Queen of Bohemia: The Life of Louise Bryant*. Boston: Houghton Mifflin, 1996.

Drake, William. *The First Wave: Women Poets in America, 1915–1945*. New York: Macmillan, 1987.

Drinnon, Anna Maria, and Richard Drinnon, eds. *Nowhere at Home: Letters from Exile of Emma Goldman and Alexander Berkman*. New York: Schocken Books, 1975.

Duberman, Martin. *Paul Robeson: A Biography*. New York: The New Press, 1989.

Durham, Weldon, ed. *American Theatre Companies: 1888–1930*. New York: Greenwood Press, 1987.

Egan, Leona Rust. *Provincetown as a Stage: Provincetown, the Provincetown Players, and the Discovery of Eugene O'Neill*. Orleans, Mass.: Parnassus Imprints, 1994.

Faderman, Lillian. *Odd Girls and Twilight Lovers: A History of Lesbian Life in Twentieth-Century America*. New York: Penguin Press, 1991.

Fallon, Gabriel. "The Abbey Theatre Acting Tradition." In *The Story of the Abbey Theatre*, ed. Sean McCann, 101–25. London: New English Library, 1967.

Faludi, Susan. *Backlash: The Undeclared War against American Women*. New York: Doubleday, 1991.

Farnham, Emily. *Charles Demuth: Behind a Laughing Mask*. Norman: Oklahoma University Press, 1971.

Field, Andrew. *Djuna: The Life and Times of Djuna Barnes*. New York: Putnam, 1983.

Fishbein, Leslie. *Rebels in Bohemia: The Radicals of "The Masses," 1911–1917*. Chapel Hill: University of North Carolina Press, 1982.

Foster, Joseph. *D. H. Lawrence in Taos*. Albuquerque: University of New Mexico Press, 1972.

Gardner, Virginia. *"Friend and Lover": The Life of Louise Bryant*. New York: Horizon Press, 1982.

Garrison, Dee. *Mary Heaton Vorse: The Life of an American Insurgent*. Philadelphia: Temple University Press, 1989.

———, ed. *Rebel Pen: The Writings of Mary Heaton Vorse*. New York: Monthly Review Press, 1985.

Gelb, Arthur, and Barbara Gelb. *O'Neill*. 1962. New York: Harper and Row, 1973.

———. *O'Neill: Life with Monte Cristo*. New York: Applause, 2000.

Gelb, Barbara. *So Short a Time: A Biography of John Reed and Louise Bryant*. New York: Norton, 1973.

Gilder, Rosamond. *Enter the Actress: The First Women in the Theatre*. Freeport, N.Y.: Books for Libraries Press, 1931.

Gillespie, Patti P. "Feminist Theatre: A Rhetorical Phenomenon." *Quarterly Journal of Speech* 64 (1978): 286–94.

Goldman, Arnold. "The Culture of the Provincetown Players." *Journal of American Studies* 12 (December 1978): 291–310.

Gurko, Miriam. *Restless Spirit: The Life of Edna St. Vincent Millay.* New York: Crowell, 1962.

Hahn, Emily. *Mabel.* Boston: Houghton Mifflin, 1977.

———. *Romantic Rebels: An Informal History of Bohemianism in America.* Boston: Houghton, 1977.

Handlin, Oscar. *The Americans.* Boston: Little, Brown, 1963.

Hart, Lynda, ed. *Making a Spectacle: Feminist Essays on Contemporary Women's Theatre.* Ann Arbor: University of Michigan Press, 1989.

Heller, Adele, and Lois Rudnick, eds. *1915: The Cultural Moment.* New Brunswick, N.J.: Rutgers University Press, 1991.

Hennigan, Shirlee. "The Woman Director in the Contemporary Professional Theatre." Ph.D. diss., Washington State University, 1983.

Herring, Philip. *Djuna: The Life and Work of Djuna Barnes.* New York: Viking, 1995.

Hewitt, Barnard. *Theatre U.S.A: 1665–1957.* New York: McGraw-Hill, 1959.

Hicks, Granville. *John Reed: The Making of a Revolutionary.* New York: Macmillan, 1936.

Hicks, John D. *Normalcy and Reaction, 1921–1933: An Age of Disillusionment.* Washington, D.C.: American Historical Association, 1960.

Hoffman, Marilyn Friedman. *Marguerite and William Zorach: The Cubist Years, 1915–1918.* Manchester, N.H.: Currier Gallery of Art, 1987.

Housley, Helen. "The Female Director's Odyssey: The Broadway Sisterhood." Unpublished paper, 1991.

———. "To Inherit the Wind: Margo Jones as Director." Ph.D. diss., University of Maryland, 1991.

Humphrey, Robert E. *Children of Fantasy: The First Rebels of Greenwich Village.* New York: Wiley, 1978.

Katz, Mary Jane. *The Many Lives of Otto Kahn.* New York: Macmillan, 1963.

Kenealy, Arabella. *Feminism and Sex-Extinction.* New York: Dutton, 1920.

Kuchta, Ronald A., ed. *Provincetown Painters: 1890s–1970s.* Visual Arts Publications, 1977.

Larabee, Ann E. "Death in Delphi: Susan Glaspell and the Companionate Marriage." *Mid-American Review* 2 (1987): 93–106.

———. "First-Wave Feminist Theatre, 1890–1930." Ph.D. diss., Graduate School of New York at Binghamton, 1988.

Leavitt, Dinah. *Feminist Theatre Groups.* Jefferson, N.C.: McFarland, 1980.

Lingeman, Richard. *Theodore Dreiser: An American Journey, 1908–45.* New York: Putnam, 1986.

Little, Stuart. *Off-Broadway: The Prophetic Theatre.* New York: Coward, McCann, and Geoghegan, 1972.

Makowsky, Veronica. *Susan Glaspell's Century of American Women.* New York: Oxford University Press, 1993.

Malpede, Karen. *Women in Theatre: Compassion and Hope.* New York: Drama Book Specialists, 1981.

Manthey-Zorn, Otto, ed. *Nietzsche: An Anthology of His Works.* New York: Washington Square Press, 1964.

Marcaccio, Michael D. *The Hapgoods: Three Earnest Brothers.* Charlottesville: University Press of Virginia, 1977.

*Marguerite Zorach: The Early Years, 1908–1920.* Washington, D.C.: Smithsonian Institution Press, National Collection of Fine Arts, 1973.

Mariani, Paul. *William Carlos Williams: A New World Naked.* New York: McGraw-Hill, 1981.

May, Henry. *The End of American Innocence.* New York: Oxford University Press, 1959.

McArthur, Benjamin. *Actors and American Culture, 1880–1920.* Philadelphia: Temple University Press, 1984.

McCausland, Elizabeth. *Marsden Hartley.* Minneapolis: Minnesota University Press, 1952.

McTeague, James. *Before Stanislavsky: American Professional Acting Schools and Acting Theory, 1875–1925.* Metuchen, N.J.: Scarecrow Press, 1993.

Molesworth, Charles. *Marianne Moore: A Literary Life.* New York: Atheneum, 1990.

Muncy, Robyn. *Creating a Female Dominion in American Reform, 1890–1935.* New York: Oxford University Press, 1991.

Nehls, Edward. *D. H. Lawrence: A Composite Biography.* Madison: University of Wisconsin Press, 1959.

Nicholson, Linda. *Gender and History: The Limits of Social Theory in the Age of the Family.* New York: Columbia Press, 1986.

Noe, Marcia. *Susan Glaspell: Voice from the Heartland.* Macomb: Western Illinois University Press, 1983.

O'Neill, William L. *Echoes of Revolt: "The Masses," 1911–1917.* Chicago: Quadrangle, 1966.

———. *Everyone Was Brave: A History of Feminism in America.* Chicago: Quadrangle/New York Times Book Co., 1969.

———. *The Last Romantic: A Life of Max Eastman.* New York: Oxford University Press, 1978.

Owen, Bobbi. *Costume Design on Broadway.* New York: Greenwood Press, 1987.

———. *Scenic Design on Broadway: Designers and Their Credits, 1915–1990.* New York: Greenwood Press, 1991.

Ozieblo, Barbara. "Rebellion and Rejection: The Plays of Susan Glaspell." In *Modern American Drama: The Female Canon,* ed. June Schlueter, 66–76. Rutherford, N.J.: Fairleigh Dickinson University Press, 1990.

———. *Susan Glaspell: A Critical Biography.* Chapel Hill: University of North Carolina Press, 2000.

————, ed. *The Provincetown Players: A Choice of the Shorter Works*. Sheffield, England: Sheffield Academic Press, 1994.

Papke, Mary. *Susan Glaspell: A Research and Production Sourcebook*. Westport, Conn.: Greenwood Press, 1993.

Parry, Albert. *Garrets and Pretenders: A History of Bohemianism in America*. New York: Dover, 1933.

Paul, Norman. "Copeau Looks at the American Stage." *Educational Theatre Journal* 29 (March 1977): 67–69.

Postlewait, Thomas, and Bruce A. McConachie, eds. *Interpreting the Theatrical Past*. Iowa City: University of Iowa Press, 1989.

Price, Julia S. *The Off-Broadway Theatre*. New York: Scarecrow Press, 1962.

Ranald, Margaret Loftus. *The Eugene O'Neill Companion*. Westport, Conn.: Greenwood Press, 1984.

Robinson, Alice M., Vera Mowry Roberts, and Milly S. Barranger, eds. *Notable Women in the American Theatre: A Biographical Dictionary*. New York: Greenwood Press, 1989.

Rosenstone, Robert A. *Romantic Revolutionary: A Biography of John Reed*. New York: Knopf, 1975.

Rudnick, Lois. *Mabel Dodge Luhan: New Woman, New Worlds*. Albuquerque: University of New Mexico Press, 1984.

Sarlós, Robert K. "Dionysus in 1915: A Pioneer Theatre Collective." *Theatre Research International* 3 (October 1977): 33–53.

————. *Jig Cook and the Provincetown Players: Theatre in Ferment*. Amherst: University of Massachusetts Press, 1982.

————. "Nina Moise Directs Eugene O'Neill's *The Rope*." *Eugene O'Neill Newsletter* 6, no. 3 (Winter 1982): 9–12.

————. "Producing Principles and Practices of the Provincetown Players." *Theatre Research/Recherches Theatrales* 10 (1969): 89–102.

————. "The Provincetown Players: Experiments in Style." Ph.D. diss., Yale University, 1965.

————. "Susan Glaspell and Jig Cook: Rule Makers and Rule Breakers." In *1915: The Cultural Moment*, ed. Adelle Heller and Lois Rudnick, 250–60. New Brunswick, N.J.: Rutgers University Press, 1991.

————. "Wharf and Dome: Materials for the History of the Provincetown Players." *Theatre Research/Recherches Theatrales* 10 (1970): 163–78.

Schneir, Miriam, ed. *Feminism: The Essential Historical Writings*. New York: Vintage Books, 1972.

Schuler, Catherine. *Women in Russian Theatre: The Actress in the Silver Age*. New York and London: Routledge, 1997.

Schwartz, Judith. *Radical Feminists of Heterodoxy*. Lebanon, N.H.: New Victoria Publishers, 1982.

Scott, Anne Firor. *Natural Allies: Women's Associations in American History*. Urbana and Chicago: University of Illinois Press, 1991.

Sheaffer, Louis. *O'Neill: Son and Playwright.* Boston: Little, Brown, 1968.

———. *O'Neill: Son and Artist.* Boston: Little, Brown, 1973.

Sievers, David. *Freud on Broadway.* New York: Hermitage House, 1955.

Smith, Sharon. *Women Who Make Movies.* New York: Hopkinson and Blake, 1975.

Snitow, Ann, Christine Stansell, and Sharon Thompson, eds. *Powers of Desire.* New York: Monthly Review Press, 1983.

Sochen, June. *Movers and Shakers: American Women Thinkers and Activists: 1900–1970.* New York: New York Times Book Co., 1973.

———. *The New Woman: Feminism in Greenwich Village, 1919–1920.* New York: Quadrangle Books, 1972.

———, ed. *The New Feminism in Twentieth-Century America.* London: D. C. Heath, 1971.

Stannard, Una. *Mrs. Man.* San Francisco: Germanbooks, 1977.

Taylor, Karen Malpede. *People's Theatre in Amerika.* New York: Drama Book Specialists, 1972.

Trimberger, Ellen Kay. "The New Woman and the New Sexuality: Conflict and Contradiction in the Writings and Lives of Mabel Dodge and Neith Boyce." In *1915: The Cultural Moment,* ed. Adelle Heller and Lois Rudnick, 98–116. New Brunswick, N.J.: Rutgers University Press, 1991.

———, ed. *Intimate Warriors: Portraits of a Modern Marriage, 1899–1944.* New York: Feminist Press, 1991.

Vilhauer, William W. "A History and Evaluation of the Provincetown Players." Ph.D. diss., University of Iowa, 1965.

Waterman, Arthur E. *Susan Glaspell.* New York: Twayne, 1966.

Watson, Steven. *Strange Bedfellows: The First American Avant-Garde.* New York: Abbeville Press, 1991.

Wertheim, Frank. *The New York Little Renaissance: Iconoclasm, Modernism, and Nationalism in American Culture.* New York: New York University Press, 1976.

Wexler, Alice. *Emma Goldman: An Intimate Life.* New York: Pantheon Books, 1984.

White, Palmer. *Elsa Schiaparelli: Empress of Fashion.* London: Aurum Press, 1986.

Woll, Allen, ed. *Dictionary of the Black Theatre.* Westport, Conn.: Greenwood Press, 1983.

# Index

# About the Author

Cheryl Black is Assistant Professor of Theatre at the University of
Missouri–Columbia.